THE
STATE IN
CAPITALIST
SOCIETY

THE
STATE IN
CAPITALIST
SOCIETY

Ralph Miliband

Basic Books, Inc., Publishers

New York

To the memory of
C. Wright Mills

Contents

Preface

As its title indicates, this book is concerned with the nature and role of the state in what are often referred to as 'advanced capitalist societies'. For reasons which are explained in the Introduction, I believe that these societies, despite their many diversities, have enough basic features in common to provide a general context for a study of the role which the state plays in them. Other types of society raise altogether different questions in relation to the state, and I have not attempted to deal with them here.

The structure of the book is as follows: Chapter 1 is mainly concerned with a survey of the major economic and social characteristics of advanced capitalist societies. Chapter 2 examines in greater detail the pattern of economic power which is to be found in them. Chapter 3 outlines the main institutions of the 'state system' and the social composition of the 'state elite'. Chapter 4 discusses the purpose and role of governments in the context of advanced capitalism; and chapter 5 considers the part played by the civil service, the military and the judiciary. Chapter 6 deals with the role of the state in the competition between different 'interests' in capitalist society. Chapters 7 and 8 discuss various 'agencies of legitimation', including parties, the mass media and education. Finally, chapter 9 suggests some of the directions in which the political regimes of advanced capitalism are moving.

I am grateful to the following friends and colleagues who have kindly read this book in draft and who have made useful criticisms and suggestions: Ernest Gellner, H. G. R. Greaves,

J.A.G. Griffith, W.L. Guttsman, Marcel Liebman, Robert Looker, John Saville, John Westergaard and Ernest Wohlgemuth. My greatest debt is to my wife, whose criticism and encouragement have been invaluable.

I am also grateful to the Research Division of the Government Department of the London School of Economics, which made it possible for me to avail myself of the research services of Miss Ann Marcus for a period of four months; to Miss Marcus herself for the valuable work she did for me in that time; to the Louis M. Rabinowitz Foundation which enabled me to take a term's leave from my teaching duties; to Mrs Linda Snowden, who typed and retyped with exemplary patience and skill; and to the staff of the British Library of Political and Economic Science for their helpfulness.

Since the views expressed in this book are rather controversial, it may be worth emphasising that I alone am responsible for everything which appears in the following pages.

The London School of Economics   R.M.
and Political Science

THE
STATE IN
CAPITALIST
SOCIETY

I

Introduction

I

More than ever before men now live in the shadow of the state. What they want to achieve, individually or in groups, now mainly depends on the state's sanction and support. But since that sanction and support are not bestowed indiscriminately, they must, ever more directly, seek to influence and shape the state's power and purpose, or try and appropriate it altogether. It is for the state's attention, or for its control, that men compete; and it is against the state that beat the waves of social conflict. It is to an ever greater degree the state which men encounter as they confront other men. This is why, as social beings, they are also political beings, whether they know it or not. It is possible not to be interested in what the state does; but it is not possible to be unaffected by it. The point has acquired a new and ultimate dimension in the present epoch: if large parts of the planet should one day be laid waste in a nuclear war, it is because men, acting in the name of their state and invested with its power, will have so decided, or miscalculated.

Yet, while the vast inflation of the state's power and activity in the advanced capitalist societies with which this book is concerned has become one of the merest commonplaces of political analysis, the remarkable paradox is that the state itself, as a subject of political study, has long been very unfashionable. A vast amount of work has, in the last few decades, been pro-duced on government and public administration, on elites and bureaucracy, on parties and voting behaviour, political authority and the conditions of political stability, political mobilisation and political culture, and much of this has of course dealt with or touched on the nature and role of the state. But as an institution, it has in recent times received far less attention than its importance deserves. In the early 1950s a prominent American political scientist wrote that 'neither the state nor power is a concept that serves to bring together political research'.[1] However it may be with the concept of power, this view, as regards the state, appears to have been generally accepted by 'students of politics' working in the field of Western political systems.

This, however, does not mean that Western political scientists and political sociologists have not had what used to be called a 'theory of the state'. On the contrary, it is precisely the theory of the state to which they do, for the most part, subscribe which helps to account for their comparative neglect of the state as a focus of political analysis. For that theory *takes as resolved* some of the largest questions which have traditionally been asked about the state, and makes unnecessary, indeed almost precludes, any special concern with its nature and role in Western-type societies.

A theory of the state is also a theory of society and of the distribution of power in that society. But most Western 'students of politics' tend to start, judging from their work, with the assumption that power, in Western societies, is competitive, fragmented and diffused: everybody, directly or through organised groups, has some power and nobody has or can have too much of it. In these societies, citizens enjoy universal suffrage, free and regular elections, representative institutions, effective citizen rights, including the right of free speech, association and opposition; and both individuals and groups take ample advantage of these rights, under the protection of the law, an independent judiciary and a free political culture.

As a result, the argument goes, no government, acting on behalf of the state, can fail, in the not very long run, to respond to the wishes and demands of competing interests. In the end, everybody, including those at the end of the queue, get served. In the words of a leading exponent of this democratic-pluralist view, here is a political system in which 'all the active and legitimate groups in the population can make themselves

[1] D. Easton, *The Political System*, 1953, p. 106.

heard at some crucial stage in the process of decision'.[1] Other pluralist writers, Professor Dahl has also noted,

... suggest that there are a number of loci for arriving at political decisions; that business men, trade unions, politicians, consumers, farmers, voters and many other aggregates all have an impact on policy outcomes; that none of these aggregates is homogeneous for all purposes; that each of them is highly influential over some scopes but weak over many others; and that the power to reject undesired alternatives is more common than the power to dominate over outcomes directly.[2]

Another writer, who is himself a critic of the pluralist thesis, summarises it as follows in relation to the United States:

Congress is seen as the focal point for the pressures which are exerted by interest groups throughout the nation, either by way of the two great parties or directly through lobbies. The laws issuing from the government are shaped by the manifold forces brought to bear upon the legislature. Ideally, Congress merely reflects these forces, combining them – or 'resolving' them, as the physicists say – into a single social decision. As the strength and direction of private interests alters, there is a corresponding alteration in the composition and activity of the great interest groups – labour, big business, agriculture. Slowly, the great weathervane of government swings about to meet the shifting winds of opinion.[3]

This view has received its most extensive elaboration in, and in regard to, the United States. But it has also, in one form or another, come to dominate political science and political sociology, and for that matter political life itself, in all other advanced capitalist countries. Its first result is to exclude, by definition, the notion that the state might be a rather special institution, whose main purpose is to defend the predominance in society of a particular class. There are, in Western societies, no such predominant classes, interests or groups. There are only competing blocs of interests, whose competition, which is sanctioned and guaranteed by the state itself, ensures that power *is* diffused and balanced, and that no particular interest is able to weigh too heavily upon the state.

[1] R. A. Dahl, *A Preface to Democratic Theory*, 1965, pp. 137–8.
[2] R. A. Dahl, *et al.*, *Social Science Research on Business: Product and Potential*, 1959, p. 36.
[3] R. P. Woolf, *A Critique of Pure Tolerance*, 1965, p. 11.

It is of course true, many of those who uphold this view agree, that there are elites in different economic, social, political, administrative, professional and other pyramids of power. But these elites altogether lack the degree of cohesion required to turn them into dominant or ruling classes. In fact, 'elite pluralism', with the competition it entails between different elites, is itself a prime guarantee that power in society *will* be diffused and not concentrated.

In short, the state, subjected as it is to a multitude of conflicting pressures from organised groups and interests, cannot show any marked bias towards some and against others: its special role, in fact, is to accommodate and reconcile them all. In that role, the state is only the mirror which society holds up to itself. The reflection may not always be pleasing, but this is the price that has to be paid, and which is eminently worth paying, for democratic, competitive and pluralist politics in modern industrial societies.

This dominant pluralist view of Western-type societies and of the state does not, it may also be noted, preclude a critical attitude to this or that aspect of the social order and of the political system. But criticism, and proposals for reform, are mainly conceived in terms of the improvement and strengthening of a system whose basically 'democratic' and desirable character is held to be solidly established. While there may be a good deal which is wrong with them, these are *already* 'democratic' societies, to which the notion of 'ruling class' or 'power elite' is absurdly irrelevant.

The strength of this current orthodoxy has helped to turn these claims (for they are no more than claims) into solid articles of political wisdom; and the ideological and political climate engendered by the Cold War has tended to make subscription to that wisdom a test not only of political intelligence but of political morality as well. Yet, the general acceptance of a particular view of social and political systems does not make it right. One of the main purposes of the present work is in fact to show in detail that the pluralist-democratic view of society, of politics and of the state in regard to the countries of advanced capitalism, is in all essentials wrong – that this view, far from providing a guide to reality, constitutes a profound obfuscation of it.

Notwithstanding the elaboration of various elite theories of power, by far the most important alternative to the pluralist-democratic view of power remains the Marxist one. Indeed, it could well be argued that the rapid development of pluralist-democratic political sociology after 1945, particularly in the United States, was largely inspired by the need to meet the 'challenge of Marxism' in this field more plausibly than conventional political science appeared able to do.

Yet Marxist political analysis has long suffered from marked deficiencies. Democratic pluralism may be, as will be argued here, running altogether in the wrong grooves. But Marxist political analysis, notably in relation to the nature and role of the state, has long seemed stuck in its own groove, and has shown little capacity to renew itself.

Marx himself, it may be recalled, never attempted a systematic study of the state. This was one of the tasks which he hoped to undertake as part of a vast scheme of work which he had projected in the 1850s but of which volume I of *Capital* was the only fully finished part.[1] However, references to the state in different types of society constantly recur in almost all his writings; and as far as capitalist societies are concerned, his main view of the state throughout is summarised in the famous formulation of the *Communist Manifesto*: 'The executive of the modern state is but a committee for managing the common affairs of the whole bourgeoisie'. In one form or another the concept this embodies reappears again and again in the work of both Marx and Engels; and despite the refinements and qualifications they occasionally introduced in their discussion of the state – notably to account for a certain degree of independence which they believed the state could enjoy in 'exceptional circumstances'[2] – they never departed from the view that in capitalist society the state was above all the coercive instrument of a ruling class, itself defined in terms of its ownership and control of the means of production.[3]

[1] See K. Marx to F. Lassalle, 22 February 1858, and K. Marx to F. Engels, 2 April 1858, in *Selected Correspondence*, Moscow, n.d., pp. 125, 126.

[2] See below, p. 93.

[3] See, e.g. Marx twenty-two years after the *Communist Manifesto*: 'At the same pace at which the progress of modern industry developed, widened, intensified the class antagonism between capital and labour, the state power assumed more and more the character of the national power of capital over labour, of a public

For the most part, Marxists everywhere have been content to take this thesis as more or less self-evident; and to take as their text on the state Lenin's *State and Revolution*, which is now half a century old and which was in essence both a restatement and an elaboration of the main view of the state to be found in Marx and Engels and a fierce assertion of its validity in the era of imperialism.[1] Since then, the only major Marxist contribution to the theory of the state has been that of Antonio Gramsci, whose illuminating notes on the subject have only fairly recently come to gain a measure of recognition and influence beyond Italy.[2] Otherwise, Marxists have made little notable attempt to confront the question of the state in the light of the concrete socio-economic *and* political *and* cultural reality of actual capitalist societies. Where the attempt has been made, it has suffered from an over-simple explanation of the inter-relationship between civil society and the state. Even though that 'model' comes much closer to reality than democratic-pluralist theory, it requires a much more thorough elaboration than it has hitherto been given: Paul Sweezy was scarcely exaggerating

force organised for social enslavement, of an engine of class despotism' (K. Marx, 'The Civil War in France', in K. Marx and F. Engels, *Selected Works*, 1950, vol. 1, p. 496); and Engels, 'The modern state, no matter what its form, is essentially a capitalist machine, the state of the capitalists, the ideal personification of the total national capital ... an organisation of the particular class which was *pro-tempore* the exploiting class, an organisation for the purpose of preventing any interference from without with the existing conditions of production, and therefore, especially, for the purpose of forcibly keeping the exploited classes in the conditions of oppression corresponding with the given mode of production (slavery, serfdom, wage-labour)' F. Engels, *Socialism: Utopian and Scientific, ibid.*, vol. 2, pp. 136, 138). This was written in 1887. It is the same view which is of course elaborated in *The Origin of the Family, Property and the State* of 1881, and in many of Engels' later writings.

[1] E.g., 'Imperialism – the era of bank capital, the era of gigantic capitalist monopolies, the era of the transformation of monopoly capital into state-monopoly capitalism – has particularly witnessed an unprecedented strengthening of the "state machine" and an unprecedented growth of its bureaucratic and military apparatus, in connection with the increase in repressive measures against the proletariat in the monarchical as well as the freest republican countries' (V. I. Lenin, *State and Revolution*, 1941, p. 27). Similarly, 'the forms of the bourgeois state are extremely varied, but in essence they are all the same; in one way or another, in the last analysis, all these states are inevitably the *dictatorship of the bourgeoisie*' (*ibid.*, p. 29. Italics in text).

[2] The only important study of Gramsci in English so far is J. M. Cammett's *Antonio Gramsci and the Origins of Italian Communism*, 1967; but see also J. Merrington, 'Theory and Practice in Gramsci's Marxism' in *The Socialist Register, 1968*.

when he noted some years ago that 'this is the area in which the study of monopoly capitalism, not only by bourgeois social scientists but by Marxists as well, is most seriously deficient'.[1] The purpose of the present work is to make a contribution to remedying that deficiency.

II

The countries which will be considered here are very different from each other in a multitude of ways. They have different histories, traditions, cultures, languages and institutions. But they also have in common two crucial characteristics: the first is that they are all highly industrialised countries; and the second is that the largest part of their means of economic activity is under private ownership and control. These combined characteristics are what makes them advanced capitalist countries in the first place and what distinguishes them radically from under-industrialised countries, such as India or Brazil or Nigeria, even though there too the means of economic activity are predominantly under private ownership and control; and from countries where state ownership prevails, even though some of them, like the Soviet Union, Czechoslovakia and the German Democratic Republic, are also highly industrialised. The criterion of distinction, in other words, is the level of economic activity combined with the mode of economic organisation.

The same combined characteristics of advanced capitalist countries also serve to reduce the significance of the other differences which are to be found between them. Joseph Schumpeter once noted that

... social structures, types and attitudes are coins that do not readily melt: once they are formed they persist, possibly for centuries; and since different structures and types display different degrees of ability to survive, we almost always find that actual group or national behaviour more or less departs from what we should

[1] S. Tsuru (ed.), *Has Capitalism Changed?*, 1961, p. 88. Note, however, a major attempt at a theoretical elaboration of the Marxist 'model' of the state, which appeared when the present work was nearing completion, namely N. Poulantzas, *Pouvoir Politique et Classes Sociales*, 1968.

expect it to be if we tried to infer from the dominant forms of the productive process.[1]

This is quite true. Yet, when all such national differences and specificities have been duly taken into account, there remains the fact that advanced capitalism has imposed many fundamental uniformities upon the countries which have come under its sway, and greatly served to attenuate, though not to flatten out, the differences between them. As a result, there has come about a remarkable degree of similarity, not only in economic but in social and even in political terms, between these countries: in many basic ways they inhabit to an increasing degree material and mental worlds which have much in common. As one recent writer puts it:

There are big differences between the key institutions and economic methods of one country and another. The differences are often the subject of sharp ideological cleavages. Yet when the total picture is examined, there is a certain uniformity in the texture of their societies. In terms of what they do, rather than of what they say about it, and even more markedly in terms of their behaviour over a period of years, the similarities are striking.[2]

The most important of these similarities, in economic terms, have already been noted: these are societies with a large, complex, highly integrated and technologically advanced economic base, with industrial production accounting for the largest part by far of their gross national product, and with agriculture constituting a relatively small area of economic activity;[3] and they are also societies in which the main part of economic activity is conducted on the basis of the private ownership and control of the means to such activity.

In regard to the latter point, it is of course the case that advanced capitalist countries now have an often substantial 'public sector', through which the state owns and administers a wide range of industries and services, mainly but not exclusively of an 'infra-structural' kind, which are of vast importance to

[1] Quoted in R. Bendix, *Nation-Building and Citizenship*, 1964, p. 8.
[2] A. Schonfield, *Modern Capitalism*, 1965, p. 65.
[3] Thus, the percentage of gross domestic product originating in agriculture in 1961 was 4 per cent for the United States and Britain, 6 per cent for Federal Germany and 9 per cent for France; the figure for Japan in 1960 was 15 per cent. (B. H. Russett *et al.*, *World Handbook of Political and Social Indicators*, 1964, pp. 163–4).

their economic life; and the state also plays in all capitalist economies an ever-greater economic role by way of regulation, control, coordination, 'planning', and so forth. Similarly, the state is by far the largest customer of the 'private sector'; and some major industries could not survive in the private sector without the state's custom and without the credits, subsidies and benefactions which it dispenses.

This state intervention in every aspect of economic life is nothing new in the history of capitalism. On the contrary, state intervention presided at its birth or at least guided and helped its early steps, not only in such obvious cases as Germany and Japan but in every other capitalist country as well;[1] and it has never ceased to be of crucial importance in the workings of capitalism, even in the country most dedicated to *laissez faire* and rugged individualism.[2] Nevertheless, the scale and pervasiveness of state intervention in contemporary capitalism is now immeasurably greater than ever before, and will undoubtedly continue to grow; and much the same is also true for the vast range of social services for which the state in these societies has come to assume direct or indirect responsibility.[3]

The importance of the 'public sector' and of state intervention in economic life generally is one of the reasons which have been advanced in recent years for the view that 'capitalism' had become a misnomer for the economic system prevailing in these countries. Together with the steadily growing separation between the ownership of capitalist enterprise and its management,[4] public intervention, it has been argued, has radically transformed the capitalism of the bad old days: these countries, as Mr Crosland among others once put it, have become 'post-capitalist' societies, different in kind from what they were in the past, and even as recently as the second world war.

This belief, not simply in the occurrence of major changes in the structure of contemporary capitalism, which are not in question, but in its actual transcendence, in its evolution into an altogether *different* system (and, needless to say, a much *better*

[1] See, e.g. Barrington Moore Jr, *Social Origins of Dictatorship and Democracy*, 1966.
[2] See, e.g. P. K. Crosser, *State Capitalism in the Economy of the United States*, 1960, and G. Kolko, *The Triumph of Conservatism*, 1963.
[3] For a convenient survey, see Schonfield, *Modern Capitalism*.
[4] See below, pp. 28 ff.

one), forms a major element in the pluralist view of Western societies. *This* economic system, unlike the old, is not only differently managed: it has also seen the emergence, in Professor Galbraith's phrase, of effective 'countervailing power' to the power of private capital; and it has also been transformed by state intervention and control. The need to abolish capitalism has, because of all this, conveniently disappeared; the job, for all practical purposes, has already been done. The central problem of politics no longer revolves, in Professor Lipset's words, 'around the changes needed to modify or destroy capitalism and its institutions'; the 'central issue' is rather 'the social and political conditions of bureaucratised society';[1] or as Professor Lipset also writes, 'the fundamental political problems of the industrial revolution have been solved: the workers have achieved industrial and political citizenship; the conservatives have accepted the welfare state; and the democratic left has recognised that an increase in overall state power carried with it more dangers to freedom than solutions for economic problems'.[2] In other words, 'Down with Marx and up with Weber'. And the same belief in the radical transformation of capitalist society has also served to buttress the currently fashionable argument that the really fundamental division in the world is that between 'industrialised' and 'under-industrialised' societies.[3]

It will be argued in later chapters that this belief in the passage of capitalism and of its deficiencies into the historical limbo is exceedingly premature. But the point which needs to be made at the outset, as an essential preliminary corrective, is that notwithstanding the existence of a 'public sector' these are societies in which by far the largest part of economic activity is still dominated by private ownership and enterprise: in *none* of

[1] S.M.Lipset, 'Political Sociology', in R.K.Merton (ed.), *Sociology Today*, 1959, p. 9.

[2] S.M.Lipset, *Political Man*, 1963, p. 406. See also Professor Talcott Parsons: 'Through industrial development under democratic auspices, the most important legitimately-to-be expected aspirations of the "working class" have in fact been realised' (T.Parsons, 'Communism and the West. The Sociology of the Conflict', in A. and E.Etzioni (eds.), *Social Change*, 1964, p. 397).

[3] See for instance Raymond Aron's rejection of 'l'opposition socialisme et capitalisme' and his view of 'socialisme et capitalisme, comme deux modalités d'un même genre, la société industrielle' (R.Aron, *Dix-Huit Leçons sur la Société Industrielle*, 1962, p. 50).

them does the state own more than a subsidiary part of the means of production.[1] In this sense at least, to speak – as is commonly done – of 'mixed economies' is to attribute a special and quite misleading meaning to the notion of mixture.[2] Nor, as will be shown later, has state intervention, regulation and control in economic life, however important it may be, affected the operation of capitalist enterprise in the manner suggested by 'post-capitalist' theorists. Whatever ingenious euphemism may be invented for them, these are still, in all essentials and despite the transformations which they have undergone, authentically capitalist societies.

In all advanced capitalist countries there is to be found a vast scatter of individually or corporately owned small and medium-sized enterprises, running into millions of economic units,[3] constituting a distinct and important part of their economic landscape, and profoundly affecting their social and political landscape as well. No doubt, economic trends are against small and medium-sized business, and many such enterprises are in one way or another dependent upon and subsidiary to large-scale concerns. But their importance in the life of these societies

[1] See, e.g. J.F. Dewhurst *et al.*, *Europe's Needs and Resources. Trends And Prospects in Eighteen Countries*, 1961, pp. 436–42, esp. tables 13–17; also P. Lowell, 'Lessons from Abroad', in M. Shanks (ed.), *Lessons of Public Enterprise*, 1963.

[2] While 'the mixed economy' carries the strongly apologetic implication that capitalism is *really* a thing of the past, 'state monopoly capitalism', which is used in Communist literature to describe advanced capitalism, is intended, on the contrary, to stress the alliance of powerful capitalist forces with the state. The formula, however, is ambiguous, in that it tends to obscure the degree to which 'monopoly capitalism' remains, and is helped by the state to remain, a private affair.

[3] In the United States, Professor C. Kaysen notes, 'there are currently some 4·5 million business enterprises .. more than half of these are small unincorporated firms in retail trade and service. Corporations formed only 13 per cent of the total number; 95 per cent of the unincorporated firms had fewer than twenty employees' (C. Kaysen, 'The Corporation: How Much Power? What Scope', in E. S. Mason (ed.) *The Corporation in Modern Society*, 1960, p. 86). In France, firms employing one to ten workers accounted for 98·3 per cent of all enterprises in 1896, and the percentage in 1958 was still 95·4 per cent. On the other hand, while small firms employed 62·7 per cent of all wage-earners in 1896, this total had dropped to 20 per cent in 1958 (E. Mandel, *Traité d'Economie Marxiste*, 1963, vol. 2, p. 11). According to the Japanese Population Census of 1960, small manufacturers in Japan numbered 2,750,000, of whom only 360,000 were employers. 1,210,000 employed no one at all, and 860,000 employed only members of their own family. There were also 3,440,000 small tradesmen (H. Tamuna, 'Changes in Factors Conditioning the Urban Middle Class', in *Journal of Social and Political Ideas in Japan*, 1963, no. 2, p. 82).

remains considerable and ought not, whether from an economic, social or political point of view, be obscured by the ever greater importance of the giant corporation. The political history of these countries would undoubtedly have been radically different had the concentration of economic power been as rapid and as relentless as Marx thought it must become. In fact, as Professor E. S. Mason has noted for the United States, 'the largest corporations have grown mightily, but so has the economy'.[1]

Nevertheless, advanced capitalism *is* all but synonymous with giant enterprise; and nothing about the economic organisation of these countries is more basically important than the increasing domination of key sectors of their industrial, financial and commercial life by a relatively small number of giant firms, often interlinked. 'A few large corporations,' Professor Carl Kaysen remarks, again in regard to the United States, 'are of overwhelmingly disproportionate importance in our economy, and especially in certain key sectors of it. Whatever aspect of their economic activity we measure – employment, investment, research and development, military supply – we see the same situation.'[2] In the same vein, Professor Galbraith also writes that

... nothing so characterises the industrial system as the scale of the modern corporate enterprise. In 1962 the five largest industrial corporations in the United States, with combined assets in excess of $36 billion, possessed over 12 per cent of all assets used in manufacturing. The fifty largest corporations had over a third of all manufacturing assets. The five hundred largest had well over two-thirds. Corporations with assets in excess of $10,000,000, some two hundred in all, accounted for about 80 per cent of all resources used in manufacturing in the United States. In the mid 1950s, twenty-eight corporations provided approximately 10 per cent of all employment in manufacturing, mining and retail and wholesale trade. Twenty-three corporations provided 15 per cent of all employment in manufacturing. In the first half of the decade (June 1950–June 1956) a hundred firms received two-thirds by value of all defence contracts; ten firms received one-third. In 1960 four corporations accounted for an estimated 22 per cent of all industrial research and development expenditure. Three hundred and eighty-four corpora-

---

[1] Mason, *The Corporation in Modern Society*, p. 10.
[2] Kaysen, *ibid.*, p. 86.

tions employing five thousand or more workers accounted for 55
per cent of these expenditure; 260,000 firms employing fewer than
a thousand accounted for only 7 per cent.[1]

Much the same kind of story is told for other advanced
capitalist countries. Thus, Mr Kidron notes that

> ... in Britain, one hundred and eighty firms employing one-third
> of the labour force in manufacturing accounted for one-half of
> net capital expenditure in 1963; seventy-four of these, with ten
> thousand or more workers each, for two-fifths. Two hundred firms
> produce half manufacturing exports; a dozen as much as a fifth.
> So it is in Germany where the hundred biggest firms were respon-
> sible for nearly two-fifths of industrial turnover, employed one-
> third of the labour force and shipped one-half of manufacturing
> exports in 1960; and where the top fifty had increased their share of
> sales to 29 per cent from 18 per cent in 1954. And so it is almost
> everywhere, the only major exception being France, the traditional
> home of small units; but even there mergers are changing the scene
> fast.[2]

There is every reason to think that this domination of capitalist economies by giant enterprise will become even more
marked in the coming years, not least because state intervention
itself tends, directly or indirectly, to accelerate the process,[3]
notwithstanding the often-expressed intention to protect small
business and to oppose monopoly.

The enormous *political* significance of this concentration of
private economic power in advanced capitalist societies,
including its impact upon the state, is one of the main concerns
of this study. But it must also be noted that the giant corporation is not simply a national phenomenon, affecting only the
economic and political life of separate countries. As long ago
as 1848, Marx and Engels noted in the *Communist Manifesto* the
relentlessly international drives of capitalism and its compulsive
disregard of national boundaries. But this has now assumed

[1] J. K. Galbraith, *The New Industrial State*, 1967, pp. 74–5.

[2] M. Kidron, *Western Capitalism since the War*, 1968, p. 14. In relation to France,
one writer observes that 'mises à part les sociétés dépendantes de l'Etat, une cin-
quantaine de groupes seulement jouent dans l'économie un rôle moteur' (M.
Drancourt, *Les Clés du Pouvoir*, 1964, p. 14). For a general survey of monopolistic
concentration, see Mandel, *Traité d'Economie Marxiste*, vol. 1, chapter 12.

[3] See, e.g. the setting up of the Industrial Reorganisation Corporation by the
Labour government in Britain, with the specific purpose of encouraging mergers.

altogether new dimensions. For it is another major feature of
contemporary capitalism that a growing number of the largest
firms in the capitalist world are assuming an ever more pronounced trans-national character, in terms of ownership and
management. Much of this is the result of the acquisition by
American corporations of a rapidly expanding stake in the
economic life of other advanced capitalist countries, often to the
point of actual control of the latter's major enterprises and
industries.[1] This has aroused a certain degree of national
resistance here and there, but not so as to provide a decisive
check to the process.[2]

At the same time, a similar process of capitalist internationalisation has recently gathered force in Western Europe, sometimes in opposition to American penetration, more often in
conjunction with it. New and formidable capitalist complexes
are thus coming into being in Western Europe, whose trans-
national character has very large implications not only in
economic terms but in political terms as well.[3] The European
Economic Community is one institutional expression of this
phenomenon and represents an attempt to overcome, within
the context of capitalism, one of its major 'contradictions',
namely the constantly more marked obsolescence of the
nation-state as the basic unit of international life.

But advanced capitalism is also international in another,
more traditional sense, namely in that large-scale capitalist
enterprise is deeply implanted in the under-industrialised
areas of the world. The achievement of formal political
independence by these vast zones of exploitation, together with
revolutionary stirrings in many of them, have made the
preservation and the extension of these capitalist interests more
expensive and more precarious than in the past. But for the
present, this Western stake in Latin America, the Middle East,

---

[1] For a recent survey of this massive American implantation in Western Europe,
see J.J.Servan-Schreiber, *Le Défi Américain*, 1967, part I. For Britain, see also J.
Dunning, *American Investment in the British Manufacturing Industry*, 1958, and J.
McMillan and B.Harris, *The American Take-Over of Britain*, 1968.

[2] As a token of the force of this process, and of the irresistible attractions it has for
local capitalist interests, note for instance its advance in Gaullist France, notwithstanding the so-called 'anti-Americanism' of the General.

[3] On which see, e.g. E.Mandel, 'International Capitalism and "Supra-Nation-
ality"', in *The Socialist Register, 1967*.

Africa and Asia remains very large indeed,[1] weighs very deeply upon the foreign policies of capitalist states, and is in fact one of the dominant elements, if not *the* dominant element, of present-day international relations.

III

The common economic characteristics of advanced capitalism provide the countries concerned with a broadly similar 'economic base'. But this 'economic base' also helps to bring about, and is indeed mainly responsible for bringing about, very notable similarities in their social structure and class distribution.

Thus, there is to be found in all these countries a relatively small number of people who own a markedly disproportionate share of personal wealth, and whose income is largely derived from that ownership.[2] Many of these wealthy people also control the uses to which their assets are put. But to an increasing extent, this control is vested in people who though they may themselves be wealthy (and in fact generally are) do not themselves own more than a small part or even sometimes any of the assets which they control and manage. Taken together, here is the class which Marxists have traditionally designated as the 'ruling class' of capitalist countries. Whether owners and controllers *can* thus be assimilated will be discussed in the next chapter; and whether it is in any case appropriate to speak of a 'ruling class' at all in relation to these countries is one of the main themes of this study. But it is at least possible at this stage to note the existence of economic elites which, by virtue of ownership or control or both, do command many of the most important sectors of economic life.

Again, these are countries in which the other end of the social scale is occupied by a working class mostly composed of

[1] See, e.g. P.A. Baran, *The Political Economy of Growth*, 1957; H. Magdoff, 'Economic Aspects of US Imperialism', in *Monthly Review*, 1966, vol. 18, no. 6; and 'The Age of Imperialism' in *Monthly Review*, 1968, vol. 20, nos. 5 and 6; M. Barratt Brown, *After Imperialism*, 1963; and P. Jalée, *The Pillage of the Third World*, 1968, and *Le Tiers Monde dans l'Economie Mondiale*, 1968.

[2] See chapter 2.

industrial workers, with agricultural wage-earners forming a steadily decreasing part of the labour force.[1] In other words, the principal form assumed by the 'relations of production' in these countries is that between capitalist employers and industrial wage-earners. This is one of the main elements of differentiation between advanced capitalist societies and collectivist societies on the one hand, and the pre-industrial societies of the 'Third World' on the other.

Like other classes, the working class of advanced capitalist societies has always been, and remains, highly diversified; and there are also important differences in the internal composition of the working class of one country as compared to another. Yet, and notwithstanding these differences, inside countries and between them, the working class remains everywhere a distinct and specific social formation by virtue of a combination of characteristics which affect its members in comparison with the members of other classes.[2] The most obvious of these characteristics is that here are the people who, generally, 'get least of what there is to get', and who have to work hardest for it. And it is also from their ranks that are, so to speak, recruited the unemployed, the aged poor, the chronically destitute and the sub-proletariat of capitalist society. For all the insistence of growing or achieved 'classlessness' ('we are all working class now') the proletarian condition remains a hard and basic fact in these societies, in the work process, in levels of income, in opportunities or lack of them, in the whole social definition of existence.

The economic and political life of capitalist societies is *primarily* determined by the relationship, born of the capitalist mode of production, between these two classes – the class which on the one hand owns and controls, and the working class on the other. Here are still the social forces whose confrontation most powerfully shapes the social climate and the political system of advanced capitalism. In fact, the political process in these societies is mainly *about* the confrontation of these forces, and is intended to sanction the terms of the relationship between them.

At the same time, it would clearly be misleading to assign a

[1] For some relevant figures, see Russett *et al.*, *World Handbook*, pp. 177–8.
[2] See chapter 2.

merely figurative role to other classes and social formations in capitalist society. They are in fact of considerable importance, not least because they significantly affect the relations between the two 'polar' classes. These are societies of extremely high social density, as might be expected from their economic structure. This high social density naturally finds expression in political terms as well, and greatly helps to prevent the political polarisation of capitalist societies.

The main point to be noted here, however, is that these societies do present a roughly similar social structure, not only in terms of their 'polar' classes but in regard to other classes as well.

Thus, one may distinguish in all capitalist societies a large and growing class of professional people – lawyers, accountants, middle-rank executives, architects, technicians, scientists, administrators, doctors, teachers, etc. – who form one of the two main elements of a 'middle class', whose role in the life of these societies is of great importance, not only in economic terms but in social and political ones too.

The other element of this 'middle class' is associated with small and medium-sized enterprise, to whose numerical importance reference has already been made. Here too there is much disparity, since within this class are to be found business-men employing a few workers and also owners or part-owners of fairly sizeable enterprises of every kind; and to this class may also be assimilated small or medium labour-employing farmers.[1]

But despite such disparities, this business class may also be taken as a distinct element of the socio-economic structure of advanced capitalism: it cannot be assimilated economically and socially with the owners and controllers of large-scale enterprise, or with self-employed shopkeepers, craftsmen and artisans.

The latter have, as a class, been numerically worst affected by the development of capitalism. In all advanced capitalist countries the proportion of self-employed has shown a marked, in some cases a dramatic decrease, as for instance in the United States where it declined from 40·4 per cent in 1870 to 13·3 per cent in 1954.[2]

[1] Large landowners, on the other hand, are more appropriately grouped with the owners and controllers of large-scale enterprise.

[2] K. Mayer, 'Changes in the Social Structure of the United States', in *Transactions of the Third World Congress of Sociology*, 1965, vol. 3, p. 70. For other leading capitalist countries, see Mandel, *Traité d'Economie Marxiste*, vol. 1, pp. 197–8.

Even so, this class of self-employed tradesmen, craftsmen and artisans is still a long way from extinction. One of the constant features in the history of capitalism is, in fact, the tenacious resistance of the 'small man' (and this is also true of the small businessman) to absorption into the ranks of the other-employed, notwithstanding the fact that the rewards are generally small and the toil and nagging anxiety often un-remitting. Here too the direction of the trend should not obscure the continuing existence of this class, one important consequence of which is that it continues to afford, at least to some members of the working classes, a route of escape from the proletarian condition.

The steady decline of the independent self-employed artisan and shopkeeper has been paralleled by the extraordinary growth of a class of office workers, with which may be grouped the sales force of advanced capitalism. This is the class which has absorbed a constantly larger proportion of the labour force, and the inflation of its numbers in the last hundred years is in fact the greatest occupational change which has occurred in capitalist economies.[1]

Werner Sombart's description of this element of the labour force as a class of 'quasi-proletarians' is as apt now for the larger part of it as it was half a century ago. Together with the working class it constitutes the main element of what may properly be called the subordinate classes of advanced capitalist societies. At the same time, its career prospects, conditions of work, status and style of life are on the whole higher than those of the industrial working class;[2] and its own view of itself as definitely *not* of the working class – often its dislike and recoil from it – has had important consequences for the political life of these societies in that it has helped further to prevent the political coalescence of the subordinate classes into anything like a political bloc.

[1] In some countries it constitutes at least a quarter and in the United States a third of the employed population. See e.g. M. Crozier, 'Classes sans Conscience ou Préfiguration de la Société sans Classes', in *Archives Européennes de Sociologie*, 1960, vol. 1, no 2, p. 236; also R. Dahrendorf, 'Recent Changes in the Class Structure of European Societies', in *Daedalus*, Winter 1964, p. 245.

[2] See, S. M. Lipset and R. Bendix, *Social Mobility in Industrial Society*, 1959, pp. 14ff; also R. Sainsaulieu, 'Les Employés à la Recherche de leur Identité', in 'Darras', *Le Partage des Bénéfices. Expansion et Inégalités en France*, 1966.

Finally, these societies all include a lar ge number of 'cultural workmen' – writers, journalists, critics, preachers, poets, intellectuals of one sort or other, who may either be included, in the case of the established and more or less affluent, in the professional middle class, or, for the rest, among independent craftsmen or white collar workers. But this assimilation may be unduly arbitrary and may also tend to obscure the particular role such people play in the life of these societies.[1]

This brief enumeration does not account for every economic, social and occupational group in advanced capitalist society. It does not include, for instance, a sizeable criminal element, of a more or less professional kind, whose role in certain fields of economic activity, notably in the United States, is not negligible. Nor does it include a student population of by now vast and still growing importance numerically and in political terms as well. No more than cultural workmen are these elements readily 'placed' in the social structure.

But the largest omission is that of the people who are professionally concerned with the actual running of the state, either as politicians, or as civil servants, judges and military men. This omission, which is deliberate and which will be made good in later chapters, is not due to the fact that such people are 'classless'. It is rather that their place in the social and political system is of crucial importance in the analysis of the relation of the state to society, and cannot be briefly summarised at this stage.

It may also be noted that the above enumeration reveals nothing about the degree of consciousness which their members have concerning their class position, the particular ideological and political attitudes which that consciousness (or lack of it) may engender, or – consequently – about the actual relations between classes. These are obviously important questions, particularly for the bearing they have on the political process itself. But any answer to these questions must proceed from an initial identification of who the actors in that process actually are. And the need, it should be added, is not less real because many of the actors may not, as it were, know their lines, or because they insist on acting the 'wrong' part. As C. Wright Mills put it.

[1] See chapters 7 and 8.

... the fact that men are not 'class conscious', at all times and in
all places does not mean that 'there are no classes' or that 'in America
everybody is middle class'. The economic and social facts are one
thing. Psychological feelings may or may not be associated with
them in rationally expected ways. Both are important, and if
psychological feelings and political outlooks do not correspond to
economic or occupational class, we must try to find out why, rather
than throw out the economic baby with the psychological bath, and
so fail to understand how either fits into the national tub.[1]

The remark obviously holds also for capitalist countries other
than the United States.

But the point is not only that these countries do have identifiable social classes, whatever the latter's degree of consciousness
of themselves; it is also that the social divisions enumerated
earlier are *common* to all advanced capitalist countries. No doubt
there are variations, of greater or lesser magnitude; but nowhere
are these of a kind to make for *radically* different social structures.

This becomes particularly obvious if comparison is made between these countries, on the one hand, and under-industrialised
or collectivist countries on the other. Thus, many of the classes
which are found in the countries of advanced capitalism are
also found in countries of the Third World, for instance large
property owners, or small businessmen and small traders, or
professional men, or white collar employees, or industrial
workers. But they are found there in altogether different
proportions, most obviously, as already noted, as between
industrial and agricultural workers; or between large-scale
entrepreneurs (where, apart from foreign enterprises, they
exist at all) and large landowners. A class which is of major
importance in advanced capitalism is thus marginal or all but
absent in the conditions of under-industrialisation; while
classes which are of subsidiary importance in the former – for
instance landowners and peasants – are often the major
elements of the social equation in the latter.

The same point, for different reasons, is also true for the
societies of the collectivist world. The official view that these are
societies made up of 'workers, peasants and intellectuals' can
hardly be taken as an exhaustive description of their social
structure. But whatever classification is attempted for them

[1] C. W. Mills, *Power, Politics and People*, ed. by I. L. Horowitz, 1962, p. 317.

must take into account the absence of a class of capitalist owners and employers and the presence, at the apex of the social pyramid, of groups whose pre-eminence derives from a particular political system which also fundamentally affects every other part of the social system. As compared with the countries of advanced capitalism, whatever their own differences from each other, these are essentially different worlds.

While advanced capitalism may thus be said to provide a broadly similar socio-economic environment for the political life of the countries where it prevails, that political life itself has often been exceedingly dissimilar.

This is not only the case in terms of the manifest differences between them in regard to such matters as the relative strength of the executive *vis-à-vis* the legislature, or the existence in some of a two-party system and in others of a multi-party one, or of federal as distinct from unitary arrangements, or of strong versus weak judiciaries. Much more dramatically, advanced capitalism has in the twentieth century provided the context for Nazi rule in Germany and for Stanley Baldwin in Britain, for Franklin Roosevelt in the United States and for the particular brand of authoritarianism which prevailed in Japan in the 1930s. Capitalism, experience has shown again and again, can produce, or if this is too question-begging a phrase can accommodate itself to, many different types of political regime, including ferociously authoritarian ones. The notion that capitalism is incompatible with or that it provides a guarantee against authoritarianism may be good propaganda but it is poor political sociology.

However, while the broadly similar socio-economic structures of advanced capitalism cannot *necessarily* be associated with a particular type of political regime and particular political institutions, they have nevertheless *tended* to do so: and since the second world war at least, *all* advanced capitalist countries have had regimes distinguished by political competition on a more-than-one party basis, the right of opposition, regular elections, representative assemblies, civic guarantees and other restrictions on the use of state power, etc. It is this type of regime which Marx and Engels described, and which Marxists have continued to describe, as 'bourgeois democratic', and which is more familiarly described as simply 'democratic'. The first description is intended to suggest that these are regimes in which an economically dominant class rules *through* democratic institutions, rather than by way of dictatorship; the second is based, *inter alia*, on the claim that they are regimes in which, precisely because of their democratic institutions, no class or group is able to assure its permanent political predominance. The following chapters are intended to elucidate the strength of these respective contentions. At this stage, however, the point to note is that, whether they are thought to be 'bourgeois democratic' or simply 'democratic', these societies do have crucial similarities not only in economic but in political terms as well. It is on this basis that they lend themselves, despite their many specific features, to what may be described as a general political sociology of advanced capitalism.

2

Economic Elites and Dominant Class

In the Marxist scheme, the 'ruling class' of capitalist society is that class which owns and controls the means of production and which is able, by virtue of the economic power thus conferred upon it, to use the state as its instrument for the domination of society. In opposition to this view, the theorists of liberal democracy (and often of social democracy as well) have denied that it was possible to speak in any really meaningful way of *a* capitalist class at all, and that such economic power as could be located in capitalist society was so diffuse, fragmented, competitive, and so much subject to a multitude of counter-vailing checks as to render impossible its hegemonic assertion *vis-à-vis* the state or society. At the most, one might speak, as we noted in the last chapter, of a plurality of competing political and other elites, incapable by the very fact of their competitive plurality, their lack of cohesion and common purpose, of forming a dominant class of any kind.

The first requirement, therefore, is not to determine whether an economically dominant class does wield decisive economic power in these societies. It is rather to determine whether such a class exists at all. Only after this has been decided does it become possible to discuss its political weight.

I

In a famous passage of his Introduction to *Democracy in America*, Alexis de Tocqueville informs the reader that the whole book was written 'under the impression of a kind of religious dread

produced in the author's mind by the contemplation of this
irresistible revolution which has advanced for so many centuries
in spite of all obstacles'.[1] He was of course referring to the
advance of democratic egalitarianism.

That was more than a hundred and thirty years ago. Since
then, men in every generation have echoed de Tocqueville's
belief that equality was irresistibly on the march. Particularly
since the end of the second world war, the view has been most
insistently fostered that a relentless bulldozer was working away
with immense force in all advanced capitalist countries and
bringing into being levelled, egalitarian societies. 'With the
tradition of Stoic-Christian ethics behind it,' one sociologist
writes, 'egalitarianism represents the most potent socio-
political solvent of modern times.'[2] Other writers have attributed the egalitarian drive to less ethereal, more mundane
causes, such as industrialisation, popular pressures, democratic
institutions, etc.; but the belief in the force and effectiveness of
that drive, however varied the causes, has been one of the most
common and pervasive themes of postwar social and political
writing, and may without exaggeration be described as one of
the great 'idées-forces' of the age, which has served to prop up
vast theories about 'mass society', the 'end of ideology', the
transformation of working-class life and consciousness, the
nature of democratic politics in Western societies, and much
else besides. But while there is nothing very new about this
notion of conquering egalitarianism, it was, until recently,
mainly conservative writers who tended to stress how far the
bulldozing process had gone and to bemoan what they held to
be its disastrous consequences. In our time, however, they have
been joined by a multitude of writers who would strongly reject
the conservative label, but who have also proclaimed the actual
or imminent arrival of equality, not however to bemoan it, but
to welcome it. Thus, a whole school of British social-democratic
'revisionists', echoing conservative writers, made it their business in the postwar years to persuade the British labour movement of the dramatic advance towards equality which was
supposed to have occurred in that period.[3]

[1] A. de Tocqueville, *De la Démocratie en Amérique*, 1951, vol. 1, p. 4.
[2] J. H. Meisel, *The Myth of the Ruling Class: Gaetano Mosca and the Elite*, 1962, p. 6.
[3] For a survey of this effort, see J. Saville, 'Labour and Income Redistribution'
in *The Socialist Register, 1965*.

More recent evidence, however, has served to show, in Professor Titmuss's words, that 'we should be much more hesitant in suggesting that any equalising forces at work in Britain since 1938 can be promoted to the status of a "natural law" and projected into the future . . . there are other forces, deeply rooted in the social structure and fed by many institutional factors inherent in large-scale economies, operating in reverse directions'.[1] For the United States, it has been suggested by Professor Kolko that there was 'no significant trend towards income equality' in that country between 1910 and 1959;[2] and another American writer, who strongly contests this view in regard to the earlier part of that period, yet notes that 'in the absence of remedial action, this nation may soon be faced with an increase in the disparity of incomes. We may then discover that our "social revolution" has not only been marking time for twenty years, but that it is also beginning to move backwards'.[3]

Such findings would be much less significant if *existing* economic inequalities were not already very large in advanced capitalist countries: it could then plausibly be argued that, a high degree of equalisation having been achieved at some stage in the past, it was hardly surprising and of no really great moment that further equalisation should not proceed rapidly.

But this cannot be argued, for the fact is that there do exist in these countries very large differences in the distribution of income;[4] and also what Professor Meade has recently called 'a really fantastic inequality in the ownership of property'.[5]

The most obvious example of this latter form of inequality is provided by Britain, where 1 per cent of the population owned 42 per cent of personal wealth in 1960, 5 per cent owned 75 per cent and 10 per cent owned 83 per cent.[6] As for the United

---

[1] R. Titmuss, *Income Distribution and Social Change*, 1965, p. 198. See also R. Blackburn, 'The Unequal Society', in R. Blackburn and A. Cockburn (eds), *The Incompatibles. Trade Union Militancy and the Consensus*, 1967.

[2] G. Kolko, *Wealth and Power in America*, 1962, p. 13.

[3] H. P. Miller, *Rich Man, Poor Man*, 1964, p. 54.

[4] See e.g. Miller, *ibid.*, p. 12.

[5] J. E. Meade, *Efficiency, Equality and the Ownership of Property*, 1964, p. 27. See also J. Revell, *Changes in the Social Distribution of Property in Britain during the Twentieth Century*, 1965.

[6] *Ibid.*, p. 27. The figures for 1911–13 were 69 per cent, 87 per cent and 92 per cent respectively. See also *The Economist*, 'Still no Property-Owning Democracy', 15 January 1966, for figures which suggest even greater inequality.

States, one study notes that the share of wealth accruing to the top 2 per cent of American families in 1953 amounted to 29 per cent (instead of 33 per cent in 1922);[1] and that 1 per cent of adults owned 76 per cent of corporate stock, as compared with 61·5 per cent in 1922.[2] In Britain, only 4 per cent of the adult population held any shares in commercial or industrial companies in the mid-1960s, while in 1961 1 per cent of the adult population owned 81 per cent of privately owned company shares and almost all the rest was owned by the top 10 per cent.[3] Even if it is true that share ownership is now somewhat wider than in the past, this hardly warrants the belief in 'People's Capitalism'. For not only is share ownership still extremely restricted, but also very unbalanced in the sense that the vast majority of shareholders hold very little, while a relatively small number have extremely large holdings.[4]

In short, these are countries where, notwithstanding all levelling proclamations, there continues to exist a relatively small class of people who own large amounts of property in one form or other, and who also receive large incomes, generally derived wholly or in part from their ownership or control of that property.[5]

[1] R. J. Lampman, *The Share of Top Wealth-Holders in National Wealth*, 1962, p. 26.

[2] *Ibid.*, p. 209.

[3] H. F. Liddell and D. G. Tipping, 'The Distribution of Personal Wealth in Britain', in *Bulletin of the Oxford University Institute of Statistics*, 1961, vol. 3, no. 1, p. 91; see also *The Economist*, 'Shareholders: Why so Few', 2 July 1966. The latter also notes that Britain is 'well ahead of Europe. Statistics on European share-holdings are non-existent. But it is safe to say that in Europe investment is largely confined to the comparatively rich' (p. 52).

[4] See e.g. V. Perlo, ' "The People's Capitalism" and Stock-Ownership', in *American Economic Review*, 1958, vol. 48, no. 3.

[5] For Britain, e.g. the 10 per cent of the population which owned 83 per cent of total personal wealth in 1960 received 99 per cent of personal income (before tax) received from property (Meade, *Efficiency, Equality and the Ownership of Property*, p. 27). It is also quite certain that income tax returns greatly understate actual income receipts. For the United States, one writer has observed that 'the record has been unbelievably bad; the revenue service estimates that about $3·3 billion in dividends and interest – much of it paid to wealthy families – goes scot free of taxation in the most blatant kind of cheating operation. This cost to the government in tax revenue is something between $800 million and $1 billion a year' (H. Rowen, *The Free Enterprisers. Kennedy, Johnson and the Business Establishment,* 1964, p. 52). The same author also notes that, according to an Inland Revenue Report of 1961, '48 per cent of returns claiming expense account deductions were faulty, and two-thirds of all deductions disallowed were actually personal expenses and not *bona fide* business items' (*ibid.*, p. 56).

But these are not only countries with a small class of wealthy people: they also include a very large class of people who own very little or next to nothing,[1] and whose income, mostly derived from the sale of their labour, spells considerable material constriction, actual poverty, or destitution.

Poverty, as is often said (not least by people who are not themselves afflicted by it), is a fluid concept. But it is now much more difficult than it was some years ago, when the 'affluent society' was invented, to deny the existence in the societies of advanced capitalism of poverty and deprivation on a huge scale and often of an extreme kind. Since the early 1960s there has appeared enough evidence in regard to countries like Britain, the United States and France to show beyond any question that here is no marginal or residual phenomenon but an endemic condition which affects a substantial part of their populations.[2]

Much has recently been made of the 'consumer revolution' in these countries, and of the 'assimilation of life styles' between classes which it is supposed to have inaugurated.[3] But this insistence on changing consumption patterns is doubly misleading: first, because it systematically understates the vast differences which do continue to exist, both quantitatively and qualitatively, in the consumption possibilities of the working

---

[1] In 1959–60, 87·9 per cent of British taxpayers owned 3·7 per cent of total wealth, the average 'wealth' held being £107 (*The Economist*, 'Still no Property Owning Democracy', 15 January 1966, p. 218).

[2] Thus, the findings of an official Conference on Economic Progress in the United States which reported in 1962 have been summarised as follows: 'Thirty-four million people in families and four million unattached individuals [that is, unattached economically to a family unit] lived in poverty; thirty-seven million people in families and two million unattached individuals lived in deprivation. The total of seventy-seven million comprised two-fifths of the US population in 1960' (H. Magdoff, 'Problems of United States Capitalism', in *The Socialist Register, 1965*, p. 73). 'Deprivation' was held by the Conference to include people living above the stark poverty level but below what a Labour Department investigation found to be a 'modest but adequate' worker's family budget (*ibid.*, p. 73). See also J. N. Morgan, *et al.*, *Income and Welfare in the United States*, 1962; M. Harrington, *The Other America*, 1962; and P. Baran and P. Sweezy, *Monopoly Capital*, 1966. For Britain, see, e.g. B. Abel-Smith and P. Townsend, *The Poor and the Poorest*, 1965; and P. Townsend, *Poverty, Socialism and Labour in Power*, 1967. For France, see P. M. de la Gorce, *La France Pauvre*, 1965.

[3] For a critique of this thesis, see J. H. Goldthorpe and D. Lockwood, 'Affluence and the British Class Structure', in *Sociological Review*, vol. 10, no 2, 1963; and D. Lockwood, 'The "New Working Class"', in *European Journal of Sociology*, vol. 1, no. 2, 1960.

classes and of other classes;[1] and secondly, because access to more goods and services, however desirable it is, does not basically affect the place of the working class in society and the relationship of the world of labour to the world of capital. It may well be true, as Serge Mallet writes, that 'dans les centres de vacances de la Côte d'Azur, de Sicile et de Grèce, de jeunes métallos partagent les bungalows "tahitiens" de filles de directeurs. Ils achètent les mêmes disques et dansent les mêmes rythmes'.[2] But whatever the holiday relationships between 'jeunes metallos' and 'filles de directeurs' may be, the relationship of the former to the 'directeurs' themselves remains the same. Even if the outward and visible manifestations of class were not as conspicuous as they do in fact remain, it would still be quite unwarranted to interpret this as evidence of the erosion, let alone the dissolution, of class divisions which are firmly rooted in the system of ownership of advanced capitalist societies. To achieve their dissolution or even their serious erosion would take rather more than working-class access to refrigerators, television sets, cars, or even 'tahitian' bungalows on the Riviera; and more even than death duties, progressive taxation, and a host of other measures denounced and deplored by the rich as ruinous and crippling, yet which have had no radical impact upon economic inequality—not very surprisingly since this system of ownership operates on the principle that 'to him who hath shall be given', and provides ample opportunities for wealth to beget more wealth.[3]

II

It cannot be seriously disputed that a relatively small class of people do own a very large share of wealth in advanced capitalist countries, and that they do derive many privileges

[1] See e.g. A. Pizzarno, 'The Individualistic Mobilisation of Europe', in *Daedalus*, Winter 1964, pp. 217ff.

[2] S. Mallet, *La Nouvelle Classe Ouvrière*, 1963, p. 8.

[3] 'In real life capitalisms it has taken the utmost efforts of the 90 per cent of the population to prevent their share of the national product from falling, and so to enable their standard of life to rise with the rise of productivity . . . capitalism has in fact an innate tendency to extreme and ever-growing inequality. For how other-

from that ownership. On the other hand, it has often been argued that ownership is now a fact of diminishing significance, not only because it is hinged by a multitude of restrictions – legal, social and political – but also because of the constantly growing separation between the ownership of private wealth and resources and their actual control. Control, the familiar argument goes, has passed or is passing, in crucially important areas of economic life, into the hands of managers who do not themselves own more, at best, than a small part of the assets they command. Thus, while ownership may still confer certain privileges, it no longer affords a decisive element of economic or political power. This, it is said, is a further reason for rejecting not only the notion of a 'ruling class' based upon the ownership of the means of production but of a 'capitalist class' as well. This managerial argument requires further consideration.

That managerialism represents an important phenomenon in the evolution of capitalism is not in doubt. A hundred years ago, Marx had already drawn attention, on the basis of the growth of joint stock enterprise, to 'the transformation of the actually functioning capitalist into a mere manager, administrator of other people's capital, and of the owner of capital into a mere owner, a mere money capitalist'.[1] But Marx was then pointing (with remarkable prescience) to a phenomenon that was then only in its early stages. Since then, and particularly in the last few decades, this separation of ownership and control, at least in large-scale enterprises, has become one of the most important features in the internal organisation of capitalist enterprise.

At the same time it is entirely incorrect to suggest or to imply, as is constantly done, that this process is all but complete, and thus to ignore the continuing importance of what Jean Meynaud calls 'un vigoureux capitalisme familial',[2] not only in regard to small and medium-sized enterprises but to very large ones as well. Thus, it has recently been noted about the United States that 'in approximately one hundred and fifty companies on the current *Fortune* list [i.e. of the five hundred

wise could all these cumulatively equalitarian measures which the popular forces have succeeded in enacting over the last hundred years have done little more than hold the position constant?' (J. Strachey, *Contemporary Capitalism*, 1956, pp. 150–1).

[1] Marx, *Capital*, vol 3, 1962, p. 427.

[2] J. Meynaud, *La Technocratie*, 1964, p. 131.

largest industrial corporations] controlling ownership rests in the hands of an individual or of the members of a single family';[1] and the author adds, not unreasonably, that 'the evidence that 30 per cent of the five hundred largest industrials are clearly controlled by identifiable individuals, or by family groups ... suggests that the demise of the traditional American proprietor has been slightly exaggerated and that the much-advertised triumph of the organisation is far from total'.[2] Similarly, 'at least ten family-controlled companies rank among the top hundred, and several of these are actively owner-managed';[3] and 'approximately seventy family-named companies among the five hundred are still controlled by the founding family'.[4]

These are large qualifications. But it is nevertheless true that at the head of the largest, most dynamic and most powerful concerns of the system are now to be found, and will increasingly be found, managers and executives who owe their position not to ownership but to appointment and co-option. The trend is uneven but it is also very strong and quite irreversible; the alternative to it is not an impossible return to owner-management but public or social ownership and control.

It has, of course, long been recognised that the managerial element is very largely immune from the control and even from the effective pressure of individual shareholders; and the bigger the enterprise, the more dispersed its ownership, the more complete is that immunity likely to be. 'In practice', Adolf Berle writes of the United States, though the point is of general application, 'institutional corporations are guided by tiny, self-perpetuating oligarchies. These in turn are drawn from and judged by the group opinions of a small fragment of America – its business and financial community ... The only real control which guides or limits their economic and social actions is the real, though undefined and tacit, philosophy of the men who compose them'.[5]

From this view of the managerial element as free from the direct pressures of the owners of the property which it controls, it is but a short step to the claim that these managers constitute a

[1] R. Sheehan, 'Proprietors in the World of Big Business', in *Fortune*, 15 June 1967, p. 178.
[2] *Ibid.*, p. 178.　　　[3] *Ibid.*, p. 180.　　　[4] *Ibid.*, p. 182.
[5] A. A. Berle, *The XXth Century Capitalist Revolution*, 1960, p. 180.

distinct economic and social grouping, with impulses, interests or motivations fundamentally different from and even antagonistic to the interests of mere owners – in fact, that they constitute a new class, destined, in the earliest and more extreme versions of the theory of 'managerial revolution', to be not only the repositories of corporate power but to become the rulers of society.

But the theory of managerial capitalism is not only based upon the notion that managers are moved by considerations other than those of owners. It also generally tends, implicitly or quite often explicitly, to claim that managerial motives and impulses are necessarily *better*, less 'selfish', more socially 'responsible', more closely concerned with the 'public interest', than old-style owner capitalism. Thus, the classic statement of the theory of managerialism—Berle and Means' *The Modern Corporation and Private Property* – suggested as early as 1932 that, if the 'corporate system' was to survive, it was 'almost inevitable ... that the "control" of the great corporations should develop into a purely neutral technocracy balancing a variety of claims by various groups in the community and assigning to each a portion of the income stream *on the basis of public policy rather than private cupidity*';[1] and this, they said, was in fact what was already happening. This view has been pushed very hard ever since, so much so that it has now become part of the dominant ideology to represent large-scale capitalist enterprise, as, in Professor Carl Kaysen's phrase, 'the soulful corporation'.[2]

[1] A. A. Berle and G. C. Means, *The Modern Corporation and Private Property*, 1932, p. 356 (my italics).

[2] 'No longer the agent of proprietorship seeking to maximise return on investment', Professor Kaysen writes, 'management sees itself as responsible to stockholders, employees, customers, the general public, and, perhaps, most important, the firm itself as an institution .. there is no display of greed or graspingness; there is no attempt to push off on to workers or the community at large part of the social costs of the enterprise. The modern corporation is a soulful corporation' (C. Kaysen, 'The Social Significance of the Modern Corporation', in *American Economic Review*, May 1957, vol. 47, no. 2, pp. 313–14). See also C. A. R. Crosland, *The Conservative Enemy*, 1962, pp. 88–9: 'Now perhaps most typical amongst very large firms, is the company which pursues rapid growth and high profits – but subject to its "sense of social responsibility" and its desire for good public and labour relations ... Its goals are a "fair" rather than a maximum profit, reasonably rapid growth, and the warm glow which comes from a sense of public duty.' See also F. X. Sutton *et al.*, *The American Business Creed*, 1956, *passim*. For some French versions of the same notion, see, e.g. H. W. Ehrmann, *Organised Business in France*, 1957, *passim*, and R. Barre, 'Le "Jeune Patron" tel qu'il se voit et tel qu'il voudrait être', in *Revue Economique*, 1958, no. 6, pp. 896–911.

The importance of this kind of claim is obvious. For the decisions which the men concerned are called upon to take in the running of vast and powerful industrial, financial and commercial enterprises affect, not only their own organisations, but a much wider area as well, often encompassing the whole of society. But if they are quite as soulful as they are claimed to be, and so deeply conscious, as managers, of their wider, public responsibilities, they may then plausibly be described as eminently trustworthy of the power which accrues to them from the control of corporate resources – indeed as their natural and most suitable custodians; and it can therefore be more easily argued that these responsible men should not be subjected to an undue and unnecessary degree of state 'interference'. No doubt, a substantial measure of state intervention in economic life is now inevitable and even desirable; but even this should only be undertaken on the basis of close cooperation between, on the one hand, ministers and civil servants officially entrusted with the safeguard of the 'public interest', and representatives of business, themselves pulsating with the same concern, on the other. Nor, on the same line of argument, is it surprising that, during the 'revisionist' controversies of the 1950s inside the Labour Party, the opponents of nationalisation should have discovered, in the words of a major policy document of 'Gaitskellite' inspiration, that 'under increasingly professional managements, large firms are as a whole serving the nation well'.[1]

In considering such claims, and the implications which are drawn from them, it may be worth remembering that very similar claims were also made by and on behalf of the now much abused old-style capitalist. Thus, Professor Bendix notes that 'the emergence of the entrepreneurial class as a political force gave rise to an essentially new ideology ... the entrepreneurial claim to authority was changed from a denunciation of the poor and a mere denial of well-publicised abuses into a claim based on moral leadership and authority on behalf of the national interest'.[2] In this perspective, there is little that is new in the propaganda of managerialism, save perhaps in intensity and volume.

---

[1] *Industry and Society*, 1957, p. 48.

[2] R. Bendix, 'The Self-Legitimation of an Entrepreneurial Class in the Case of England', in *Zeitschrift für die Gesammter Staatswissenschaft*, 1954, p. 48. See also the same author's *Work and Authority in Industry*, 1956.

Also, the sharp contrast often drawn in regard to profit between the obsessionally maximising classical capitalist entrepreneur and the coolly detached, public spirited, professional manager, would seem to do the former much injustice.

For the classical entrepreneur's motives and impulses were surely quite as various, complex and possibly contradictory as those of the modern corporate manager. In a famous passage of *Capital*, Marx speaks of the capitalist as being caught in a 'Faustian conflict between the passion for accumulation and the desire for enjoyment',[1] – and 'enjoyment' may here be taken to include a multitude of aims which conflicted with accumulation, or which were felt to be at least as important as profit. An early study of managerial behaviour suggested that 'the most important spurs to action by the businessman, other than the desire for goods for direct want-satisfaction, are probably the following: the urge for power, the desire for prestige and the related impulse of emulation, the creative urge, the propensity to identify oneself with a group and the related feeling of group loyalty, the desire for security, the urge for adventure and for "playing the game" for its own sake, and the desire to serve others ...'[2] Whatever may be thought of this extensive catalogue, it must be obvious that every one of its items would apply just as much to the traditional owner-entrepreneur as to the non-owning manager. Again, an English sociologist writes that whereas under family capitalism the goal of industrial enterprise was 'very definitely defined as profit for the owners of the enterprise, under the present system the goal has become fused with others, perhaps latent earlier, such as productivity, expansion and innovation, with no very clear idea whether they are interrelated or contradictory to one another'.[3] But it seems a very curious notion that the 'family capitalist' was not (or is not) extremely concerned with productivity, expansion and innovation, and that he failed (or fails) to see these as 'fused' with profit.

The 'Faustian conflict' of which Marx spoke no doubt also rages in the breast of the modern corporate manager, even

---

[1] Marx, *Capital*, vol. 1, p. 594.

[2] R. A. Gordon, *Business Leadership in the Large Corporation*, 1945, p. 305.

[3] J. A. Banks, 'The Structure of Industrial Enterprise in Industrial Society', in P. Halmos (ed.), *The Development of Industrial Societies*, 1965, p. 50.

though it may assume a variety of new and different forms. Nevertheless, like the vulgar owner-entrepreneur of the bad old days, the modern manager, however bright and shiny, must also submit to the imperative demands inherent in the system of which he is both master and servant; and the first and most important such demand is that he should make the 'highest possible' profits. Whatever his motives and aims may be, they can only be fulfilled on the basis of his success in this regard. The single, most important purpose of businessmen, whether as owners or managers, must be the pursuit and achievement of the 'highest possible' profits for their own enterprises. Indeed, an economic elite dripping with soulfulness would not, in the nature of the system, know how to pursue a different purpose. For the main, if not the only frame of reference for that elite and for all businessmen, is the individual firm and the profits which can be made for it. This is what, ultimately, their power is for, and to it must be subordinated all other considerations, including the public welfare.

This is not a matter of 'selfishness' in the soul of the entrepreneur or manager; or rather, that 'selfishness' is inherent in the capitalist mode of production and in the policy decisions it dictates.

Like old-style capitalism, managerial capitalism is an atomised system which continues to be marked, which is in fact more than ever marked, by that supreme contradiction of which Marx spoke a hundred years ago, namely the contradiction between its ever more *social* character and its enduringly *private* purpose. It is absurd to think that businessmen, of whatever kind, who are, willy nilly, the main instruments of that contradiction, should also be able to overcome it by some 'soulful' effort of will. For them to do so must entail the denial of the very purpose of their activity, which is the achievement of private profit. As Baran and Sweezy put it, 'profits, even though not the ultimate goal, are the necessary means to all ultimate goals. As such, they become the immediate, unique, unifying, quantitative aim of corporate policies, the touchstone of corporate rationality, the measure of corporate success'.[1] Indeed, the modern manager may well be more vigorous in his pursuit of profit than the old style entrepreneur, because, as

[1] Baran and Sweezy, *Monopoly Capital*, p. 40.

another writer suggests, with 'the rapidly growing use of economists, market analysts, other types of specialists and management
consultants by our larger businesses ... profit-oriented rationality
is more and more representative of business behaviour'.[1]

On this view, shareholders in managerially-controlled
enterprises have no reason to fear that their interests will be
sacrificed on alien altars. Tension may well occur between
managers and shareholders, and may occasionally erupt into
conflict. Shareholders, for instance, may feel that managers are
insufficiently dividend-conscious, or too generous to themselves
by way of emoluments, or too ready to spend money for
purposes not immediately and obviously related to the making
of profit; and managers for their part may feel that shareholders,
or at least those of them who take the trouble to make themselves heard, are a grasping, ignorant and short-sighted
lot. But these are tactical differences within a strategic consensus, and there is anyway precious little that shareholders can
normally do to make effective what discontent they may feel,
save of course to get rid of their shares. Be that as it may, the
fact remains that in any sense that seriously matters it is not
true that the managerial function alienates those who perform
it from those on whose behalf it is performed; the differences of
purpose and motivation which may exist between them are
overshadowed by a basic community of interests.

In any case, the notion of separation can, in terms of
managerial ownership, be pushed much too far. For, as has
often been observed, managers are often large stockholders in
their enterprises. In the United States, Kolko writes, 'the
managerial class is the largest single group in the stockholding
population, and a greater proportion of this class owns stock
than any other'.[2] Moreover, managers are also able, by way
of stock options, to increase their holdings on the most favourable terms.[3] The largest part of managerial income may not

---

[1] J. S. Early, 'Contribution to the discussion on the impact of some new developments in economic theory; exposition and evaluation', in *American Economic Review*,
May 1957, vol. 47, no. 2, pp. 333–4.

[2] Kolko, *Wealth and Power in America*, p. 67. See also C. W. Mills, *The Power Elite*,
1956, pp. 121–2, and D. Villarejo, 'Stock Ownership and the Control of Corporations', in *New University Thought* (Autumn 1961 and Winter 1962), vol. 2, pp. 33–77
and pp. 45–65.

[3] 'A recent study by the National Industrial Conference Board shows that 73
per cent of 215 top executives during the period 1950–60 gained at least 50,000

be derived from share ownership or depend upon such ownership, but managers are hardly likely, all the same, to treat
their shareholdings at any given moment as of negligible
interest.[1] In this light, the picture of the manager as 'separated'
from the resources he controls appears rather overdrawn.

Moreover, high salaries are the common characteristic of the
upper layers of management, in many cases very high salaries
indeed. Thus, one writer notes that 'for leading corporate
executives [in the United States] salaries over a quarter million
dollars annually are fairly common, and higher ones are not
exactly rare. These are exclusive of stock bonuses and stock
options at reduced rates which may effectively double the
executive's income'.[2] Again, of nine hundred top American
executives studied by *Fortune* magazine, 80 per cent were found
to earn more than 50,000 dollars annually, excluding shares,
pensions and retirement provisions, expense accounts, etc.;[3]
and Kolko gives a figure of 73,600 dollars as the median income
for the highest paid seventeen hundred corporation executives
in the United States in 1958.[4] The upper layers of management
may not do quite so well in other advanced capitalist countries,
but they are nevertheless everywhere in the uppermost reaches
of the income pyramid.

Finally, it should also be noted that the social origin of the
managerial element in these countries is generally the same as

dollars through the use of stock options, that 32 per cent gained 250,000 dollars,
and that 8 per cent gained at least 1,000,000 dollars' (R. C. Heilbroner, 'The View
from the Top. Reflections on a Changing Business Ideology', in E. F. Cheit (ed.),
The Business Establishment, 1964, p. 25). By 1957, option plans had been instituted
by 77 per cent of the manufacturing corporations listed in the New York or
American Stock Exchanges (E. F. Cheit, 'The New Place of Business. Why Managers Cultivate Social Responsibility', in Cheit, *ibid.*, p. 178). Kolko also notes
that 'in early 1957, twenty-five General Motors officers owned an average of 11,500
shares each. Collectively their holdings would have been inconsequential if they
had chosen to try and obtain control of G. M. through their stocks. Yet each of these
men had a personal share of roughly half a million dollars in the company . . .'
(*Wealth and Power in America*, p. 65).

[1] As Mr Sheehan remarks, 'Chairman Frederic C. Donner, for example, owns
only 0·017 per cent of G. M.'s outstanding stock, but it was worth about $3,917,000
recently. Chairman Lynn A. Townsend owns 0·117 per cent of Chrysler, worth
about $2,380,000. Their interest in the earnings of those investments is hardly an
impersonal one' ('Proprietors in the World of Big Business', p. 242).

[2] W. E. Moore, *The Conduct of the Corporation*, 1962, p. 13.

[3] S. Keller, *Beyond the Ruling Class*, 1963, p. 224.

[4] Kolko, *Wealth and Power in America*, p. 66.

that of other men of high income and large property. For the
United States, one writer notes, 'as regards the recruitment
of modern industrial managers, three separate studies have
shown roughly the same thing: the majority of the managers of
the biggest corporations come from upper-middle- and upper-
class families, and had fathers in business concerns'.[1] For
Western Europe, Mr Granick observes that 'a major feature of
Continental business, although not particularly of British, is
that all layers of management come primarily from the
bourgeoisie, and that they think and act in terms of private
property which they themselves own'.[2] The exclusion of Britain
from this general pattern does not seem justified. It may well be,
in Mr Guttsman's words, that 'a considerable proportion of
managers has always been recruited from men who had
entered industry on the factory floor – not all of them necessarily the sons of working class families'.[3] But it has also recently
been noted that 64 per cent of the executives of the one hundred
largest British companies bore that significant hallmark of
membership of the upper and upper-middle classes, namely that
they attended public schools.[4] It is obviously the case that 'as
the social scale is ascended chances of getting on the board
greatly improve, from being practically negligible at the bottom
to being extremely good at the top'.[5]

All in all, there would therefore seem to be no good reason to

---

[1] Keller, *Beyond the Ruling Class*, p. 63.
[2] D. Granick, *The European Executive*, 1962, p. 30.
[3] W. L. Guttsman, *The British Political Elite*, 1963, p. 333.
[4] H. Glennerster and R. Pryke, *The Public Schools*, 1965, p. 17.
[5] R. V. Clements, *Managers. A Study of their Career in Industry*, 1958, pp. 83–4.
A recent French study also notes that 'la plupart des dirigeants sont issus de la
bourgeoisie' (N. Delefortrie-Soubeyroux, *Les Dirigeants de l'Industrie Française*,
1961, p. 51). For Japan, the largest proportion by far of business leaders is drawn
from fathers who were themselves executives or owners of large enterprises, with
the sons of landlords and small businessmen second and sons of labourers nowhere
(J. C. Abegglen and H. Mannari; 'Leaders of Modern Japan: Social Origins and
Mobility', in *Economic Development and Cultural Change*, vol. 9, no. 1, part 2 (October
1960), table I, p. 112.) R. P. Dore also notes 'the total absence in the Japanese
sample of the sons of manual labourers and tenant farmers in the recruitment of
contemporary Japanese business leaders' (R. E. Ward and D. A. Rustow (eds.),
Political Modernisation in Japan and Turkey, 1964, p. 203). In the Swedish case, a
survey made in 1958 showed that 3·5 per cent of the directors of industrial enterprises with more than five hundred employees came from the working class, and
that this percentage had been shrinking since the late 1940s (G. Therborn, 'Power
in the Kingdom of Sweden', *International Socialist Journal*, 1965, vol. 2, no. 7, p. 60).

accept as valid the thesis that advanced capitalism has produced a managerial and corporate 'new class', radically or even
substantially distinct from large-scale capitalist owners. In the
passage of *Capital* devoted to the managerial phenomenon,
Marx speaks of the divorce of ownership from management as
'the abolition of the capitalist mode of production within the
capitalist mode of production, and hence a self-dissolving
contradiction, which *prima facie* represents a mere phase of
transition to a new form of production'.[1] A mere phase of
transition it no doubt is. But it is not the managers who will be
the grave-diggers of the old order and who will bring into being
a 'new form of production'. Nor of course did Marx cast the
managers in this unlikely role. Managerialism means that the
most important elements of capitalist property have now grown
too large to be both wholly owned and efficiently run by owner-
entrepreneurs. But it does not in any sense mean the transcendence of capitalism.[2] In the words of Jean Meynaud, 'les
facteurs rapprochant les patrons de style familial et les managers
professionnels sont bien plus forts que les éléments susceptibles
de les diviser: les premiers comme les seconds sont des dirigeants
capitalistes'.[3] The point is just as valid in the field of 'industrial
relations' as in any other. Like all other large employers of
labour, managers in charge of complex, multi-process enterprises have an obvious interest in smooth labour relations and
in the 'routinisation' of conflict inside the firm; and in seeking
to achieve this, they may well see the unions as allies rather
than opponents – or rather as both. But whatever else this may

---

[1] Marx, *Capital*, vol. 1, p. 429.

[2] Professor Galbraith, it may be noted here, has recently argued that managerial
power has actually passed to the 'technostructure', which comprises a 'very large'
group of people, extending 'from the most senior officials of the corporation to
where it meets, at the outer perimeter, the white and blue collar workers whose
function is to conform more or less mechanically to instructions and routine'
(Galbraith, *The New Industrial State*, p. 71). 'It is not the managers who decide.
Effective power of decision is lodged deeply in the technical, planning and other
specialised staffs' (*ibid.*, p. 69). On the evidence, this thesis seems to me to lack any
serious warrant, as I have argued in 'Professor Galbraith and American Capitalism', *The Socialist Register, 1968*.

[3] J. Meynaud, *La Technocratie*, 1964, p. 169. In the article quoted earlier, Mr
Sheehan similarly concludes: 'Very few executives argue that the managers of a
widely held company run their business any differently from the proprietors of a
closely held company'; 'it is unrealistic to assume that because a manager holds
only a small fraction of his company's stock he lacks the incentive to drive up the
profits' ('Proprietors in the World of Big Business', pp. 183, 242).

mean, there is no good evidence that it has caused managerially-run enterprises to be organised differently from owner-managed ones.[1] In both, the work process remains one of domination and subjection: the industrial armies of advanced capitalism, whoever their employers may be, continue to function inside organisations whose patterns of authority they have had no share in bringing into being, and to the determination of whose policies and purposes they have made no contribution.

III

Managers, we have just seen, are mainly drawn from the propertied and professional classes. But this is only one example of a process of recruitment to the ranks of wealth and to the command posts of advanced capitalist society which is typical of these systems – notwithstanding the familiar claim that these are fluid, socially open societies, with a rapid 'circulation of elites'.

In fact, elite recruitment in these societies has a distinctly hereditary character. Access from the working classes into the middle and upper classes is generally low. There is, as Mr Westergaard notes, 'a good deal of movement of individuals between the different strata' but 'much of this movement covers fairly short distances in social space, involves shifts within either the manual or the non-manual group far more often than between them, and is characterised by sharp and persistent inequalities in the distribution of opportunities'.[2] Studies on the basis of data up to 1960 have found that the number of sons of manual workers who were able to make what

---

[1] See, e.g., Serge Mallet, *La Nouvelle Classe Ouvrière*, for some interesting case studies of labour relations in some of the most up-to-date enterprises in France. In one of these studies, Mallet notes that 'the managers and technocrats who run Bull are not theoreticians of neo-capitalism; in no way do they seek to play the rôle of pioneers of labour relations and they use, wherever they are able, the usual methods of direction and discipline...' (p. 81). See also R. Blauner, *Alienation and Freedom. The Factory Worker and his Industry* (1964).

[2] J. Westergaard, 'The Withering Away of Class. A Contemporary Myth', in P. Anderson and R. Blackburn (eds.), *Towards Socialism*, 1965, p. 89. See also, for this intra-class movement, as opposed to inter-class mobility, R. Bendix and S. M. Lipset, *Social Mobility in Industrial Society*, 1964, chapter 1.

Professor Miller calls 'the big leap' into higher business and independent professional occupations was mostly well under 5 per cent, with a high figure of nearly 8 per cent for the United States.[1] It may not be essential, in order to achieve material or professional success, to be born of wealthy or even of well-to-do parents: but it is certainly an enormous advantage, rather like joining a select club, membership of which offers unrivalled opportunities for the consolidation and enhancement of the advantages which it in any case confers.[2]

In a sense, it might even be argued that the spread of managerialism tends to reinforce the advantage of what Harold Laski used to call the careful selection of one's parents. For access to the upper layers of capitalist enterprise of the managerial type increasingly requires, as owner capitalism did not, certain formal educational qualifications which are very much more easily obtained by the children of the well-to-do than by other children – and this is also the case for all other professional qualifications.[3] Educational qualifications are obviously not enough to reach the top layers of management and may still, quite often, be unnecessary. But the trend is clearly towards the professionalisation of business, at least in the sense that getting a start in this particular race increasingly requires the kind of formal educational qualifications which are to be obtained in universities or equivalent institutions; and this is even more true for other elite positions.

But these institutions are still far more accessible to children of upper- and middle-class parents than to children of parents from other classes. Thus one general survey noted a few years ago that:

... the composition of the student body is, in its essentials, the same throughout Western Europe. The upper class and upper-middle class, however defined, are never less than a large minority

---

[1] S. M. Miller, 'Comparative Social Mobility', in *Current Sociology*, 1960, vol. 9, no. 1, pp. 39–40. See also D. V. Glass (ed.), *Social Mobility in Britain* (1954).

[2] 'Self-recruitment – that is, the invisible hand of the family – certainly plays an even larger part in the careers of top people than it does in society in general' (R. Dahrendorf, 'Recent Changes in the Class Structure of European Societies, in *Daedalus*, Winter 1964, p. 235).

[3] Nor is the point irrelevant to politics. As Professor Meynaud notes, 'an education concluded at the primary school level is a serious handicap to a would-be candidate for Parliament' (J. Meynaud, 'The Parliamentary Profession', in *International Social Science Journal*, 1961, vol. 13, no. 4, p. 520).

(45 per cent in Holland) and usually a substantial majority (56 per cent in Sweden, with over 80 per cent in the Mediterranean countries). The balance is chiefly made up by the children of salaried employees, small businessmen and the farming community – the working class, even where it is equally prosperous or nearly so, is poorly represented – at the most 10 per cent to 15 per cent, and more usually 4 per cent to 8 per cent.[1]

For Federal Germany, Professor Dahrendorf has said that:

... until recently only 5 per cent of all German university students came from families which in the total occupational structure account for just over 50 per cent. This proportion has now risen to just over 6 per cent, but this is still exceedingly low.[2]

Two French authors, for their part, have observed that:

... an approximate calculation of chances of access to university according to the father's profession shows that these are of the order of less than 1 per cent for the sons of agricultural wage-earners to nearly 70 per cent for the sons of businessmen and to more than 80 per cent for members of the liberal professions. These statistics clearly demonstrate that the educational system operates, objectively, a process of elimination which is the more thorough as one reaches the most unprivileged classes.[3]

For Britain, the Robbins Report noted in 1963 that:

... the proportion of young people who enter full-time higher education is 45 per cent for those whose fathers are in the 'higher professional' group, compared with only 4 per cent for those whose fathers are in skilled manual occupations.[4]

A comparative survey which included the United States, Federal Germany and France in the postwar years also noted that:

[1] A. Kerr, *Universities of Europe*, 1962, p. 51. For Britain, however, see fn. 2, p. 43.
[2] R. Dahrendorf, 'The Crisis in German Education', in *Journal of Contemporary History*, 1967, vol. 2, no. 3, p. 143.
[3] P. Bourdieu and J. C. Passeron, *Les Héritiers*, 1964, pp. 13–14. See also M. Praderie, 'Héritage Social et Chances d'Ascension' in 'Darras', *Le Partage des Bénéfices*, and H. Girard, *La Réussite Sociale en France*, 1961, pp. 345ff.
[4] *Higher Education*, Cmd. 2154, 1963, p. 51. Two British sociologists have also noted that 'at the extreme of the scale an unskilled manual worker's daughter has a chance of only one in five or six hundred of entering a university – a chance a hundred times lower than if she had been born into a professional family' (A. Little and J. Westergaard, 'The Trend of Class Differentials in Educational Opportunity in England and Wales', in *British Journal of Sociology*, 1964, vol. 15, no. 4, pp. 307–8).

... the general picture ... is one of definite inequalities in opportunities for higher education. The non-farm, non-labour sectors of society supply from three-fifths up to over nine-tenths of the students though this group is a small fraction of any society.[1]

Bendix and Lipset wrote in 1959 about the United States that:

... as in other countries, the overwhelming majority of American university students are children of businessmen, well-to-do farmers, or professionals,[2]

while another writer remarked in 1961 that:

... the odds are almost even that the middle-class American child will get through college, and twelve to one against the working-class child.[3]

This upper- and middle-class predominance in higher education is hardly surprising. Such education requires an earlier preparation which working-class children are least likely to receive. In most cases, these children attend schools which are, in Mr Meyer's apt phrase, 'custodial institutions', where they await the time when school-leaving regulations allow them to assume the role for which their class circumstances destined them from birth, namely that of hewers of wood and drawers of water. What Professor Dahrendorf says in this connection about Federal Germany is of wider application:

German society [he writes] is sometimes described by sociologists, and often believed by our politicians to be virtually classless and it is generally said in political debate that obviously in the modern world, these classes and social strata have disappeared and nowadays everybody has the same opportunity as everyone else and so on. This, it seems to me, turns out to be, if one studies the educational problem, a remarkably ideological view of German society and one which in itself reflects the hope of preserving conditions in which the ambitions of people are limited more or less to their own social sphere, their own social range.[4]

---

[1] C. A. Anderson, 'The Social Status of University Students in Relation to the Type of Economy: an International Comparison', in *Transactions of the Third World Congress of Sociology*, 1956, vol. 5, pp. 51–2.
[2] Bendix and Lipset, *Social Mobility in Industrial Society*, p. 94.
[3] M. Meyer, *The Schools*, 1961, p. 116.
[4] R. Dahrendorf, 'The Crisis in German Education', p. 144. See also H. Adam, 'Social Mobility through Education?' in *International Socialist Journal*, 1964, vol. 1, p. 4.

Of coure, many teachers do seek and are able to fulfil a positive educational role. But the fact remains that working-class children have to contend with an immeasurably less favourable environment than their upper- and middle-class contemporaries, and are subject to a multitude of economic, social and cultural handicaps.[1]

Nevertheless, working-class children do, despite all obstacles, gain access to higher education in steadily growing numbers,[2] not least because advanced capitalism requires better trained personnel than an older industrial system. But as an OECD Report noted in 1967, 'educational expansion *per se* has not necessarily lessened differential participation between classes'.[3] And as higher education spreads, so does an old distinction *between* the institutions which provide it assume a new importance. Some institutions offer much greater facilities of every kind than others, enjoy a much higher prestige than others, and are much more likely to provide recruits for the command posts of society. These establishments, entry to which naturally requires more stringent qualifications than others, are also much more likely to be accessible to upper- and middle-class students than to working-class ones.

Those who fear a 'meritocratic' society in which everyone, starting more or less equally, would be judged on 'merit' alone, need not therefore be unduly alarmed: the race is still rigged – against the working-class competitors.

Even if all this is ignored, it also has to be remembered that a university qualification only offers a *start* in the post-university race. But here too, the race is rigged. For a number of other

[1] See, e.g. J. W. B. Douglas, *The Home and the School*, 1964; J. Floud *et al.*, *Social Class and Education Opportunity*; Bendix and Lipset, *Social Mobility in Industrial Society*, pp. 94–5, fn. 24; *Higher Education*, Appendix I (Cmd 2154–I), part 2, *Factors Influencing Entry to Higher Education*, and Part 3, *The Pool of Ability*; P. Bourdieu, 'La Transmission de l'Héritage Culturel' in 'Darras', *Le Partage des Bénéfices*; and A. Girard, 'Selection for Secondary Education in France', in A. H. Halsey, J. Floud, C. A. Anderson (eds.), *Education, Economy and Society*, 1961, pp. 186ff.

[2] Thus, reporting a UNESCO conference of European Ministers of Education in November 1967, *The Times* correspondent noted that 'over a quarter of the British university population are the sons and daughters of manual workers. This compares with 14 per cent in Sweden, 8·3 per cent in France, and 5·3 per cent in West Germany' (*The Times*, 20 November 1967).

[3] Organisation for Economic Cooperation and Development, *Social Objectives in Educational Planning*, 1967, p. 307.

factors intervene, and materially affect career patterns. One of
these is the network of 'connections' which links members of the
elite groups; in contrast, working-class families do not, on the
whole, have very good connections.

Nor, it might be added, does a greater 'equality of opportunity' have in any case much to do with genuine equality,
given the context in which it occurs. It may enable more
working-class children to reach 'the top'. But this, far from
destroying the class hierarchies of advanced capitalism, helps to
strengthen them. The infusion of new blood into the upper
layers of the economic and social pyramid may present a
competitive threat to individuals who are already there, but is
no threat to the system itself. Even a far more 'meritocratic'
way to the top, grafted to the existing economic system, would
only ensure that a larger number of people of working-class
origin would occupy the top rungs of the *existing* system. This
may be thought desirable, but it would not cause its transformation into a *different* system.

The point, however, remains fairly academic. For the upper
and middle class in these societies, including its entrepreneurial
and managerial element, is still largely self-recruiting and
therefore to a marked degree socially cohesive. Indeed that
class is in one sense now *more* socially cohesive than in the past.
A hundred years ago, the aristocracy still formed a class sharply
distinct, economically and socially, from other classes in most
advanced capitalist societies. Since then, aristocrats have
everywhere been increasingly assimilated to the world of industrial, financial and commercial enterprise and undergone a
process of 'bourgeoisification' which may not yet, in certain
respects, be complete but which is nevertheless very far
advanced. True, aristocracy still carries a good deal of *cachet*,
but the business classes are no longer conscious of being *parvenu*
and socially inferior to any other group or class, even in countries such as Germany and Japan where common businessmen
were until recently greatly overshadowed, in social terms, by an
aristocratic class.

'Before the first world war', Mr Granick notes, 'German
business had utterly failed to establish its prestige within the
upper classes ... between the wars, business became much more
prestigious ... by the 1950s, for the first time in German history,

the traditional pre-industrial upper classes had lost their importance';[1] and a Japanese writer notes of Japan that 'today those who engage in commerce and industry are considered the pillars of the community and find easy entry into the most respected levels of society. Seekers of wealth no longer need be apologetic, for their number is legion. The change in the ethos is but one measure of the rise of business to a position of dominance in the national life'.[2] This process has been somewhat masked in Britain, where successful entrepreneurs have been able to supplement capitalist cash with aristocratic *cachet*, but here too, wealth is an accepted passport to rank.

Similarly, successful entrepreneurs and managers of working-class origin are easily assimilated into the propertied class, both in their style of life and in their outlook. Some may retain a lingering sense of their antecedents, but this is unlikely to be of great consequence, socially or ideologically. Wealth, in this restricted sense at least, is the great leveller.

But wealth is also a great leveller in ideological and political terms. Schumpeter once noted that 'class members ... understand one another better ... look out into the same segment of the world, with the same eyes, from the same point of view, in the same direction'.[3] The point need not be pushed too far. There are other influences than class membership which produce ideological and political congruity between men; and conversely, class membership may not produce such congruity at all. Obviously, members of the propertied classes are often divided over a multitude of specific policies and issues, not to speak of differences in religion and culture.

But neither should *this* point be pushed too far. Professor

---

[1] Granick, *The European Executive*, p. 30. Another writer similarly observes that 'World War II brought the demise of such rival elite groups as the Prussian landed gentry, the officer corps, and the aristocracy. After a few setbacks at the beginning, during the last decade the power of the entrepreneur has risen rapidly, and he can now consider himself an influential person' (G. Braunthal, *The Federation of German Industry in Politics*, 1965, p. 58).

[2] N. Ike, *Japanese Politics*, 1958, p. 82. Another writer notes that 'the top bracket of business executives has largely superseded the older *zaibatsu* families and has become the principal elite in postwar Japan' (A. B. Cole, *Japanese Society and Politics: The Impact of Social Stratification and Mobility on Politics*, 1956, p. 86).

[3] J. Schumpeter, 'Social Classes in an Ethnically Homogeneous Environment', in *Imperialism. Social Classes*, 1955, p. 109.

Aron has ironically complained that one of his 'disappoint-ments' was to discover that those who, 'in the Marxist repre-sentation of the world were supposed to determine the course of events', had in fact 'most often no political conceptions' [*sic*]; 'in regard to most of the great questions discussed in France in the last ten years, it was impossible to say what French capital-ists, large, medium and small, what the "monopolists" and the men of the trusts wanted. I have met some representatives of this "accursed race" and I have never known them to have a definite and unanimous opinion, either on the policy to be followed in Indo-China, or on the policy to be followed in Algeria'.[1]

This is surely a very superficial view. For what divisions there may have existed among the French economic elites about Indo-China or Algeria occurred inside a field of *conservative* options, and severely excluded any other. There may have been some among the members of these elites who wished for rapid decolonisation but history, somehow, does not record a massive degree of pressure on the part of any segment of the French bourgeoisie on behalf of the Vietnamese and Algerian libera-tion struggles – or for the nationalisation of private enterprise, or for a major redistribution of wealth, or for a radical exten-sion of social benefits, or for an extension of trade union rights; and so forth.[2]

Specific differences among dominant classes, however genuine they may be in a variety of ways, are safely contained within a particular ideological spectrum, and do not preclude a basic political consensus in regard to the crucial issues of economic and political life. One obvious manifestation of this fact is the support which dominant classes accord to conserva-tive parties. As will be further discussed later, different segments

[1] R. Aron, *Sociologie des Sociétés Industrielles. Esquisse d'une Théorie des Régimes Politiques*, 1958, p. 81.

[2] In a recent book on Federal Germany, Professor Dahrendorf, like Professor Aron in the case of France, strongly insists on the lack of ideological and political cohesion of the German elites. But he then goes on to refer to the 'agreement by the elites to alter as little as possible the present structures' (R. Dahrendorf, *Society and Democracy in Germany*, 1968, p. 275). This might be thought not to be a bad basis of cohesion. 'Those at the top of German society', he also suggests, 'are essentially strangers to each other' (p. 271). But these 'strangers' have an excellent means of recognition, namely their common wish 'to alter as little as possible the present structures'.

of these classes may support different and competing conservative parties: but they do not very much tend to support anti-conservative ones. In fact, dominant classes have so far fulfilled a great deal better than the proletariat Marx's condition for the existence of a 'class for itself', namely that it should be conscious of its interests as a class: the rich have always been far more 'class conscious' than the poor. This does not mean that they have always known how best to safeguard their interests – classes, like individuals, make mistakes – though their record from this point of view, at least in advanced capitalist countries, is not, demonstrably, particularly bad. But this too does not affect the point that beyond all their differences and disagreements, men of wealth and property have always been fundamentally united, not at all surprisingly, in the defence of the social order which afforded them their privileges. As Professor Kolko puts it for the United States:

... the signal fact of American business history is the consensus among businessmen, of varying degrees of importance and in different industries, that the capitalist system is worth maintaining in one form or another; this has resulted in a general attitude that has not necessarily been opposed to decisive innovation in the economic sphere, but which has opposed radical economic programmes that might, in the process of altering the concentration of economic power, also undermine the stability, if not the very existence of the status quo.[1]

Nor, it should be added, is there the slightest evidence to suggest that the managerial element in capitalist society deviates in any respect from this underlying agreement on the need to preserve and strengthen the private ownership and control of the largest possible part of society's resources, and, as was noted earlier, on the need to enhance to the highest possible point the profits which accrue from that ownership and control.

Even so, it may readily be granted that there does exist a plurality of economic elites in advanced capitalist societies; and that despite the integrating tendencies of advanced capitalism these elites constitute distinct groupings and interests, whose competition greatly affects the political process. This 'elite pluralism' does not, however, prevent the separate elites in

[1] Kolko, *The Triumph of Conservatism*, p. 12.

capitalist society from constituting a dominant economic class, possessed of a high degree of cohesion and solidarity, with common interests and common purposes which far transcend their specific differences and disagreements.

In the context of the present study, the most important of all questions raised by the existence of this dominant class is whether it also constitutes a 'ruling class'. The question is not whether this class has a *substantial* measure of political power and influence. No one can seriously deny that it has: at least, no one should be taken seriously who does deny it. The question is a different one altogether, namely whether this dominant class also exercises a much greater degree of power and influence than any other class; whether it exercises as *decisive* degree of political power; whether its ownership and control of crucially important areas of economic life also insures its control of the means of political decision-making in the particular political environment of advanced capitalism. This brings us back to the nature and role of the state in these societies.

3

The State System and the State Elite

There is one preliminary problem about the state which is very seldom considered, yet which requires attention if the discussion of its nature and role is to be properly focused. This is the fact that 'the state' is not a thing, that it does not, as such, exist. What 'the state' stands for is a number of particular institutions which, together, constitute its reality, and which interact as parts of what may be called the state system.

The point is by no means academic. For the treatment of one part of the state – usually the government – as the state itself introduces a major element of confusion in the discussion of the nature and incidence of state *power;* and that confusion can have large political consequences. Thus, if it is believed that the government is in fact the state, it may also be believed that the assumption of governmental power is equivalent to the acquisition of state power. Such a belief, resting as it does on vast assumptions about the nature of state power, is fraught with great risks and disappointments. To understand the nature of state power, it is necessary first of all to distinguish, and then to relate, the various elements which make up the state system.

It is not very surprising that government and state should often appear as synonymous. For it is the government which speaks on the state's behalf. It was the state to which Weber was referring when he said, in a famous phrase, that, in order to be, it must 'successfully claim the monopoly of the legitimate use of physical force within a given territory'. But 'the state' cannot claim anything: only the government of the day, or its duly empowered agents, can. Men, it is often said, give their allegiance not to the government of the day but to the state. But the state, from this point of view, is a nebulous entity; and while men may choose to give their allegiance to it, it is to the government that they are required to give their obedience. A defiance of its orders is a defiance of the state, in whose name the government alone may speak and for whose actions it must assume ultimate responsibility.

This, however, does not mean that the government is necessarily strong, either in relation to other elements of the state system or to forces outside it. On the contrary, it may be very weak, and provide a mere façade for one or other of these other elements and forces. In other words, the fact that the government does speak in the name of the state and is formally *invested* with state power, does not mean that it effectively *controls* that power. How far governments do control it is one of the major questions to be determined.

A second element of the state system which requires investigation is the administrative one, which now extends far beyond the traditional bureaucracy of the state, and which encompasses a large variety of bodies, often related to particular ministerial departments, or enjoying a greater or lesser degree of autonomy – public corporations, central banks, regulatory commissions, etc. – and concerned with the management of the economic, social, cultural and other activities in which the state is now directly or indirectly involved. The extraordinary growth of this administrative and bureaucratic element in all societies, including advanced capitalist ones, is of course one of the most obvious features of contemporary life; and the relation of its leading members to the government and to society is also crucial to the determination of the role of the state.

Formally, officialdom is at the service of the political executive, its obedient instrument, the tool of its will. In actual fact it is nothing of the kind. Everywhere and inevitably the administrative process is also part of the political process; administration is always political as well as executive, at least at the levels where policy-making is relevant, that is to say in the upper layers of administrative life. That this is so is not necessarily due to administrators' desire that it should be so. On the contrary, many of them may well wish to shun 'politics' altogether and to leave 'political' matters to the politicians;

or alternatively to 'depoliticise' the issues under discussion. Karl Mannheim once noted that 'the fundamental tendency of all bureaucratic thought is to turn all problems of politics into problems of administration'.[1] But this, for the most part, merely means that political considerations, attitudes and assumptions are incorporated, consciously or not, into the 'problems of administration', and correspondingly affect the nature of administrative advice and action. Officials and administrators cannot divest themselves of all ideological clothing in the advice which they tender to their political masters, or in the independent decisions which they are in a position to take. The power which top civil servants and other state administrators possess no doubt varies from country to country, from department to department, and from individual to individual. But nowhere do these men *not* contribute directly and appreciably to the exercise of state power. If the regime is weak, with a rapid ministerial turnover, and with no possibility of sustained ministerial direction, as happened under the French Fourth Republic, civil servants will step into the vacuum and play an often dominant part in decision-making. But even where the political executive is strong and stable, top administrators are still able to play an important role in critical areas of policy by tendering advice which governments often find it very difficult, for one reason or another, to discount. However much argument there may be over the nature and extent of bureaucratic power in these societies, the range of possibilities must exclude the idea that top civil servants can be reduced to the role of mere instruments of policy. As Professor Meynaud notes, 'the establishment of an absolute separation between the political and administrative sectors has never represented much more than a simple juridical fiction of which the ideological consequences are not negligible'.[2]

Some of these considerations apply to all other elements of the state system. They apply for instance to a third such element, namely the military, to which may, for present purposes, be added the para-military, security and police forces of the state, and which together form that branch of it mainly concerned with the 'management of violence'.

---

[1] K. Mannheim, *Ideology and Utopia*, 1952, p. 105.
[2] Meynaud, *La Technocratie*, p. 68.

In most capitalist countries, this coercive apparatus con-
stitues a vast, sprawling and resourceful establishment, whose
professional leaders are men of high status and great influence,
inside the state system and in society. Nowhere has the inflation
of the military establishment been more marked since the
second world war than in the United States, a country which
had previously been highly civilian-oriented.[1] And much the
same kind of inflation has also occurred in the forces of 'internal
security', not only in the United States; it is probably the case
that never before in any capitalist country, save in Fascist Italy
and Nazi Germany, has such a large proportion of people been
employed on police and repressive duties of one kind or another.

Whatever may be the case in practice, the formal constitutional position of the administrative and coercive elements is to
serve the state by serving the government of the day. In contrast,
it is not at all the formal constitutional duty of judges, at least
in Western-type political systems, to serve the purposes of their
governments. They are constitutionally independent of the
political executive and protected from it by security of tenure
and other guarantees. Indeed, the concept of judicial independence is deemed to entail not merely the freedom of
judges from responsibility to the political executive, but their
active duty to protect the citizen *against* the political executive
or its agents, and to act, in the state's encounter with members
of society, as the defenders of the latter's rights and liberties.
This, as we shall see, can mean many different things. But in
any case, the judiciary is an integral part of the state system,
which affects, often profoundly, the exercise of state power.

So too, to a greater or lesser degree, does a fifth element of the
state system, namely the various units of sub-central government. In one of its aspects, sub-central government constitutes
an extension of central government and administration, the
latter's antennae or tentacles. In some political systems it has
indeed practically no other function. In the countries of advanced capitalism, on the other hand, sub-central government
is rather more than an administrative device. In addition to
being agents of the state these units of government have also
traditionally performed another function. They have not only
been the channels of communication and administration from

[1] See Mills, *The Power Elite*, chapter 8.

the centre to the periphery, but also the voice of the periphery, or of particular interests at the periphery; they have been a means of overcoming local particularities, but also platforms for their expression, instruments of central control and obstacles to it. For all the centralisation of power, which is a major feature of government in these countries, sub-central organs of government, notably in federal systems such as that of the United States, have remained power structures in their own right, and therefore able to affect very markedly the lives of the populations they have governed.

Much the same point may be made about the representative assemblies of advanced capitalism. Now more than ever their life revolves around the government; and even where, as in the United States, they are formally independent organs of constitutional and political power, their relationship with the political executive cannot be a purely critical or obstructive one. That relationship is one of conflict *and* cooperation.

Nor is this a matter of division between a pro-government side and an anti-government one. *Both* sides reflect this duality. For opposition parties cannot be wholly uncooperative. Merely by taking part in the work of the legislature, they help the government's business. This is one of the main problems of revolutionary parties. As they enter existing parliamentary bodies, so are they also compelled, however reluctantly, to take a share in their work which cannot be purely obstructive. They may judge the price worth paying. But by entering the parliamentary arena they make at least a particular political game possible, and must play it according to rules which are not of their own choosing.

As for government parties, they are seldom if ever single-minded in their support of the political executive and altogether subservient to it. They include people who, by virtue of their position and influence must be persuaded, cajoled, threatened or bought off.

It is in the constitutionally-sanctioned performance of this cooperative and critical function that legislative assemblies have a share in the exercise of state power. That share is rather less extensive and exalted than is often claimed for these bodies. But, as will be further argued presently, it is not, even in an epoch of executive dominance, an unimportant one.

These are the institutions – the government, the administration, the military and the police, the judicial branch, sub-central government and parliamentary assemblies—which make up 'the state', and whose interrelationship shapes the form of the state system. It is these institutions in which 'state power' lies, and it is through them that this power is wielded in its different manifestations by the people who occupy the leading positions in each of these institutions – presidents, prime ministers and their ministerial colleagues; high civil servants and other state administrators; top military men; judges of the higher courts; some at least of the leading members of parliamentary assemblies, though these are often the same men as the senior members of the political executive; and, a long way behind, particularly in unitary states, the political and administrative leaders of sub-central units of the state. These are the people who constitute what may be described as the state elite.

Of course, the state system is not synonymous with the political system. The latter includes many institutions, for instance parties and pressure groups, which are of major importance in the political process, and which vitally affect the operation of the state system. And so do many other institutions which are not 'political' at all, for instance, giant corporations, Churches, the mass media, etc. Obviously the men who head these institutions may wield considerable power and influence, which must be integrated in the analysis of political power in advanced capitalist societies.

Yet while there are many men who have power outside the state system and whose power greatly affects it, they are not the actual repositories of state power; and for the purpose of analysing the role of the state in these societies, it is necessary to treat the state elite, which does wield state power, as a distinct and separate entity.

It is particularly necessary to do so in analysing the relationship of the state to the economically dominant class. For the first step in that analysis is to note the obvious but fundamental fact that this class is involved in a *relationship* with the state, which cannot be *assumed*, in the political conditions which are typical of advanced capitalism, to be that of principal to agent. It may well be found that the relationship is very close indeed and that the holders of state power are, for many different reasons, the agents of private economic power – that those who wield that power are also, therefore, and without unduly stretching the meaning of words, an authentic 'ruling class'. But this is precisely what has to be *determined*.

II

Writing in 1902, Karl Kautsky observed that 'the capitalist class rules but does not govern', though he added immediately that 'it contents itself with ruling the government'.[1] This is the proposition which has to be tested. But it is obviously true that the capitalist class, as a class, does not actually 'govern'. One must go back to isolated instances of the early history of capitalism, such as the commercial patriciates of cities like Venice and Lübeck, to discover direct and sovereign rule by businessmen.[2] Apart from these cases, the capitalist class has generally confronted the state as a separate entity – even, in the days of its rise to power, as an alien and often hostile element, often under the control and influence of an established and landowning class, whose hold upon the state power had to be broken by revolution, as in France, or by erosion, as in England in the nineteenth century,[3] that process of erosion being greatly facilitated, in the English case, by the constitutional and political changes wrought by violence in the seventeenth century.[4]

Nor has it come to be the case, even in the epoch of advanced capitalism, that businessmen have themselves assumed the major share of government. On the other hand, they have generally been well represented in the political executive and in other parts of the state system as well; and this has been particularly true in the recent history of advanced capitalism.

This entry of businessmen in the state system has often been greatly underestimated. Max Weber, for instance, believed that industrialists had neither the time nor the particular qualities

[1] K. Kautsky, *The Social Revolution*, 1903, p. 13.
[2] See, e.g. O. C. Cox, *The Foundations of Capitalism*, 1959.
[3] See, e.g. J. D. Kingsley, *Representative Bureaucracy*, 1944.
[4] On which see, e.g. Barrington Moore Jr, *Social Origins of Dictatorship and Democracy*, chapter 1.

required for political life;[1] and Schumpeter wrote of the 'industrialist and merchant' that 'there is surely no trace of any mystic glamour about him which is what counts in the ruling of men. The stock exchange is a poor substitute for the Holy Grail ... A genius in the business office may be, and often is, utterly unable outside of it to say boo to a goose – both in the drawing-room and on the platform. Knowing this he wants to be left alone and to leave politics alone'.[2] Less dramatically but no less definitely, Raymond Aron has more recently written of businessmen that 'they have governed neither Germany, nor France, nor even England. They certainly played a decisive role in the management of the means of production, in social life. But what is characteristic of them as a socially dominant class is that, in the majority of countries, they have not themselves wanted to assume political functions'.[3]

Businessmen themselves have often tended to stress their remoteness from, even their distaste for, 'politics'; and they have also tended to have a poor view of politicians as men who, in the hallowed phrase, have never had to meet a payroll and who therefore know very little of the *real* world – yet who seek to interfere in the affairs of the hard-headed and practical men whose business it is to meet a payroll, and who therefore do know what the world is about. What this means is that businessmen, like administrators, wish to 'depoliticise' highly contentious issues and to have these issues judged according to the criteria favoured by business. This may look like an avoidance of politics and ideology: it is in fact their clandestine importation into public affairs.

In any case, the notion of businessmen as remote from political affairs, in a direct and personal way, greatly exaggerates their reluctance to seek political power; and equally underestimates how often the search has been successful.

In the United States, businessmen were in fact the largest single occupational group in cabinets from 1889 to 1949; of the total number of cabinet members between these dates, more than 60 per cent were businessmen of one sort or another.[4] Nor

---

[1] R. Bendix, *Max Weber; An Intellectual Portrait*, 1960, p. 436.
[2] J. Schumpeter, *Capitalism, Socialism and Democracy*, 1950, pp. 137–8.
[3] R. Aron, *La Lutte des Classes*, 1964, p. 280.
[4] H. D. Lasswell, *et al.*, *The Comparative Study of Elites* , 1952, p. 30.

certainly was the business membership of American cabinets less marked in the Eisenhower years from 1953 to 1961.[1] As for members of British cabinets between 1886 and 1950, close to one-third were businessmen, including three prime ministers – Bonar Law, Baldwin and Chamberlain.[2] Nor again have businessmen been at all badly represented in the Conservative cabinets which held office between 1951 and 1964. And while businessmen have, in this respect, done rather less well in some other advanced capitalist countries, nowhere has their representation been negligible.

But the government itself is by no means the only part of the state system in which businessmen have had a direct say. Indeed, one of the most notable features of advanced capitalism is precisely what might be called without much exaggeration their growing colonisation of the upper reaches of the administrative part of that system.

State intervention has gone further and assumed more elaborate institutional forms in France than anywhere else in the capitalist world.[3] But both in the elaboration of the French Plans and in their execution, men belonging to the world of business, and particularly of big business, have enjoyed a marked, almost an overwhelming preponderance over any other occupational or 'sectional' group. As Mr Schonfield notes, 'in some ways, the development of French planning in the 1950s can be viewed as an act of voluntary collusion between senior civil servants and the senior managers of big business. The politicians and the representatives of organised labour were both largely passed by'.[4]

Much the same kind of business predominance over other economic groups is to be found in the financial and credit

---

[1] See, e.g. Mills, *The Power Elite*, pp. 232ff.

[2] Lasswell, *et al.*, *The Comparative Study of Elites*, p. 30. See also Guttsman, *The British Political Elite*, pp. 92ff.

[3] Even here, however, the notion of 'planning' ought not to be invested with too positive a meaning: see, e.g., J. Sheahan, *Promotion and Control of Industry in Post-War France*, 1963, who notes that 'throughout the 1950's, the French technique of planning used a mild system of differential favours to secure cooperation, but attached no direct penalties to the refusal to cooperate' (p. 181); the same author also describes French 'planners' as a 'group of well intentioned and intelligent people trying to help clarify alternatives for government and business' (p. 181).

[4] Schonfield, *Modern Capitalism*, p. 128.

institutions of the state,[1] and in the nationalised sector.[2] The creation of that sector has often been thought of as removing an important area of economic activity from capitalist control and influence. But quite apart from all the other forces which prevent a subsidiary nationalised sector from being run on other than orthodox lines, there is also the fact that business has carved out an extremely strong place for itself in the directing organs of that sector; or rather, that business has been invited by governments, whatever their political coloration, to assume a major role in the management and control of the public sector.[3] In comparison, representatives of labour have appeared as very poor parents indeed – not, it should be added, that the entry of a greater number of 'safe' trade union leaders would make much difference to the orientation of institutions which are, in effect, an integral part of the capitalist system.

The notion that businessmen are not directly involved in government and administration (and also in parliamentary assemblies[4]) is obviously false. They are thus involved, ever more closely as the state becomes more closely concerned with economic life; wherever the state 'intervenes', there also, in an exceptionally strong position as compared with other economic groups, will businessmen be found to influence and even to determine the nature of that intervention.

It may readily be granted that businessmen who enter the state system, in whatever capacity, may not think of themselves as representatives of business in general or even less of their own industries or firms in particular.[5] But even though the *will* to think in 'national' terms may well be strong, businessmen involved in government and administration are not very likely, all the same, to find much merit in policies which appear to run

[1] For Britain see, e.g. S. Wilson and T. Lupton, 'The Social Background and Connections of "Top Decision-Makers" ', in *The Manchester School of Economic and Social Studies*, vol. 27, 1959.

[2] See, e.g. *Universities and Left Review, The Insiders* (n.d.); C. Jenkins, *Power at the Top*, 1959; and J. Hughes, *Nationalised Industries in the Mixed Economy*, 1960.

[3] A typical recent example being the appointment by the Wilson government of an eminent businessman, with no Labour connections, to head the newly-nationalised (or rather re-nationalised) Steel Corporation.

[4] See below, p. 66.

[5] Note, however, the conclusion reached by a Senate investigating committee that, in the Second World War, 'dollar-a-year men (as they were then called) were "persons with axes to grind" and "lobbyists" ' (D. C. Blaisdell, *American Democracy under Pressure*, 1950, p. 190).

counter to what they conceive to be the interests of business, much less to make themselves the advocates of such policies, since they are almost by definition most likely to believe such policies to be inimical to the 'national interest'. It is much easier for businessmen, where required, to divest themselves of stocks and shares as a kind of *rite de passage* into government service than to divest themselves of a particular view of the world, and of the place of business in it.

Notwithstanding the substantial participation of businessmen in the business of the state, it is however true that they have never constituted, and do not constitute now, more than a relatively small minority of the state elite as a whole. It is in this sense that the economic elites of advanced capitalist countries are not, properly speaking, a 'governing' class, comparable to pre-industrial, aristocratic and landowning classes. In some cases, the latter were able, almost, to dispense with a distinct and fully articulated state machinery and were themselves practically the state.[1] Capitalist economic elites have not achieved, and in the nature of capitalist society could never achieve, such a position.

However, the significance of this relative distance of business-men from the state system is markedly reduced by the social composition of the state elite proper. For businessmen belong, in economic and social terms, to the upper and middle classes – and it is also from these classes that the members of the state elite are predominantly, not to say overwhelmingly, drawn. The pattern is monotonously similar for all capitalist countries and applies not only to the administrative, military and judicial elites, which are insulated from universal suffrage and political competition, but to the political and elective ones as

---

[1] Thus, Professor Habbakuk writes of England in the eighteenth century that 'the English landowners were the governing class of the country. Ministers were drawn usually from the great families and though the property qualifications imposed by the Act of 1711 were easily evaded, the normal social and political processes ensured that most MP's came from landed families. Local government likewise was in the hands, not of a bureaucracy, but of Justices of the Peace, who were generally landowners. The land tax was administered by the same class, and even in those departments which were staffed by professionals, the more important and dignified posts were often filled from landowning families' (H.J.Habbakuk, 'England', in A.Goodwin (ed.), *The European Nobility in the 18th Century*, 1953, pp. 11–12). Landed families, it should also be noted, predominated in the Army, the Navy and the Church.

well, which are not. Everywhere and in all its elements the
state system has retained, socially speaking, a most markedly
upper- and middle-class character, with a slowly diminishing
aristocratic element at one end, and a slowly growing working-
class and lower-middle-class element at the other. The area of
recruitment is much more narrow than is often suggested. As
Professor Dahrendorf notes, 'the "middle class" that forms the
main recruiting ground of the power elite of most European
countries today, often consists of the top 5 per cent of the
occupational hierarchy in terms of prestige, income and
influence'.[1]

One main reason for this bourgeois predominance in the
appointive institutions of the state system has already been
discussed in relation to the economic and social hierarchies
outside that system, namely that children born of upper- and
middle-class parents have a vastly better chance of access than
other children to the kind of education and training which is
required for the achievement of elite positions in the state
system. Greatly unequal opportunities in education also find
reflection in the recruitment to the state service, since qualifications which are only obtainable in institutions of higher
education are a *sine qua non* for entry into that service.

Thus in France the main means of entry to top administrative
positions is the Ecole Nationale d'Administration. But Professor
Meynaud notes that in the year 1962, fifty-six out of seventy-one
university students who were successful in the examinations for
admission to the E.N.A. belonged by social origin to 'la partie
la plus favorisée de la population'; and of the twenty-two
successful candidates from the civil service itself, ten belonged
to the same class. Of the university students who presented
themselves, there was not a single one whose parents were
workers or peasants. 'Dans l'ensemble,' Meynaud comments,
'la sélection sociale de la haute fonction publique reste essen-
tiellement inégalitaire. Autrement dit, malgré la réforme de
1945, la "démocratisation" demeure très limitée.'[2] The same

---

[1] Dahrendorf, 'Recent Changes in the Class Structure of European Societies',
p. 238.

[2] Meynaud, *La Technocratie*, p. 51. Another writer notes that for the years 1952–8,
about 60 per cent of the 547 successful candidates for admission to the E.N.A.
belonged to 'les milieux à la fois les moins nombreux et les plus élevés dans la
hiérarchie sociale, fonctionnaires des catégories A1 et 2, cadres et chefs d'entreprise'

is also true of the French military[1] and of the French judiciary.[2]

Not of course that France is notably more 'undemocratic' in this respect than other capitalist countries. Thus the bulk of British higher civil servants has to a remarkable degree continued to be drawn from a narrowly restricted segment of the population, much of it public school and Oxbridge educated;[3] and the same marked upper- and middle-class bias has remained evident in the higher reaches of the British army[4] and the judiciary.[5]

The picture is not appreciably different for the United States, where the kind of inequality of educational opportunity which was mentioned in the last chapter has also helped to narrow the area of recruitment to the state service. As Professor Matthews notes:

Those American political decision-makers[6] *for whom this information is available* are, with very few exceptions, sons of professional men, proprietors and officials, and farmers. A very small minority were sons of wage-earners, low salaried workers, farm labourers or tenants ... the narrow base from which political decision-makers appear to be recruited is clear.[7]

In the case of the United States military it has also been noted that:

(A. Girard, *La Réussite Sociale en France*, 1961, p. 308). See also F. Bon and M. A. Burnier, *Les Nouveaux Intellectuels*, 1966; T. B. Bottomore, 'Higher Civil Servants in France', in *Transactions of the Second World Congress of Sociology*, 1953; and P. Lalumière, *L'Inspection des Finances*, 1959.

[1] See, e.g. R. Girardet, *La Crise Militaire Française 1945-1962*, 1964, pp. 39-46. Another writer notes, however, that 'in regard to social origins the centre of gravity for the army officer corps as a whole, following a pattern typical for a period of low military prestige, had probably sunk to the lower-middle class by the late 1950s. Yet in the higher grades the middle and upper bourgeoisie, and to a lesser degree the noble aristocracy, were still well represented, though in decline' (J. S. Ambler, *The French Army in Politics 1945-1962*, p. 134).

[2] See, e.g. Girard, *La Réussite Sociale en France*, p. 336.

[3] See, e.g. R. K. Kelsall, *The Higher Civil Servants in Britain*, 1955; Wilson and Lupton, 'Top Decision Makers', in *The Manchester School of Economics and Social Studies*, vol. 27, 1959; and 'Recruitment to the Civil Service', 6th Report of the Committee on Estimates, H. C. 308, 1964-5.

[4] See, e.g. J. Harvey and K. Hood, *The British State*, 1958, pp. 112ff.

[5] No less than 76 per cent of judges in 1956 had been educated at public schools (Glennerster and Pryke, *The Public Schools*, p. 17). See also 'Well-Bred Law' in *The Sunday Times*, 18 August 1963.

[6] 'Political decision-makers' here includes 'high level civil servants'.

[7] D. R. Matthews, *The Social Background of Political Decision-Makers*, 1954, pp. 23-4 (italics in text).

... on the whole, the high officers of the army and navy have been men of the upper-middle rather than truly higher or definitely lower classes. Only a very small percentage of them are of working-class origin.[1]

As for Supreme Court Justices, it has been remarked that:

... throughout American history there has been an overwhelming tendency for presidents to choose nominees for the Supreme Court from among the socially advantaged families ... In the earlier history of the Court he very likely was born in the aristocratic gentry class, although later he tended to come from the professional upper-middle class.[2]

The same kind of upper- and middle-class preponderance is yet again encountered in Federal Germany:

... while less than 1 per cent of the present population of the Federal republic [one writer notes] carries a 'von' in the family name, the bearers of aristocratic titles may actually have increased among senior civil servants. Senior civil servants claiming descent from working-class families remain as conspicuous by their absence as ever.[3]

Similarly, Professor Dahrendorf notes that:

... despite the break up of the old monopoly and the consequent dwindling significance of nobility, German elite groups from 1918 to the present [including the state elite] have been consistently recruited to a disproportionately great extent from middle and higher groups of the service class and the middle class as well as from their own predecessors in elite positions.[4]

---

[1] Mills, *The Power Elite*, p. 192. Professor Janowitz also notes that 'American military leaders traditionally have come from the more privileged strata' (M. Janowitz, *The Professional Soldier*, 1960, p. 69). He also adds that 'however, recent trends in their social background supply striking confirmation of the decline of the relatively high social origins of the military, and its transformation into a more socially heterogenous group' (p. 89). But this 'more socially heterogeneous group' still leaves men born in the 'business, professional and managerial' classes with a crushing preponderance over those born in the 'white collar' and 'worker' class (see *ibid.*, table 14, p. 91).

[2] J.R. Schmidhauser, 'The Justices of the Supreme Court – A Collective Portrait', in *Midwest Journal of Political Science*, 1959, vol. 3, p. 45.

[3] L.J. Edinger, 'Continuity and Change in the Background of German Decision-Makers', in *Western Political Quarterly*, 1961, vol. 14, p. 27.

[4] Dahrendorf, *Society and Democracy in Germany*, p. 228.

And much the same story is told for Sweden[1] and Japan.[2]

While inequality of educational opportunity, based on social class, helps to account for this pattern, there are other factors which contribute to its formation. Here too, as in the case of access to elite positions outside the state system, there is also the matter of connections. Certainly, the more spectacular forms of nepotism and favouritism associated with an unregenerate aristocratic and pre-industrial age are not part of the contemporary, middle-class, competitive state service: the partial liberation of that service from the aristocratic grip was indeed one of the crucial aspects of the extension of bourgeois power in the state and society. But it would, all the same, be highly unrealistic to think that even in an examination-oriented epoch membership of a relatively narrow segment of the population is not a distinct advantage, not only in terms of entry into the higher levels of the state service, but also, and hardly less important, of chances of upward movement inside it. Such membership affords links of kinship and friendship, and generally enhances a sense of shared values, all of which are helpful to a successful career. Two French authors put the point well, and what they say can scarcely be thought to apply exclusively to France:

If a student of modest origin has successfully negotiated his university course, the entrance examination of the E.N.A. and even, why not, the final examination where the 'cultural' sifting is perhaps more severe than on entry, he will not, nevertheless, be on the same level as the offspring of great bourgeois families or of high officials: the spirit of caste and personal family relations will constantly work against him when promotions are made (at the highest level, promotion is more uncertain than at lower ones).[3]

Those who control and determine selection and promotion at the highest level of the state service are themselves most likely to be members of the upper and middle classes, by social origin or by virtue of their own professional success, and are likely to

---

[1] 'The number of workers' sons among the politico-bureaucratic top echelons has diminished from 10 per cent in 1949 to 9 per cent in 1961, whereas the percentage of sons of big businessmen went up from 12 per cent to 17 per cent (Therborn, *Power in the Kingdom of Sweden*, p. 59).

[2] See, e.g. Abegglen and Mannari, 'Leaders of Modern Japan: Social Origins and Mobility'.

[3] Bon and Burnier, *Les Nouveaux Intellectuels*, p. 165.

carry in their minds a particular image of how a high-ranking
civil servant or military officer ought to think, speak, behave
and react; and that image will be drawn in terms of the class to
which they belong. No doubt, the recruiters, aware of the pressures and demands of a 'meritocratic' age, may consciously try
to correct their bias; but they are particularly likely to overcome it in the case of working-class candidates who give every
sign of readiness and capacity to adapt and conform to class-
sanctioned patterns of behaviour and thought.[1] 'Rough
diamonds' are now more acceptable than in the past, but they
should preferably show good promise of achieving the right
kind of smoothness.

Max Weber claimed that the development of bureaucracy
tended 'to eliminate class privileges, which include the appropriation of means of administration and the appropriation of
authority as well as the occupation of offices on an honorary
basis or as an avocation by virtue of wealth'.[2] But this singularly
underestimates the degree to which existing class privileges help
to restrict this process, even though they do not arrest it
altogether.

It is undoubtedly true that a process of social dilution has
occurred in the state service, and has brought people born in the
working classes, and even more commonly in the lower-middle
classes, into elite positions inside the state system. But to speak
of 'democratisation' in this connection is somewhat misleading.
What is involved here is rather a process of 'bourgeoisification'
of the most able and thrusting recruits from the subordinate
classes. As these recruits rise in the state hierarchy, so do they
become part, in every significant sense, of the social class to
which their position, income and status gives them access. As
was already noted about working-class recruitment into the
economic elite, this kind of dilution does not materially affect
the class character of the state service and may indeed strength-
en it. Moreover, such recruitment, by fostering the belief that
capitalist societies are run on the principle of 'the career open
to the talents' usefully obscures the degree to which they are
not.

Given the particular hierarchies of the existing social order, it

---

[1] See also chapter 5.
[2] M. Weber, *The Theory of Social and Economic Organisation*, 1947, p. 340.

is all but inevitable that recruits from the subordinate classes into the upper reaches of the state system should, by the very fact of their entry into it, become part of the class which continues to dominate it. For it to be otherwise, the present intake would not only have to be vastly increased: the social order itself would have to be radically transformed as well, and its class hierarchies dissolved.

Social dilution of an even more pronounced kind than in the appointive institutions of the state system has also occurred in those of its institutions whose staffing depends, directly or indirectly, on election, namely the political executive and parliamentary assemblies. Thus, men of working-class or lower-middle-class origin have not uncommonly made their way into the cabinets of advanced capitalist countries – some of them have even become presidents and prime ministers; and an enormous amount of personal power has on occasion been achieved by altogether *déclassé* individuals like Hitler or Mussolini.

What significance this has had for the politics of advanced capitalism will be considered later. But it may be noted at this stage that men drawn from the subordinate classes have never constituted more than a minority of those who have reached high political office in these countries: the large majority has always belonged, by social origin and previous occupation, to the upper and middle classes.[1]

To a somewhat lesser degree, yet still very markedly, this has also been the pattern of the legislatures of advanced capitalist countries. The growth in representation of working-class parties (save of course in the United States) has brought into these assemblies, though still as a minority, men (and occasionally women) who were not only born in the working classes but who, until their election, were themselves workers or at least closely involved in working-class life; and even bourgeois

[1] See Lasswell *et al.*, *The Comparative Study of Elites*, p. 30; Guttsman, *The British Political Elite*, pp. 79ff; Matthews, *The Social Background of Political Decision-Makers*, pp. 23–4; D. Lerner, *The Nazi Elite*, 1951, p. 6; L. D. Edinger, 'Post-Totalitarian Leadership: Elites in the German Federal Republic', in *American Political Science Review*, 1960, vol. 54, no. 1, p. 70; Abegglen and Manari, 'Leaders of Modern Japan: Social Origins and Mobility' in *Economic Development and Cultural Change*, vol. 9, no. 1, Part 2 (October 1960), p. 116.

parties have undergone a certain process of social dilution. Nevertheless, these latter parties, which have generally dominated parliamentary assemblies, have remained solidly upper and middle class in their social composition, with businessmen and others connected with various kinds of property ownership constituting a sizeable and often a very substantial part of their membership.[1] In terms of class, national politics (and for that matter, sub-national politics as well)[2] has continued to be an 'activity' in which the subordinate classes have played a distinctly subsidiary role. Mr Guttsman writes for Britain that:

... if we ascend the political hierarchy from the voters upwards, we find that at each level – the membership of political parties, party activists, local political leaders, M.P.'s, national leaders – the social character of the group is slightly less 'representative' and slightly more tilted in favour of those who belong to the middle and upper levels of our society.[3]

The tilt is in fact much more than slight; and the point does not apply any the less to other countries than to Britain.

What the evidence conclusively suggests is that in terms of social origin, education and class situation, the men who have manned *all* command positions in the state system have largely, and in many cases overwhelmingly, been drawn from the world of business and property, or from the professional middle classes. Here as in every other field, men and women born into the subordinate classes, which form of course the vast majority of the population, have fared very poorly – and not only, it must be stressed, in those parts of the state system, such as administration, the military and the judiciary, which depend on appointment, but also in those parts of it which are exposed or which appear to be exposed to the vagaries of universal suffrage and the fortunes of competitive politics. In an epoch when so much is made of democracy, equality, social

[1] See, e.g. Guttsman, *The British Political Elite*, pp. 97ff; H. Berrington and S. E. Finer, 'The British House of Commons', in *International Social Science Journal*, 1961, vol. 13, no. 4, pp. 601ff; J. Blondel, *Voters, Parties and Leaders*, 1963, chapter 5; M. Dogan, 'Political Ascent in a Class Society: French Deputies 1870–1958', in D. Marvick (ed.), *Political Decision-Makers*, 1961; G. Braunthal, *The Federation of German Industry in Politics*, 1961, pp. 152ff; T. Fukutaki, *Man and Society in Japan*, 1962, p. 117.

[2] See below, pp. 171 ff.

[3] Guttsman, *The British Political Elite*, p. 27.

mobility, classlessness and the rest, it has remained a basic fact of life in advanced capitalist countries that the vast majority of men and women in these countries has been governed, represented, administered, judged, and commanded in war by people drawn from other, economically and socially superior and relatively distant classes.

4

The Purpose and Role
of Governments

The reason for attaching considerable importance to the social composition of the state elite in advanced capitalist countries lies in the strong presumption which this creates as to its general outlook, ideological dispositions and political bias. In the case of the governments of these countries, however, we can do much more than merely presume: after all, hardly a day goes by in which political leaders in charge of the affairs of their country do not press upon the public their ideas and beliefs. Much of this may conceal as much as it reveals. But a great deal remains which, together with much other evidence, notably what governments actually do, affords a clear view of what, in large terms, they are about.

At first sight, the picture is one of endless diversity between succeeding governments, and indeed inside each of them; as also between governments of different countries. Presidents, prime ministers and their colleagues have worn many different political labels (often wildly misleading), and belonged to many different parties, or occasionally to none.

This diversity of views, attitudes, programmes and policies, on an infinite number of subjects, is certainly very striking and makes for live political debate and competition. And the impression of diversity and conflict is further enhanced by the insistence of party leaders, particularly at election time, on the wide and almost impassable, or actually impassable, gulf which separates them from their opponents and competitors.

The assertion of such profound differences is a matter of great importance for the functioning and legitimation of the political system, since it suggests that electors, by voting for one or other of the main competing parties, are making a choice between fundamental and incompatible alternatives, and that they are therefore, as voters, deciding nothing less than the future of their country.

In actual fact however, this picture is in some crucial ways highly superficial and mystifying. For one of the most important aspects of the political life of advanced capitalism is precisely that the disagreements *between those political leaders who have generally been able to gain high office* have very seldom been of the fundamental kind these leaders and other people so often suggest. What is really striking about *these* political leaders and political office-holders, in relation to each other, is not their many differences, but the extent of their agreement on truly fundamental issues – as they themselves, when occasion requires, have been wont to recognise, and as large numbers of people among the public at large, despite the political rhetoric to which they are subjected, recognise in the phrase 'politicians are all the same'.[1] This is an exaggeration, of course. But it is an exaggeration with a solid kernel of truth, at least in relation to the kind of men who tend to succeed each other in office in advanced capitalist countries. Marxists put the same point somewhat differently when they say that these men, whatever their political labels or party affiliations, are bourgeois politicians.

The basic sense in which this is true is that the political office-holders of advanced capitalism have, with very few exceptions, been agreed over what Lord Balfour, in a classical formulation, once called 'the foundations of society', meaning above all the existing economic and social system of private ownership and private appropriation – Marx's 'mode of production'. Balfour was writing about Britain, and about the Whig and Tory administrations of the nineteenth century. But his point applies equally well to other capitalist countries, and to the twentieth century as well as to the nineteenth.

For it is no more than a matter of plain political history that

[1] As witnessed, for instance, by the number of people in countries like Britain and the United States who, when asked whether they believe that there are important differences between the main competing parties, tend to answer in the negative.

the governments of these countries have mostly been composed of men who beyond all their political, social, religious, cultural and other differences and diversities, have at least had in common a basic and usually explicit belief in the validity and virtues of the capitalist system, though this was not what they would necessarily call it; and those among them who have not been particularly concerned with that system, or even aware that they were helping to run a specific economic system, much in the way that they were not aware of the air they breathed, have at least shared with their more ideologically-aware colleagues or competitors a quite basic and unswerving hostility to any socialist alternative to that system.

There have, it is true, been occasions, whose significance will be considered presently, when men issued from working-class and formally socialist parties have occupied positions of governmental power, either alone or more commonly as members of coalitions, in many capitalist countries. But even though these men have quite often professed anti-capitalist convictions, they have never posed – and indeed have for the most part never wished to pose – a serious challenge to a capitalist system (or rather, as most of them would have it, a 'mixed economy'), whose basic framework and essential features they have accepted much more readily than their pronouncements in opposition, and even sometimes in office, would have tended to suggest.

In this sense, the pattern of executive power has remained much more consistent than the alternation in office of governments bearing different labels and affecting different colorations has made it appear: capitalist regimes have mainly been governed by men who have either genuinely believed in the virtues of capitalism, or who, whatever their reservations as to this or that aspect of it, have accepted it as far superior to any possible alternative economic and social system, and who have therefore made it their prime business to defend it. Alternatively, these regimes have been governed by men who, even though they might call themselves socialists, have not found the commitment this might be thought to entail in the least incompatible with the ready, even the eager, acceptance of all the essential features of the system they came to administer.

In fact, it could even be said that this basic acceptance of the capitalist order has been *more* pronounced in this century than in any previous epoch in the history of capitalism. This is not only because it is mainly conservative politicians who have dominated the political executive of their country; or because formally socialist politicans who have occupied office have been content to work the system; but also because the virtual disappearance of the landed interest and of aristocracy as a powerful economic, social and political force, and their assimilation into the ranks of business, has removed one strongly discordant voice from the councils of government. This does not mean that aristocrats themselves have ceased to occupy office; but rather that with the 'bourgeoisification' of aristocracy, a greater degree of basic consensus on the nature of the economic and social order than ever before became possible.

However, even if we leave out for the present the particular role of formally socialist power-holders, it must be stressed again that this basic consensus between bourgeois politicians does not preclude genuine and important differences between them, not only on issues other than the actual management of the economic system, but on that issue as well.

Thus, it has always been possible to make an important distinction between parties and leaders, however committed they might be to the private enterprise system, who stood for a large measure of state intervention in economic and social life, and those who believed in a lesser degree of intervention; and the same distinction encompasses those parties and men who have believed that the state must assume a greater degree of responsibility for social and other kinds of reform; and those who have wished for less.

This quarrel between strong interventionists and their opponents has been and remains a perfectly genuine one. No doubt, no serious politician – however bourgeois and convinced of the virtues of private enterprise – would now wish or be able to dismantle the main structure of state intervention; and indeed it is often the most capitalist-oriented politicians who see most clearly how essential that structure of intervention has become to the maintenance of capitalism. Even so, sufficient differences endure about the desirable extent, the character and the incidence of intervention, to make the debate around such questions (and around many other ones as well) a serious and meaningful one, upon whose outcome depends much which affects many aspects of public policy and many individual lives. From this point of view at least, competition between these men is by no means a complete sham.

But the fact nevertheless remains that these differences and controversies, even at their most intense, have never been allowed by the politicians concerned to bring into question the validity of the 'free enterprise' system itself; and even the most determined interventionists among them have always conceived their proposals and policies as a means, not of eroding – let alone supplanting – the capitalist system, but of ensuring its greater strength and stability. To a much larger extent than appearance and rhetoric have been made to suggest, the politics of advanced capitalism have been about different conceptions of how to run the *same* economic and social system, and not about radically different social systems. *This* debate has not so far come high on the political agenda.

This consensus between political office-holders is clearly crucial. The ideological dispositions which make the consensus possible may not, because of various counter-pressures, finally determine how governments will act in every particular situation. But the fact that governments accept as beyond question the capitalist context in which they operate is of absolutely fundamental importance in shaping their attitudes, policies and actions in regard to the specific issues and problems with which they are confronted, and to the needs and conflicts of civil society. The general commitment deeply colours the specific response, and affects not only the solution envisaged for the particular problem perceived, but the mode of perception itself; indeed, ideological commitment may and often does prevent perception at all, and makes impossible not only prescription for the disease, but its location.

However, political office-holders themselves do not at all see their commitment to capitalist enterprise as involving any element of class partiality. On the contrary, they are the most ardent and eloquent exponents of the view of the state, and of themselves, as above the battles of civil society, as classless, as concerned above all to serve the whole nation, the national interest, as being charged with the particular task of subduing special interests and class-oriented demands for the supreme good of all. In their thoughts and words, Hegel's exalted view of the state as the embodiment and the protector of the whole of society, of its higher reason, and of its permanent interests, lives again – particularly when they rather than their opponents are in office. 'I belong to everyone and I belong to no one', General de Gaulle said shortly after coming to power in 1958, and it would be absurd to doubt that this is indeed how the general does see himself – far, far above the interests of lesser men, be they capitalists, wage-earners, farmers, shopkeepers, the sick, the poor, the young or the old. Other political leaders may not find it easy to present themselves in quite such grandiose terms; but they do their best, and see themselves in much the same guise as the general does, even when they appear to others to exhibit the most blatant class bias in their policies and actions.

That most political leaders in positions of power do hold this view of their office, and of themselves, with sincerity and conviction need not, in general, be doubted. Indeed, to dismiss their proclamations of freedom from class bias as mere hypocrisy leads to a dangerous underestimation of the dedication and resolution with which such leaders are likely to pursue a task of whose nobility they are utterly persuaded. Men so persuaded are not easily deflected from their purpose by appeals to reason or sentiment or evidence, particularly when matters of great moment are at stake.

Opponents of capitalism believe it to be a system whose very nature nowadays makes impossible the optimum utilisation of resources for rational human ends; whose inherent character is one of compulsion, domination and parasitical appropriation; whose spirit and purpose fatally corrode all human relations; and whose maintenance is today the major obstacle to human progress.

Bourgeois politicians and governments view the system in precisely opposite terms – as most closely congruent with 'human nature', as uniquely capable of combining efficiency, welfare and freedom, as the best means of releasing human initiative and energy in socially beneficent directions, and as providing the necessary and only possible basis for a satisfactory social order.

Anyway, why speak of 'capitalism' at all, with its emotive and propagandistic evocations of a system which no longer *really* exists, and which has been replaced by an 'industrial system' in which private enterprise, though still the essential motor of the economy, is now much more 'responsible' than in the past, and whose purposes are now in any case closely supervised by the democratic state?

'Liberal democracy,' Robert Lynd wrote twenty-five years ago, 'has never dared face the fact that industrial capitalism is an intensely coercive form of organisation of society that cumulatively constrains men and all of their institutions to work the will of the minority who hold and wield economic power; and that this relentless warping of men's lives and forms of association becomes less and less the result of voluntary decisions by "bad" men or "good" men and more and more an impersonal web of coercions dictated by the need to keep "the system" running.'[1] This is even more true today than when it was first written; but the governments which manage 'liberal democracy' are mostly composed of men who *cannot* see the system in this guise, who attribute the deficiencies in it which they perceive as separate and specific 'problems', remediable within its confines – in fact *only* remediable within its confines. This is what makes it possible for politicians who are, in this fundamental respect, extreme doctrinaires, to claim that theirs is an essentially empirical, undogmatic, pragmatic, *practical* approach to affairs.

A French writer recalls de Gaulle's famous phrase, 'Toute ma vie, je me suis fait une certaine idée de la France', and comments that 'quand l'idée de la France prend corps et devient réalité, elle se confond dans son esprit tout naturellement prisonnier de son milieu avec la France des Trusts'.[2]

The comment may not be exactly accurate, since de Gaulle's 'idea' of France is certainly more complex than is allowed here. But it is quite true that this 'idea' includes, as the general's policies during and immediately after the war clearly showed and as his conduct of affairs since 1958 has also demonstrated, economic and social arrangements in which large-scale capitalist enterprise, no doubt under the watchful eye of a strong state, must play a crucially important role. With greater

---

[1] Foreword to R. A. Brady, *Business as a System of Power*, 1943, p. xii.
[2] H. Claude, *Le Gaullisme*, 1960, p. 76.

or lesser qualifications, other political leaders and governments have taken the same view, and seen capitalist enterprise as a necessary, desirable, to-be-assumed element of their society. They wish, without a doubt, to pursue many ends, personal as well as public. But all other ends are conditioned by, and pass through the prism of, their acceptance of and commitment to the existing economic system.

Given their view of that system, it is easy to understand why governments should wish to help business in every possible way, yet do not at all feel that this entails any degree of bias towards particular classes, interests and groups. For if the national interest is in fact inextricably bound up with the fortunes of capitalist enterprise, apparent partiality towards it is not really partiality at all. On the contrary, in serving the interests of business and in helping capitalist enterprise to thrive, governments are really fulfilling their exalted role as guardians of the good of all. From this standpoint, the much-derided phrase 'What is good for General Motors is good for America' is only defective in that it tends to identify the interests of one particular enterprise with the national interest. But if General Motors is taken to stand for the world of capitalist enterprise as a whole, the slogan is one to which governments in capitalist countries do subscribe, often explicitly. And they do so because they accept the notion that the economic rationality of the capitalist system is synonymous with rationality itself, and that it provides the best possible set of human arrangements in a necessarily imperfect world.

In this sense, the attitude of political office-holders to businessmen as a class or as a social type is of relatively minor importance. Their circle of relations, friends, former associates and acquaintances is much more likely to include businessmen than, say, trade union leaders; and the favourable view they take of capitalist enterprise is also likely to make them take a sympathetic view of the men who run it. Thus President Eisenhower in 1952:

I believe in our dynamic system of privately owned businesses and industries. They have proven that they can supply not only the mightiest sinews of war, but the highest standard of living in the world for the greatest number of people....But it requires someone to take these things and to produce the extraordinary statistics that the

United States with 7 per cent of the world's population produces 50
per cent of the world's manufactured goods. If that someone is to
be given a name, I believe that his name is the American businessman.[1]

Political leaders in countries less steeped in the business creed
are not often quite so naïvely gushing; and even in the United
States, presidents have on occasion taken a less enthusiastic
view of those whom one of them (admittedly long ago, and not
very seriously) denounced as 'malefactors of great wealth'. It
may well be, indeed, that many political leaders have taken a
very poor view of this or that section of business, or even
considered business as an inferior activity, from which they felt
themselves far removed.

All this, however, is of no serious consequence, given a
fundamental commitment to the system of which businessmen
are an intrinsic and major part.[2] Because of that commitment,
and because of their belief that the national interest is inextricably bound up with the health and strength of capitalist
enterprise, governments naturally seek to help business – and
businessmen. Thorstein Veblen once wrote that 'the chief –
virtually sole – concern of the constituted authorities in any
democratic nation is a concern about the profitable business of
the nation's substantial citizens'.[3] This is quite true, but not
necessarily or at all because of any particular predilection of the
'constituted authorities' for substantial citizens. The concern
goes with the general commitment.

---

[1] S. E. Harris, *The Economics of Political Parties*, 1962, p. 5. On coming to office,
President Johnson put the same point somewhat differently but, it may be surmised, with no less feeling: 'We think we have the best system. We think that
where a capitalist can put up a dollar, he can get a return on it. A manager can
get up early to work and with money and men he can build a better mousetrap.
A laborer who is worthy of his hire stands a chance of getting attention and maybe
a little profit-sharing system, and the highest minimum wages of any nation in the
world' (R. Evans and R. Novak, *Lyndon B. Johnson: The Exercise of Power*, 1966,
p. 347).
[2] Note, e.g. President Kennedy's lack of enthusiasm for businessmen in general
(A. M. Schlesinger Jr, *A Thousand Days: John F. Kennedy in the White House*, 1965,
pp. 631ff), but also his almost desperate concern to reach accommodation with
the 'business community', for which see below, chapter 6.
[3] T. Veblen, *Absentee Ownership*, 1923, pp. 36–7.

II

The first and most important consequence of the commitment which governments in advanced capitalist countries have to the private enterprise system and to its economic rationality is that it enormously limits their freedom of action in relation to a multitude of issues and problems. Raymond Aron has written that 'il va de soi qu'en régime fondé sur la propriété des moyens de production, les mesures prises par les législateurs et les ministres ne seront pas en opposition fondamentale avec les intérêts des propriétaires'.[1] This proposition, he comments, is too obvious to be instructive. It *should* perhaps be obvious. But it does not appear to be so to most Western political scientists who view the state as free from the inherent bias in favour of capitalist interests which Professor Aron's proposition implies.

That bias has immense policy implications. For the resolution, or at least the alleviation of a vast range of economic and social problems requires precisely that governments *should* be willing to act in 'fundamental opposition' to these interests. Far from being a trivial matter, their extreme reluctance to do so is one of the largest of all facts in the life of these societies. Were it to be said about a government that though faced with a vast criminal organisation it could not be expected to act in fundamental opposition to it, the observation would not be thought uninstructive about its character and role. The same is true of the proposition which Professor Aron so casually puts forward and tosses aside.

On the other hand, that proposition tends to obscure a basic aspect of the state's role. For governments, acting in the name of the state, have in fact been compelled over the years to act against *some* property rights, to erode *some* managerial prerogatives, to help redress *somewhat* the balance between capital and labour, between property and those who are subject to it. This is an aspect of state intervention which conservative writers who lament the growth of 'bureaucracy' and who deplore state

[1] R. Aron, 'Classe Sociale, Classe Politique, Classe Dirigeante', in *Archives Européennes de Sociologie*, 1960, vol. 1, no. 2, pp. 272–3.

'interference' in the affairs of society regularly overlook. Bureaucracy is indeed a problem and a danger, and the experience of countries like the Soviet Union has amply shown how greatly unrestrained bureaucratic power can help to obstruct the creation of a socialist society worthy of the name. But concentration upon the evils of bureaucracy in capitalist countries obscures (and is often intended to obscure) the fact that 'bureaucratic' intervention has often been a means of alleviating the evils produced by unrestrained private economic power.

The state's 'interference' with that power is not in 'fundamental opposition' to the interests of property: it is indeed part of that 'ransom' of which Joseph Chamberlain spoke in 1885 and which, he said, would have to be paid precisely for the purpose of *maintaining* the rights of property in general. In insisting that the 'ransom' be paid, governments render property a major service, though the latter is seldom grateful for it. Even so, it would not do to ignore the fact that even very conservative governments in the regimes of advanced capitalism have often been forced, mainly as a result of popular pressure, to take action against *certain* property rights and capitalist prerogatives.

As against this, however, must be set the very positive support which governments have generally sought to give to dominant economic interests.

Capitalist enterprise, as was noted in chapter I, *depends* to an ever greater extent on the bounties and direct support of the state, and can only preserve its 'private' character on the basis of such public help. State intervention in economic life in fact largely *means* intervention for the purpose of helping capitalist enterprise. In no field has the notion of the 'welfare state' had a more precise and apposite meaning than here: there are no more persistent and successful applicants for public assistance than the proud giants of the private enterprise system.

Nor need that assistance be of a direct kind to be of immense value to capitalist interests. Because of the imperative requirements of modern life, the state must, within the limits imposed upon it by the prevailing economic system, engage in bastard forms of socialisation and assume responsibility for many functions and services which are beyond the scope and capabilities of capitalist interests. As it does so, however, what Jean Meynaud calls 'the bias of the system' ensures that these interests will automatically benefit from state intervention. Because of the private ownership and control of a predominant part of economic life, Professor Meynaud writes:

... all the measures taken by the state to develop and improve the national economy always end up by being of the greatest benefit to those who control the levers of command of the production-distribution sector: when the state cuts tunnels, builds roads, opens up highways or reclaims swamps, it is first of all the owners of the neighbouring lands who reap the rewards...the concept of the 'bias of the system' makes it also possible to understand that the measures taken to remedy the derelictions, shortcomings and abuses of capitalism result ultimately, where successful, in the consolidation of the regime. It matters little in this respect that these measures should have been undertaken by men sympathetic or hostile to capitalist interests: thus it is that laws designed to protect the workers and directed against their exploitation by employers will be found useful to the latter by inducing them to make a greater effort to rationalise or mechanise the productive process.[1]

Governments may be solely concerned with the better running of 'the economy'. But the description of the system as 'the economy' is part of the idiom of ideology, and obscures the real process. For what is being improved is a *capitalist* economy; and this ensures that whoever may or may not gain, capitalist interests are least likely to lose.

The 'bias of the system' may be given a greater or lesser degree of emphasis. But the ideological dispositions of governments have generally been of a kind to make more acceptable to them the structural constraints imposed upon them by the system; and these dispositions have also made it easier for them to submit to the pressures to which they have been subjected by dominant interests.

Taxation offers a ready illustration of the point. As was noted in chapter 2, the economic system itself generates extremely powerful tendencies towards the maintenance and enhancement of the vast inequalities of income and wealth which are typical of all advanced capitalist societies. Given that

[1] J. Meynaud, *Rapport sur la Classe Dirigeante Italienne*, 1964, pp. 190–1.

economic system, no government can achieve redistributive miracles. But the limits of its powers in this field are nevertheless not finally fixed – despite the system's tendencies to inequality and the fierce opposition of the forces of wealth to redistributive taxation. And the fact that taxation has not, over the years, affected more deeply than it has the disparities of income and wealth in these societies must to a major extent be attributed to the attitude of governments towards inequality, to the view they take of the conflicting claims of the rich and the poor, and to their acceptance of an economic orthodoxy which has, at any particular moment of time, declared additional burdens on the rich to be fatal to 'business confidence', 'individual initiative', the propensity to invest, etc.

The same considerations apply to government intervention in 'industrial relations', the consecrated euphemism for the permanent conflict, now acute, now subdued, between capital and labour.

Whenever government have felt it incumbent, as they have done more and more, to intervene directly in disputes between employers and wage-earners, the result of their intervention has tended to be disadvantageous to the latter, not the former. On innumerable occasions, and in all capitalist countries, governments have played a decisive role in defeating strikes, often by the invocation of the coercive power of the state and the use of naked violence; and the fact that they have done so in the name of the national interest, law and order, constitutional government, the protection of 'the public', etc., rather than simply to support employers, has not made that intervention any the less useful to these employers.

Moreover, the state, as the largest of all employers, is now able to influence the pattern of 'industrial relations' by the force of its own example and behaviour: that influence can hardly be said to have created new standards in the employer-employee relationship. Nor could it have been expected to do so, given the 'business-like' spirit in which the public sector is managed.

Governments are deeply involved, on a permanent and institutionalised basis, in that 'routinisation of conflict,' which is an essential part of the politics of advanced capitalism. They enter that conflict in the guise of a neutral and independent party, concerned to achieve not the outright defeat of one side or the other but a 'reasonable' settlement between them. But the state's intervention in negotiations occurs in the shadow of its known and declared propensity to invoke its powers of coercion, against one of the parties in the dispute rather than the other, if 'conciliation' procedures fail. These procedures form, in fact, an additional element of restraint upon organised labour, and also serve the useful purpose of further dividing the trade union ranks. The state does interpose itself between the 'two sides of industry' – not, however, as a neutral but as a partisan.

Nor is this nowadays only true when industrial disputes actually occur. One of the most notable features in the recent evolution of advanced capitalism is the degree to which governments have sought to place new and further inhibitions upon organised labour in order to prevent it from exercising what pressures it can on employers (and on the state as a major employer) in the matter of wage claims. What they tend to achieve, by such means as an 'incomes policy', or by deflationary policies which reduce the demand for labour, is a *general* weakening of the bargaining position of wage-earners.[1] Here too, the policies adopted are proclaimed to be essential to the national interest, the health of the economy, the defence of the currency, the good of the workers, and so on. And there are always trade union leaders who can be found to endorse both the claims and the policies. But this does not change the fact that the main effect of these policies is to leave wage-earners in a weaker position *vis-à-vis* employers than would otherwise be the case. The *purpose*, in the eyes of political office-holders, may be all that it is said to be; but the *result*, with unfailing regularity, is to the detriment of the subordinate classes. This is why the latter, in this as in most other instances, have good reason to beware when the political leaders of advanced capitalist countries invoke the national interest in defence of their policies – more likely than not they, the subordinate classes, are about to be done. Wage-earners have always had to reckon with a hostile state in their encounter with employers. But now

[1] See, e.g., Kidron, *Western Capitalism Since the War*, pp. 190ff; 'Incomes Policy and the Trade Unions', in *International Socialist Journal*, 1964, vol. 1, no 3; and 'The Campaign Against the Right to Strike', in *ibid.*, 1964, vol. 1, no. 1.

more than ever they have to reckon with its antagonism, in
practice, as a direct, pervasive, and constant fact of economic
life. Their immediate and daily opponent remains the employer;
but governments and the state are now much more closely
involved in the encounter than in the past.

Quite naturally, this partiality of governments assumes an
even more specific, precise and organised character in relation
to all movements, groupings and parties dedicated to the
transformation of capitalist societies into socialist ones. The
manner in which governments have expressed this antagonism
has greatly varied over time, and between countries, assuming
here a milder form, there a harsher one; but the antagonism
itself has been a permanent fact in the history of all capitalist
countries. In no field has the underlying consensus between
political office-holders of different political affiliations, and
between the governments of different countries, been more
substantial and notable – the leaders of all governmental
parties, whether in office or in opposition, and including
nominally 'socialist' ones, have always been deeply hostile to
the socialist and militant left, of whatever denomination, and
governments themselves have in fact been the major protagonists against it, in their role of protectors and saviours of
society from the perils of left-wing dissidence.

In this instance too, liberal-democratic and pluralist theorists,
in their celebration of the political competition which prevails
in their societies, and in their insistence on the political neutrality of the state, quite overlook the fact that the governments
of advanced capitalist societies, far from taking a neutral view
of *socialist* competition, do their level best to make it more difficult.
In some countries, for instance Federal Germany, Communist
and other left-wing parties and organisations are suppressed
altogether, and membership made a crime punishable by law;
in others, such as the United States, left-wing organisations, of
which the Communist Party is only one, operate in conditions
of such harassment as to narrow rather drastically, in their
case, the notion of free political competition.

Nor is the state's hostility less marked in other countries,
though it may assume different forms – for instance electoral
manipulation as in France and Italy for the purpose of robbing
their Communist parties of the parliamentary representation to

which their electoral strength entitles them; the engineering of bias in the mass media, in so far as lies in the considerable and growing power of governments; and also episodic but quite brutal repression of left-wing dissenters.

Governments, in other words, are deeply concerned, whatever their political coloration, that the 'democratic process' should operate within a framework in which left-wing dissent plays as weak a role as possible.

The argument is not whether governments should or should not be neutral as between conservative and anti-conservative ideologies, movements, parties and groups. That question is not susceptible to resolution in terms of such imperatives. The argument is rather that the governments of advanced capitalist countries have never been thus neutral, and that they have for the most part used the state power on the conservative as against the anti-conservative side. And the further argument is that in so doing they have, whatever other purposes they might have wished to serve, afforded a most precious element of protection to those classes and interests whose power and privileges socialist dissent is primarily intended to undermine and destroy. Those who believe in the virtues of a social order which includes such power and privileges will applaud and support governmental partiality, and may even ask for more of it. Those who do not will not. The important point is to see what so much of political analysis obscures, often from itself, namely that this *is* what governments, in these countries, actually do.

The argument so far has centered on some of the main *internal* consequences which flow from the commitment of governments to the capitalist system. But the *external* consequences of that commitment are no less direct and important.

Here, perhaps even more than in other fields, the purposes which governments proclaim their wish to serve are often made to appear remote from specific economic concerns, let alone capitalist interests. It is the national interest, national security, national independence, honour, greatness, etc. that is their concern. But this naturally includes a sound, healthy, thriving economic system; and such a desirable state of affairs depends in turn on the prosperity of capitalist enterprise. Thus, by the same mechanism which operates in regard to home affairs, the

governments of capitalist countries have generally found that
their larger national purposes required the servicing of capitalist
interests; and the crucial place which these interests occupy in
the life of their country has always caused governments to make
their defence against foreign capitalist interests, and against
the foreign states which protect *them*, a prime consideration in
their conduct of external affairs.[1]

The whole history of Western (and Japanese) imperialism is a
clear case in point. It is certainly not true that these governments went into Africa or Asia *simply* to serve powerful economic interests. Nor did they embark upon imperialist expansion
simply because they were 'compelled' to do so by such interests.
Vast historical movements of this kind cannot be reduced to
these simplicities. But here too the many other purposes which
governments have wished to serve in their quest for empire
have involved, preeminently, the furtherance of private
economic interests. They may *really* have been concerned with
national security, the strengthening of the economic and social
fabric, the shouldering of the white man's burden, the fulfilment
of their national destiny, and so forth. But these purposes
required, as they saw it, the securing by conquest of lands
which were already or which could become zones of exploitation for their national capitalist interests, whose implantation
and expansion were thus guaranteed by the power of the state.
In this case too the fact that political office-holders were seeking
to achieve many other purposes should not obscure the fact
that, *in the service of these purposes*, they became the dedicated
servants of their business and investing classes.

The same considerations apply to the attitude of capitalist
governments towards the formally independent countries of the
Third World in which their national capitalist interests have a
stake, or might acquire one.

Thus, the attitude of the government of the United States
towards, say, Central and Latin America is not exclusively
determined by its concern to protect American investments in
the area or to safeguard the opportunity of such investments in
the future. When for instance the government of the United
States decided in 1954 that the Arbenz government in Guate-

[1] As an American Secretary of State put it in May 1914 to the National Council
of Foreign Trade, in words which have remained highly apposite: 'I can say,

mala must be overthrown,[1] it did so not merely because that government had taken 225,000 acres of land from the American-owned United Fruit Company but because that action, in the eyes of the government of the United States, provided the best possible proof of 'Communist' leanings, which made the Arbenz regime a threat to 'American security'.[2] But what this and many other similar episodes mean is that 'American security' is so interpreted by those responsible for it as to require foreign governments to show proper respect for the rights and claims of American business. This may not be the only test of a government's 'reliability'; but it is a primary one nevertheless. As a general rule, the American government's attitude to governments in the Third World, or for that matter in the whole non-socialist world, depends very largely on the degree to which these governments favour American free enterprise in their countries or are likely to favour it in the future.[3] The governments of other advanced capitalist countries are moved by a similar concern. The difference between them and the government of the United States is not in basic approach but in the scale of their foreign investments and enterprises and in their capacity to act in defence of these interests.

In this perspective, the supreme evil is obviously the assumption of power by governments whose main purpose is precisely to abolish private ownership and private enterprise, home and foreign, in the most important sectors of their economic life or in all of them. Such governments are profoundly objectionable not only because their actions adversely affect foreign-owned interests and enterprises or because they render future capitalist implantation impossible; in some cases this may be of no great economic consequence. But the objection still remains because

not merely in courtesy – but as a fact – my Department is your department; the ambassadors, the ministers and the consuls are all yours. It is their business to look after your interests and to guard your rights'. (Quoted in W. A. Williams, *The Tragedy of American Diplomacy*, 1959, p. 51).

[1] See, e.g. D. Wise and T. B. Ross, *The Invisible Government*, ch. 11, 1964.

[2] 'In the era of the Cold War, keeping Soviet power and influence out of the hemisphere, and particularly out of the Panama Canal area, was far more important to Washington than old-fashioned style banana diplomacy. But certainly the seizure of United Fruit's holdings without adequate compensation forced Eisenhower to take action' (*ibid.*, p. 170).

[3] Nor of course is this a *new* feature of American foreign policy. For its permanent importance in American history, see, e.g. W. A. Williams, *The Tragedy of American Diplomacy*, and, by the same author, *The Contours of American History*, 1961.

the withdrawal of any country from the world system of capitalist enterprise is seen as constituting a weakening of that system and as providing encouragement to further dissidence and withdrawal.

Here also lie the roots of the fierce hostility towards the Bolshevik Revolution which led the capitalist powers to try to crush it in blood – long before, incidentally, the notion of 'Soviet aggression' had become the standard justification for their policies. And here too lies the main clue to the foreign policies of these powers since the end of the second world war, indeed during that war as well.[1] The purpose, always and above all else, has been to prevent the coming into being, anywhere, of regimes fundamentally opposed to capitalist enterprise and determined to do away with it.

Western office-holders have justified their attitude to socialist regimes and movements in terms of their love of freedom, their concern for democracy, their hatred of dictatorship, and their fear of aggression. In this instance, as in most others, it is not very useful to ask whether in these proclamations they were 'sincere' or not. The important point is rather that they defined freedom in terms which made capitalist enterprise one of its main and sometimes its sole ingredient. On this basis, the defence of freedom does become the defence of free enterprise: provided *this* is safe, all else, however evil, can be condoned, overlooked and even supported.[2] Almost by definition, no

[1] See, e.g. J. Bagguly, 'The World War and the Cold War', in D. Horowitz (ed.), *Containment and Revolution*, 1967).

[2] In October 1961, President Kennedy told Cheddi Jagan, then prime minister of British Guiana, that 'we are not engaged in a crusade to force free enterprise on parts of the world where it is not relevant. If we are engaged in a crusade for anything, it is national independence. That is the primary purpose of our aid. The secondary purpose is to encourage individual freedom and political freedom. But we can't always get that; and we have often helped countries which have little personal freedom, if they maintain their national independence. This is the basic thing. So long as you do that, we don't care whether you are socialist, capitalist, pragmatist, or whatever. We regard ourselves as pragmatists' (A. M. Schlesinger Jr, *A Thousand Days*, pp. 775–6). The trouble with such sentiments is not only that they are belied by American support across the world for regimes whose 'national independence' consists in subservience to the United States, and about which the notion of 'individual freedom and political freedom' is a grotesque if not an obscene joke. Equally important is the fact that the *real* test is always a regime's attitude to capitalist and notably American enterprise. Aid to Yugoslavia, or to any other dissident Communist country, comes within the sphere of Cold War politics, and scarcely affects the main point.

regime which respects capitalist interests can be deemed hopelessly bad and must in any case be considered as inherently superior to any regime which does not. Given this attitude, it is not of major consequence that capitalist governments should have been concerned, in external relations, with more than the interests of their businessman and investors. However that may be, *these* are the interests which their policies have most consistently served.

III

As we noted earlier, there have been occasions in the political life of advanced capitalist countries when ultimate executive power has come into the hands of social democratic governments whose political commitments appeared to range them against their traditional and business elites. Save in the case of the Scandinavian countries[1] such occasions have been fairly infrequent. Much more commonly, governmental coalitions have at one time or another included, in prominent positions and in substantial numbers, social-democratic ministers and even, as in the case of France, Italy and Belgium after the second world war, Communist ones. It is therefore necessary to examine how far such episodes affect the general proposition advanced above, that, despite appearances to the contrary, executive power in the world of advanced capitalism has never in fact held any serious threat to the prevailing economic system and to its main beneficiaries.

Before proceeding with this, however, it is necessary to consider an entirely different experience, namely that of the Fascist regimes in Italy and Germany, where *déclassé*

It is also worth noting that well before 1961 British Guiana was already the subject of attention by the C.I.A., which played a major role in the downfall of Jagan and in the assumption of power by a government wholly satisfactory to the United States government – and to American capitalist enterprise.

[1] For the achievements and the shortcomings of Swedish Social Democracy, as the party of government for over three decades, in the management of a society in which the means of economic activity have remained for the most part under private management and control, see P. Anderson, 'Sweden: Mr Crosland's Dreamland', and 'Sweden II. Study in Social Democracy', in *New Left Review*, 1961, nos. 7 and 9.

adventurers, one of them a 'revolutionary socialist' in his early days, and both full of anti-capitalist and anti-bourgeois rhetoric, proclaimed it as their purpose to effect the total transformation of their societies, and held what may properly be described as absolute power for a good many years. How far, it may well be asked, does *this* experience qualify or negate the notion of fundamental congruity on the 'foundations of society' between state power and capitalist interests? The answer, it may be said at once, is – not at all. In the light of the evidence, the point would hardly need much argument, were it not for the fact that the economic and social reality of Fascism is now so often ignored or obscured.

The Fascist rhetoric of total transformation and renewal, with its anti-bourgeois resonances, is obviously important, if only because the Fascist leaders could not, without it, have acquired a mass following. Nor is it to be doubted that many of them believed with utter conviction that they were engaged on the creation of an entirely new social order.

The reality, however, was altogether different from their grandiose elucubrations; and they themselves approached their task with the absolutely firm determination *not* to attack the basic framework of that capitalist system they often reviled. As Mussolini told his Senate on 13 January 1934, more than ten years after he had assumed power:

The corporative economy respects the principle of private property. Private property completes the human personality. It is a right. But it is also a duty. We think that property ought to be regarded as a social function; we wish therefore to encourage, not passive property, but active property, which does not confine itself to enjoying wealth, but develops it and increases it. The corporative economy respects private initiative. The Charter of Labour expressly states that only when private initiative is unintelligent, nonexistent, or inefficient may the state intervene.[1]

This, at least, was one line of policy to which the Italian dictator held unswervingly.

[1] G. Salvemini, *Under the Axe of Fascism*, 1936, p. 134. Salvemini also notes that the Senate which Mussolini was addressing was 'composed of wealthy bondholders, army chiefs, high civil servants, large estate owners, big businessmen, former university professors, and successful professional men' (*ibid.*, p. 134).

As for Germany, one student of Nazism notes that:

In the confidential conversations, which culminated in his speech to the captains of the Ruhr industries on 27 January 1932, Hitler revised the economic program of the NSDAP. He had previously conceded to the small firms that his party supported private property, but he was now extending his policy by largely adopting the ideas of big business. He argued for the elimination of unions and for the managerial freedom of employers within concerns. He outlined his program of public works and rearmament, which would lead to recovery and to many orders for business concerns. These public orders would not have the effect of delegating more economic functions to the government, since the leaders of big business were to be given the task of directing the economy through the economic organisations under their control. Hitler also promised a stable government that would stay in power for a long time.[1]

And the same author also notes that:

Taken into his confidence, leading businessmen trusted Hitler and convinced themselves that the party, once in power, would provide big business with the opportunity to determine the economic policy of his government.[2]

These 'leading businessmen' who financed and supported Hitler,[3] together with many other elements of Germany's traditional elites, as their Italian equivalents had done for Mussolini, did not make a dupe's bargain. Hitler and his colleagues had not entered into alliance with them in bad faith, the better to accomplish, once in power, a revolutionary and anti-capitalist purpose. There was no such purpose, and those among his followers who thought there was and who constituted the 'left-wing' of Nazism, soon paid with their lives for their mistake. 'Vigorous encouragement of private enterprise', another recent writer notes, 'was one of the programmatic

---

[1] A. Schweitzer, *Big Business in the Third Reich*, 1964, p. 100.

[2] *Ibid*, p. 100.

[3] 'Without the formidable assistance of the industrialists, the Nazi Party would have floundered on the rocks of bankruptcy' (J. W. Wheeler-Bennett, *The Nemesis of Power. The German Army in Politics. 1918–1945*, 1953, p. 273). Note also Dr Adenauer's remark in 1949 that 'the Ruhr industry – and therein I include coal mining as well as the entire heavy industry – in the years up to 1933 used the great economic power that was concentrated there for political purposes to the detriment of the German people' (quoted by Braunthal, *The Federation of German Industry in Politics*, p. 17).

points Hitler presented to the Reichstag in March 1933'.[1]

One such 'encouragement', of immense importance to any kind of assessment of the Fascist regimes, was of course the physical destruction of all working-class defence organisations – parties, unions, cooperatives, their ancillary organisations, their press, their parliamentary representation – and the creation of new controlling bodies dominated by employers and the state. Had they done nothing else, the Fascist dictators, by the subjugation of all manifestations of working-class power and influence, would have richly earned the gratitude of employers and of the economically dominant classes generally. As Salvemini aptly puts it: 'A Socialist state would nationalise capital on the ground that it is redeeming the worker from the slavery of wages. The Fascist state has nationalised labour and hires it out to private capital at the price that it, the state, deems expedient'.[2] In so doing, these regimes also earned the gratitude of millions of wage-earners, who found employment on such terms preferable to no employment at all. But their gratitude and support does not affect the point that the Fascist conquest of power entailed an immediate and dramatic increase in the power of capital over labour. It was, after all, no small thing that 'workers who fostered class conflict ... were usually handed over without ceremony to the Gestapo', and that 'workers were now legally required to show absolute obedience and loyalty to their leader, who was in turn required to care for their welfare'.[3] This 'leader' was the employer and complaints against his failure to look after his workers' welfare could easily be construed as 'fostering class conflict'. No wonder that 'net profits rose by 433 per cent between the beginning of 1933 and the end of 1936';[4] and that, as Mr Schoenbaum notes, 'while wages

[1] D. Schoenbaum, *Hitler's Social Revolution: Class and Status in Nazi Germany 1933–1939*, 1966, p. 55. 'A Party editorial in 1939', Mr Schoenbaum also notes, 'declared free enterprise to be the very basis of Germany's socialism, and the social responsibility deriving from free enterprise the key to its realisation' (*ibid.*, p. 55).

[2] Salvemini, *Under the Axe of Fascism*, p. 138.

[3] T. W. Mason, 'Labour in the Third Reich', in *Past and Present*, no. 33 (April 1966), p. 177. See also R. A. Brady, *The Spirit and Structure of German Fascism*, 1936; F. Neumann, *Behemoth*, 1942; Schweitzer, *Big Business in the Third Reich*; and Schoenbaum, *Hitler's Social Revolution*. For labour under Italian Fascism, see Salvemini, *Under the Axe of Fascism*.

[4] Schweitzer, p. 398. Some of this was obviously due to the utilisation of previously idle plants. But, in the same author's words, 'there can be no doubt that the dictated wage markets and the lopsided job markets contributed, directly and

remained static and even fell slightly between 1934 and 1940, the average net income of income tax payers, and thus of managerial and entrepreneurial business, rose by 46 per cent'.[1] Until the war, German business only had German workers to exploit: German victory delivered into its hands millions of slave labourers from occupied Europe, who were even more helpless *vis-à-vis* their employers than their German counterparts.

Of course, business under Fascism had to submit to a far greater degree of state intervention and control than it liked, and there was no doubt a good deal about the state's economic and social policies which it found disagreeable. But businessmen themselves played a major role in the system of regulation and control, which was no small compensation – so much so, it has been said, that 'to the very end of the Nazi dictatorship the business leaders retained perhaps more power than any other elite group besides the Nazi bosses'.[2]

Nor should it be overlooked that the 'Nazi bosses' included many people who were themselves members of the business and **bourgeois** classes: 'corporate entrepreneurs and managers, skilled in industrial production and administration; the bureaucrats, skilled in interpreting the codified rules-of-the-game and applying them to concrete situations; the industrial engineers and other technologists skilled in applying knowledge to specific social goals'.[3] More generally, 'a substantial part of that Nazi elite was not only middle class, but distinctly upper class, with a notable number of high-ranking officers'.[4]

effectively, to the restoration of profits. Thus we may say that the direct controls exercised by party and state, far from being harmful to business, simultaneously exploited labour and enriched business and restored the institution of private profits' (*ibid.*, p. 398).

[1] Schoenbaum, *Hitler's Social Revolution*, p. 156.

[2] W. Deutsch and L. J. Edinger, *Germany Rejoins the Powers*, 1954, p. 99. Another writer has also noted that 'by and large, business was the one sphere in Germany in which the party did not actively proceed to introduce its own men. Those placed on inside boards of directors [*Vorstand*] because of their party connections and activities were mostly "contact men" – useful for public relations purposes, manœuvring for larger material allocations, etc. – rather than decision-makers involved in basic management' (D. Granick, *The European Executive*, p. 165). See also Schweitzer, *Big Business in the Third Reich*, pp. 43ff.

[3] D. Lerner, *The Nazi Elite*, 1951, p. 6.

[4] *Ibid.*, pp. 54ff. Note also the bourgeois and upper-class character of much of the higher element of the SS (see Schoenbaum, *Hitler's Social Revolution*, p. 239). The same class bias was characteristic of Italian Fascism: see Brady, *Business as a System of Power*, p. 81.

It is often said that Fascism is an extreme example of the state's domination of society. This is quite true. But the formula, in that it lacks social content, is misleading in two senses: first, in the sense that it obscures the degree to which the Fascist state acted in ways enormously advantageous to the business and possessing classes; but also, secondly, because it fails to take into account the fact that 'the state' continued to be largely manned by people who belonged to the traditional administrative, military and judicial elites. Indeed, the Nazi regime seems to have reversed the trend towards the 'democratisation' of the state system which had been a feature of the Weimar regime: there were for instance more aristocrats in positions of power between 1933 and 1945 than between 1918 and 1933, and fewer people of working-class origin.[1] Ultimate power of an absolute kind was in the hands of the dictators. But they had, perforce, to devolve a great deal of that power upon others. All in all, the evidence shows that the people concerned were not likely to harbour thoughts in any way dangerous to the established economic and social order.

In any case, all members of the Fascist state systems were expected to subscribe with absolute loyalty to a body of ideas which, however hollow it might be in other respects, excluded clearly and emphatically any attack on the basic framework of capitalism. Not only were dangerous thoughts not likely to be found among the men who came and went in the corridors of Fascist power. Such thoughts were positively forbidden, taboo.

But the most telling fact of all about the real nature of the Fascist systems is surely that, when they came to an end, twenty years after Mussolini's 'March on Rome' and twelve years after Hitler's assumption of the chancellorship, the economic and social structure of both countries had not been significantly changed. The classes which occupied the higher reaches of the economic and social pyramid before the Fascists came to power were still there; and so was the capitalist system which sustained these classes. Well might Franz Neumann state that 'the essence of National Socialist social policy consists in the acceptance and strengthening of the prevailing class character

---

[1] Matthews, *The Social Background of Political Decision Makers*, p. 49.

of German society'.[1] Exactly the same was true of Italy.

At the same time it is also true that the privileged classes in both Italy and Germany had to pay a high *political* price for the immense advantages which were conferred upon them by the Fascist regimes. For while they retained many positions of power and influence, they had to submit to a dictatorship over which they had no *genuine* control at all. Having helped the dictators to rob all other classes, and notably the working classes, of any semblance of power, they found their own drastically curtailed and in some crucial areas, notably foreign policy, altogether nullified. This is not a situation which an economically and socially dominant class, however secure it may feel about the ultimate intentions of its rulers, can contemplate without grave qualms, since it introduces into the process of decision-making, to which its members have been used to make a major contribution, an extremely high element of unpredictability.

It is in this perspective that must be understood the notion of the independence of the state power from all forces in civil society, to which Marx and Engels occasionally referred as possible in 'exceptional circumstances',[2] and of which Fascism, in the context of advanced capitalism, may be said to provide the furthest example. In that context, however, the concept is ambiguous in that it suggests a certain *neutrality* on the part of the state power in regard to social forces, which actual experience belies. Marx himself, writing of the *coup d'état* of Louis Bonaparte, suggested that 'only under the second Bonaparte does the state seem to have made itself completely independent';[3] 'the struggle seems to be settled in such a way that all classes, equally impotent and equally mute, fall on their knees before the rifle butt'.[4] But Marx also noted, in a famous phrase, that 'the state power is not suspended in mid-air'[5] and that Louis Napoleon's main task, his 'mission', was to 'safeguard "bourgeois order"'.[6] This is also a valid description of the 'mission' of the Fascist dictators. Nor was it the case in

---

[1] F. Neumann, *Behemoth*, 1942, p. 298.

[2] See, e.g. K. Marx, *The Eighteenth Brumaire of Louis Bonaparte*, and F. Engels, *The Origin of the Family, Private Property and the State*; and for a further discussion of the point, R. Miliband, 'Marx and the State', in *The Socialist Register 1965*.

[3] Marx, *The Eighteenth Brumaire*, in *Selected Works*, vol. 1, p. 30.

[4] *Ibid.*, p. 302.   [5] *Ibid.*, p. 302.   [6] *Ibid.*, p. 308.

Italy and Germany that *all* classes were *equally* impotent and mute under Fascism. What is true, however, is that the dictators, while working to safeguard the capitalist order, whatever their rhetoric and 'revolutionary' reforms, were also extremely well placed to determine, *on their own*, how they would do so, and to take decisions of crucial national importance quite independently.

It is the fear of such a situation arising which helps, *inter alia*, to explain why some elements of the business and traditional elites in Italy and Germany viewed the rise to power of their respective Fascist movements with unease and even hostility. Those who supported Fascism, and indeed made its accession to power possible, thought that they would buy the services of political gangsters without being dominated by them. In this, they were mistaken.

For a long time all went well and they found little to complain about as Mussolini and Hitler marched from success to success, at home, in diplomacy, and in war. The gamble appeared to have succeeded. But then came the threat of terrible retribution. For defeat in war and the collapse of the Fascist regimes raised the spectre of social revolution which they had sought to exorcise once and for all by surrendering their fate to the Fascists. In Italy, the threat came from within, in Germany from without, in the train of the advancing Russian armies.

However, the Italian and German privileged classes, having lost their Fascist masters and protectors, now found a new set of protectors in the shape of their British and American conquerors and occupiers. The Western powers were unable to do much about the postwar settlement in Eastern Europe, but they had no intention whatever of allowing radical social change in any country where they did have power to shape events, i.e. Western Europe, Greece, Japan and indeed everywhere else save Eastern Europe. Occupation by the armies of the United States and Britain amounted in effect to an absolute guarantee[1] that the existing economic and social structures would be preserved, and that any internal threat to them would be opposed, if necessary with the full force of military power, as in Greece.

---

[1] Which, it may be noted, the accession to power of a Labour government in Britain in July 1945 did nothing to make less absolute.

Indeed, defeat at the hands of the Western allies provided an additional bonus to the Italian, German and Japanese capitalist classes: it rid them of political rulers whose failure in war had turned them into encumbrances which these classes were too weak or too craven to remove themselves.

It did appear, at the end of the war, that anti-Fascism, 'de-Nazification' and the 'purge' of compromised elites might push 'democratisation' rather too far and make the return of some of these elites to positions of power and influence impossible. Similarly, there was much that was repugnant to German and Japanese business in the policies of 'decartelisation' upon which the victorious powers seemed bent. But all fears that defeat must have really drastic and irremediable consequences for the entrenched classes of the countries concerned were soon assuaged. The 'artificial revolution', as one writer has called the changes which were forced upon Germany and Japan at the end of the war, 'brought no permanent stigma to those who had led their country to ruin; neither country emerged into sovereignty with any important reservations against the employment of nationalist fanatics of the thirties and forties, even in the most responsible positions'.[1] What most opponents of Hitler in Germany wanted, the same writer suggests (perhaps unfairly to what there remained in 1945 of an authentic German socialist left), was 'a form of "palace" revolution involving the return of older elites in place of the Nazi upstarts'.[2] This is in fact what occurred, and Japanese experience was not materially different: in both countries, shifts in the power structure occurred mainly *within* a middle- and upper-class context and did not significantly affect middle- and upper-class predominance. As for 'decartelisation', it was never more than a tentative and half-hearted affair, and such efforts as were made to carry it out were correspondingly abortive.[3] A few years after the war, big business in the defeated

[1] J. D. Montgomery, *Forced to be Free. The Artificial Revolution in Germany and Japan*, 1957, p. 35. [2] *Ibid.*, p. 61.

[3] *Ibid.* See also T. A. Bisson, *Zaibatsu Dissolution in Japan*, 1949; J. B. Cohen, *Japanese Economy in War and Reconstruction*, 1949; and J. Halliday, 'Japan – Asian Capitalism', in *New Left Review*, no. 44, July–August 1967. Mr Halliday notes that 'a list of 1200 firms to be broken up was compiled; this was progressively reduced until there were only 19 firms on the list – and when nine of these had been dealt with the board set up by SCAP (composed of five prominent US businessmen) decided enough had been done' (p. 11).

countries was bigger than ever, and launched on a spectacular
course of expansion; and businessmen in both Germany and
Japan had achieved a position in society more exalted than at
any time previously.[1]

At the same time, the postwar triumphs of capitalism in
Germany, Japan and Italy were hardly a case of the Phoenix
rising from the ashes. The Phoenix had been alive and prosper-
ing throughout the years of dictatorship and terror. Defeat at
the hands of the Western powers merely gave it the chance to do
even better. For the business and other elites of these countries,
those years were not a dark hiatus between overthrow and
restoration. There was no overthrow and there was therefore no
need for restoration.

IV

Governments issued from Labour and socialist parties, or
which have included men drawn from such parties, obviously
present an altogether different case. For here are instances
where the political executive, in a number of advanced
capitalist countries, has been composed, wholly or in part, of
men representing parties and movements whose declared
purpose was the ultimate transcendance of the capitalist system
and its replacement by a socialist system based upon the
appropriation into the public domain of the largest part of the
means of production, distribution and exchange, including of
course all the most important and strategic sectors of industrial,
financial and commercial activity. And even where the fulfilment
of that purpose has been conceived, as social-democratic parties
have always conceived it, in terms of a gradual and piecemeal
process of collectivist erosion, or even where it has been

[1] This is particularly true of Japan, about which it has been noted that 'the
owners and executives of the big banks, factories and trading concerns never
attained a decisive position in prewar Japanese politics. At the peak of their
influence they were merely one wing of the ruling class, influential in economic
affairs, but insecure and lacking the power to make the great political decisions
shaping the destiny of the country. When the chips were down, following the
military resurgence of the thirties, they found themselves at a fatal disadvantage in
the struggle around the throne' (W. W. Lockwood, *The Economic Development of
apan: Growth and Structural Change*, 1954, p. 564).

abandoned altogether, these parties and movements have at least been committed to the immediate use of the state power by their governments for extensive reforms, notably in the social and economic field, designed to benefit the working classes and to eat into the power and privileges of the dominant ones.

That these governments have not achieved the transcendence of capitalism, is – or should be – obvious. But this does not by any means dispose of the question as to how far their policies and actions have in fact been at odds with the interests of the dominant classes and the business elites. The question of what they *have* achieved, of what has been the net result of their tenure of executive power, of the meaning of these 'experiments' for the nature and character of advanced capitalism and of its political system, remains relevant and needs to be probed further, the more so since it illuminates the extreme meaning, as experienced so far, which may be attributed to the notion of political competition in these systems.

The leaders of working-class parties in the countries of advanced capitalism have achieved office under one of three distinct sets of conditions.

First, they have occasionally been invited to join predominantly conservative coalitions in order to achieve 'national unity' in circumstances of grave national emergency, for instance in time of war. But since the main point of their being asked to join such coalitions was that they should *not* pursue 'partisan', 'sectional' and radical purposes, and that, even more important, they should help prevent their parties and movements from seeking to pursue them, these cases are not particularly relevant to the present discussion. Their presence in government might enable them to affect certain policies and to extract certain concessions beneficial to the working classes, but no question arises of their being able to use state power for any serious attack on the existing social order in any of its main, or even subsidiary, features.

Much the same is true of the ever more frequent occasions where representatives of social-democratic parties have entered coalitions with their conservative rivals and thus enabled the government to achieve a parliamentary majority. Even where they have obtained a substantial share of offices, and indeed where one of their number has headed the government, social-democratic ministers have generally been able to achieve little inside these hybrid formations. Far from presenting a threat to the established order, their main function has been to contain their own parties and to persuade them to accept the essentially conservative policies which they themselves have sanctioned. For the most part, participation on this basis has been a trap not a springboard.

Secondly, social-democratic leaders have in one case, that of Germany in 1918, found themselves in office as a result of their country's defeat in war and the collapse of the existing regime. But these leaders were not only not responsible for the revolutionary situation which propelled them into office; they were also desperately concerned to bring that situation to an immediate end, for which purpose they eagerly accepted the help of impeccably conservative and reactionary forces, notably the German High Command.[1] In this case too no question arises of the political executive being in any serious sense at odds with the interests of the dominant classes. On the contrary, the latter, at a time of extreme danger for them, had no more faithful, resolute and needed defenders than these leaders against any substantial erosion of their political or economic power.

The third case is that of office being achieved by social-democratic parties, as a result of a major victory at the polls.

Such victories have not, with the very doubtful exception of the Popular Front electoral victory of 1936, occurred in conditions which approximated to a revolutionary situation. But they were nevertheless only made possible by a quite definite and often very substantial shift of popular opinion in radical directions, and could at least be taken to signify a high if often vague and inchoate measure of support for the programme of reforms and the promise of a new deal which the victorious party or parties had offered in their election campaigns. Most of those who voted for these parties may not have wanted a lot more by way of radical reform than they were offered. But neither is it at all likely that they wanted less, or generally found abhorrent the notion of far-reaching social change. Those people who did

---

[1] See, e.g. F.L. Carsten, *The Reichswehr and Politics*, 1966, and Wheeler-Bennett, *The Nemesis of Power. The German Army in Politics, 1918–1945.*

find it abhorrent must be presumed to have voted for parties which could be relied on to oppose it. For the most part it is no doubt mistaken to suggest a picture of popular revolutionary fervour as the basis for electoral support of left-wing parties. But it is certainly not wrong to suggest a high degree of popular *availability* for extensive and even fundamental change.

Moreover, victory itself, followed by the accession to office of popular leaders, and their assumption, in due constitutional form, of the trappings of executive power, has always tended to enhance the belief of those who had voted for them that a new deal was indeed at hand and that great changes, favourable to the working class and concomitantly adverse to all the forces of property and privilege, were about to be introduced by 'their' government. Something like a shudder of popular expectation and hope has always tended to accompany left-wing victories at the polls, no doubt in part because such victories have on the whole been so infrequent, and have appeared to dislodge from the centre of political power society's traditional rulers; indeed because such victories are often interpreted (quite mistakenly) as actually constituting the expulsion from power of the dominant classes themselves. And these expectations, hopes and illusions have further been enhanced by the apprehension and loathing which conservative forces have tended to express, usually with great vehemence, on the morrow of their defeat.

For their part however, social-democratic leaders, in their moment of victory, and even more so after, have generally been most concerned to reassure the dominant classes and the business elites as to their intentions, to stress that they conceived their task in 'national' and not in 'class' terms, to insist that their assumption of office held no threat to business; and, in the same vein, they have equally been concerned to urge upon their followers and upon the working classes generally the virtues of patience, discipline and hard work, to warn them that electoral victory and the achievement of office by their own leaders must on no account serve as an encouragement to the militant assertion of working-class demands upon employers, propertied interests and the government itself, and to emphasise that the new ministers, faced with immense responsibilities, burdens and problems, must not be impeded in their purpose by unreasonable and unrealistic pressures. The leaders, once in office (and often before) are always more 'moderate' than their followers. Here is one variant of the 'iron law of oligarchy' which – at least in the countries of advanced capitalism – has admitted of no exception. That most of the led have with greater or lesser reluctance tended to accept their leaders' 'moderate' stance is a matter of great importance, the significance of which will be considered later. At any rate, new governments of the left have always been at great pains to *subdue* popular expectations, and to emphasise that while there was much they wished to do by way of reform, capitalist interests would find, if they did not know it already, that they were dealing with eminently reasonable and responsible men, acutely aware, unlike many of their followers, that Rome was not built in a day, and that its building must in any case be approached with the utmost circumspection.

As a token of their approach to their tasks, it is very notable that new governments of the left have very seldom embarked upon these tasks in a spirit of exuberant administrative innovation and manifested any great desire or will to cut loose from the bureaucratic web in which the state system, including the executive power, is enmeshed. There is in fact only one example in the history of advanced capitalism where a reforming administration has shown a genuine will to overcome some at least of the constrictions imposed upon it by traditional and traditionalist bureaucratic structures; and that example is not provided by a professedly left-wing government but by a government actively and explicitly dedicated to the maintenance and the restoration in health of the capitalist system, namely the presidency of Franklin Roosevelt in its famous first 'Hundred Days', and indeed for some time after.[1] In contrast, governments bearing a much more radical label have normally been content to use the administrative structures which they found ready to hand; and where they have innovated, they have also tended to staff the new bodies they have created with men who, whether drawn from the traditional bureaucracy or from outside, have seldom been known for their reforming or radical urges, let alone any socialist commitments – indeed, they have generally been men known for their impeccably conservative

---

[1] See, e.g. R. E. Sherwood, *The White House Papers of Harry L. Hopkins*, 1949, vol. I, and A. M. Schlesinger Jr, *The Coming of the New Deal*, 1958.

background and dispositions. Far from seeking to surround themselves with men ardent for reform and eager for change in radical directions, such governments have mostly been content to be served by men much more likely to exercise a restraining influence upon their own reforming propensities. However, the presence of such men at the elbow of new ministers serves an important political purpose: it demonstrates the sense of continuity which animates the new political office-holders and further helps to reassure conservative interests and forces as to their new rulers' intentions.

One reason why new governments of the left seek to provide such reassurances to these forces is that they have normally come to office in conditions of great economic, financial and social difficulty and crisis, which they have feared to see greatly aggravated by the suspicion and hostility of the 'business community'.

Such fears are well justified. But there is more than one way to deal with the adverse conditions which these new governments encounter on their assumption of office. One of them is to treat these conditions as a challenge to greater boldness, as an opportunity to greater radicalism, and as a means, rather than as an obstacle, to swift and decisive measures of reform. There is, after all, much that a genuinely radical government, firm in its purpose and enjoying a substantial measure of popular support, may hope to do on the morrow of its electoral legitimation, not despite crisis conditions but because of them. And in doing so, it is also likely to receive the support of many people, hitherto uncommitted or half-committed, but willing to accept a resolute lead.

This, however, is not how these governments have chosen to embark upon their tasks. On the contrary, they have found in the difficult conditions they inevitably faced a ready and convenient excuse for the conciliation of the very economic and social forces they were pledged to oppose, and for the reduction of their own ambitions to the point where these have ceased to hold any kind of threat to conservative forces. And the longer they have been in office, the more marked have become these tendencies. Social democratic governments have seldom if ever begun very boldly; but their later stages have generally been still more cautious and orthodox.

On the other hand, this is not at all to suggest that governments of the left have not done many things which were strongly and even bitterly resented and opposed by the dominant classes and the business elites. As a matter of fact, all governments, however conservative, have at one time or another been compelled to do such things; and it may readily be seen that governments of the left, however 'moderate', have tended to do more than others which these classes and elites disliked and opposed.

But the really important question does not concern the subjective feelings and reactions of conservative interests to reforming (or any other) governments. To focus on this aspect of the matter, in the present context, is to confuse the issue. After all, it is quite probable that no leader of a government in this century has been more hated, and even feared, by business elites than was Roosevelt in the early (and even in the later) stages of the New Deal – much more so than any social-democratic prime minister in other capitalist countries. Yet no one believes that Roosevelt sought to (or did) weaken American capitalism. On the contrary it is now evident (and it was evident to many people at the time) that the New Deal sought to, and in fact did, restore and strengthen the capitalist system, at very little cost to the dominant classes.

The important question about social-democratic and other reforming governments has to do with the objective nature of their reforms and, more generally, with the net impact of their tenure of office upon the economic and social order and upon the configuration of privilege and power in their societies. In order to gauge this, it may be best to look at the concrete record of some governments which have been committed, within the context of the constitutional regimes of advanced capitalism, to substantial measures of economic and social reform.

The first such government to require consideration is the Popular Front government of Léon Blum, brought to office as a result of the elections of 26 April and 3 May 1936. After the second ballot on the latter date, the forces of the Popular Front had won some 376 seats, with 147 seats to the Socialist Party, 106 to the moderate and bourgeois Radical-Socialist Party, and 72 to the Communist Party, the rest being shared by smaller political formations of the left. The new opposition, for its own part, had some 222 seats, dispersed over a number of more or less right-wing parties.[1] The victory of the Left was thus quite clear and unmistakable, and constituted without any doubt its biggest electoral success in the interwar years. It also constituted, or appeared to constitute, a spectacular demonstration of left-wing, radical and democratic strength against the threat of Fascism, both from inside France and from outside. Furthermore, the victory of the Popular Front was almost immediately given an entirely new dimension by the massive wave of strikes, with the occupation of enterprises by the strikers, which swept over the whole of France. It is scarcely an exaggeration to say that this 'revolution of 1936', as it has been called, was a most dramatic working-class rebellion, albeit a mainly peaceful one, against managerial authority and domination, and an equally dramatic assertion of labour demands for improved conditions.

In this sudden and potentially dangerous confrontation with labour, capital could only, given the magnitude of the movement, expect relief from one source, namely the new government itself. This it obtained in full measure, though at a price.

The Popular Front government, under the prime ministership of Léon Blum, had come into being on 4 June, one long month after the elections, and was composed of Socialists and Radicals, the Communists having rejected ministerial participation even though they promised conditional support to the new administration.

There was at least one thing over which the government and its opponents, inside Parliament and outside, were wholly agreed: the strikes and the occupation of enterprises must be brought to an end. On the eve of his appointment, the new socialist minister of the interior to be, Roger Salengro, had said: 'Let those whose task it is to lead the trade union movement do their duty. Let them hasten to put an end to this unjustified agitation. For myself, my choice is made between order and anarchy. Against whosoever it may be, I shall maintain order'.[2]

On the other hand, circumstances were not such as to enable the government to do this by force; and to give it due credit,

---

[1] G. Lefranc, *Histoire du Front Populaire*, 1965, p. 131.   [2] *Ibid.*, p. 146.

it did not contemplate any such action. What it did want was to bring the agitation to an end by peaceful means, and it achieved this, or at least created the conditions for such an outcome, by bringing capital and labour together and have them accept the famous Matignon agreements. These agreements endorsed the 40-hour week, a general increase in wages of the order of 7 to 15 per cent, and the acceptance by the employers of substantially enlarged trade union rights. In the course of the following few days and weeks, these agreements were given the force of law, together with statutory provisions for an annual fortnight's holidays with pay, the extension of compulsory schooling to the age of fourteen, the dissolution of a number of Fascist-oriented organisations, the nationalisation of the production of war material, the reform of the Bank of France, and a variety of other measures of financial and agricultural reform.

These, and some subsequent measures of reform for which the Popular Front government was responsible,[1] are not to be dismissed as altogether negligible. Yet it has recently been observed, by a writer not noticeably on the Left, that:

... the economic and social measures of the Popular Front, which were thought at the time to be quite revolutionary, seem now extraordinarily timid when compared to what has been achieved since then in France and abroad, not only by governments of the left, but also by governments making no profession whatever of radicalism.[2]

This judgement, it may be argued, takes too little account of the change of perspective which the passage of thirty years has brought about; and it may also be said that it underestimates the difficulties and the resistances which the Blum government faced.

But such arguments are only valid within the context of the government's whole orientation and purpose. *Given that orientation and purpose*, it is perfectly true that Léon Blum and his socialist colleagues (not to speak of his Radical ones) could not be expected to overcome the innumerable difficulties they faced, which were genuine enough, or to break down the resistances which stood in their path.[3] The original Popular Front pro-

[1] For which see *ibid.*, part 3.
[2] J. Baumier, *Les Grandes Affaires Françaises*, 1967, p. 35.
[3] The point is also relevant to the foreign policy of the government, and notably

gramme had envisaged an even more modest series of reforms than were eventually carried out; and the main reason, it can hardly be doubted, why the government went somewhat beyond that programme is that it found itself, on coming to office, in the midst of a social crisis of vast dimensions which it could only hope to control by immediate and tangible concessions to the working classes. Furthermore it is in the highest degree unlikely that the government's initial programme of reforms would have encountered so little opposition in the Chamber of Deputies, in the Senate (where the government was in a minority), from employers and from all conservative forces in general, had there not prevailed a situation of acute crisis. In this sense, popular militancy was the government's truest, indeed its only ally, and the best hope which Blum and his socialist colleagues had, not only of forcing through further and more extensive reforms, but of carrying their wavering or hostile Radical partners with them.

It was only on the strength of that popular militancy that they could have hoped to do a great deal more with the power they had obtained than they had originally intended. Instead, they did their best, by minimal concession and massive objurgation, to discourage militancy, and thus deprived themselves, *quite deliberately*, of their only real resource against a badly frightened, disoriented but formidable opposition. Once relieved of its immediate fears, that opposition regained its confidence and began, with ever greater effectiveness, to fight back; while the government itself began a process of retreat which was to end with its resignation in June 1937. Whether it could have achieved more in the face of the political, financial and international difficulties it confronted may be a matter for argument. What is not is that it had no wish to try. Léon Blum had made it absolutely clear, after the elections, that he intended to 'administer the bourgeois state' and to 'put into effect the Popular Front programme, not to transform the social system';[1] and that he had no intention of transforming the *exercise* of power into its *conquest*.[2] The narrowing of perspective

to its attitude to the Spanish Civil War. It supplied some military equipment and aircraft to the Republicans, but resisted all demands for greater help to them. This failed to appease the Right, and further helped to divide and demoralise the Left.

[1] D. M. Pickles, *The French Political Scene*, 1938, p. 130.
[2] Lefranc, *Histoire du Front Populaire*, p. 141. For a perceptive discussion of this

which this choice imposed upon him and his government ensured, quite apart from external contingencies, that the impact of the Popular Front 'experiment' upon the French social system would remain a very limited one and that it would not *fundamentally* affect the distribution of economic and political power in French society.

Another example of governmental power coming into the hands of men formally dedicated to the ultimate transformation of the existing social order in socialist directions is that of the Labour government which was elected in Britain in July 1945, the first occasion on which the Labour Party obtained a clear, in fact an impregnable, parliamentary majority of 146 seats over all other parties.[1]

The circumstances which attended Labour's victory were in one sense less dramatic than those which followed the Popular Front's electoral success; in another sense, more. The Labour government's assumption of office was not marked by any vast upsurge of popular agitation such as had occurred in France; but there was nevertheless, at the end of the war, a deep popular expectation of new beginnings, a widespread sense that the sacrifices and privations endured in war, and indeed during the long years before the war, must be redeemed by a thorough renewal of Britain's social fabric. It was this sentiment which had made Labour's victory possible and which presented a unique chance to the new government. Here, it might seem, was a moment of greater danger for all conservative forces than they had faced at any previous time in the long history of their supremacy over British life.

Reality was, however, very different from appearance. The conservative forces were in fact in no danger at all. Like their counterparts in relation to the Blum government, these forces could rely, with the utmost confidence, on the 'moderation' of the men to whom they had been forced by popular suffrage to surrender executive power. Here too, there was a price to be paid; but it was, all things considered, a remarkably small

distinction in Léon Blum's thought, see C. Audry, *Léon Blum ou la Politique du Juste*, 1955.

[1] The account which follows draws heavily on my *Parliamentary Socialism*, 1961, chapter 9, 'The Climax of Labourism.'

price, which left intact the main citadel of power and privilege.

By far and away the most important characteristic of the men who assumed executive power in July 1945 was the objective modesty of their ambitions, in economic and social terms. No doubt, they thought and spoke of a 'new social order' which must be built upon the ruins of war. But in *terms of basic structures*, that new social order bore a very remarkable resemblance to the old.

Perhaps the best and most significant token of that fact is that, had it been left to the Labour leaders, the Labour Party would have gone into the 1945 election campaign free from any commitment to any measure of nationalisation whatsoever, save for the half-nationalisation of the Bank of England.[1] What *they* wanted was a continuation in peace time of the controls over economic life which had been introduced during the war, i.e. a more and better regulated peace time *capitalist* economy, together with a much wider system of welfare provisions. That the Labour Government did assume power committed to a programme of nationalisation was the result of rank and file pressure before and at the 1944 Labour Party Conference.[2]

The nationalisation programme which the government did carry through during its period of office was a good deal less extensive than the Labour activists had wished, or than those who had voted for Labour in July 1945 would in all probability have been ready to support; but it was nevertheless substantial, including as it did the Bank of England, coal, gas, electricity, railways, a part of inland transport, cable and wireless, and, very half-heartedly, in the latter stages of the government's life, the iron and steel industry.

Nor is it to be denied that these were measures which the economic and political forces of conservatism more or less strongly disliked, and which a Conservative government would not have wished to adopt. In this sense it is perfectly appropriate to say that there was a certain unhingement between these forces and the Labour government on issues of considerable importance.

On the other hand, there are a number of considerations which need, in this context, to be taken into account. One of them was expressed by *The Economist* in November 1945, after

[1] *Ibid.*, pp. 276–7.   [2] *Ibid.*, pp. 277–8.

the government had announced its nationalisation proposals, except for iron and steel. 'An avowedly Socialist Government, with a clear parliamentary majority', it wrote, 'might well have been expected to go several steps further ... If there is to be a Labour Government, the programme now stated is almost the least it could do without violating its election pledges'.[1] In other words, the government had introduced a *minimal* programme, for which capitalist interests, however much they might resent it, could well, in the circumstances of the period, be grateful.

Secondly, it is hardly irrelevant to the issue that some of the nationalisation measures proposed and carried through by the government had been advocated or at least endorsed by Conservative and Liberal politicians as early as the first world war; and that, as Professor Brady has noted, a number of such nationalisation measures had been recommended 'by Conservative dominated fact-finding and special investigating committees'.[2]

Thirdly, and perhaps most important, the government could scarcely have been more generous to the interested parties in regard to the all-important question of compensation: all in all, capitalist interests made an excellent bargain, in many instances a much better one than they could have made had they been left in command of their property.

Finally, the exceedingly conventional, bureaucratic and 'businesslike' manner in which the government envisaged the administration of the nationalised industries, combined with its appointment of men drawn from large-scale enterprise to their boards, helped to ensure that the enlarged 'public sector', far from proving in any sense an embarrassment – let alone a threat – to the private sector, would in fact become an exceedingly useful adjunct to it.

In this light, it is easier to understand Attlee's recollection that 'there was not much real opposition to our nationalisation proposals, only iron and steel roused much feeling'.[3] For all the talk of a 'mixed economy' which these measures engendered,

---

[1] *The Economist*, 24 November 1945, p. 239.

[2] R. A. Brady, *Crisis in Britain. Plans and Achievements of the Labour Government.* 1950, p. 41.

[3] C. R. Attlee, *As It Happened*, 1954, p. 165.

not to mention the often-expressed view that Britain, because of them, had undergone a 'socialist revolution', all nice and peaceful, nationalisation not only did not weaken British capitalism; in some essential regards it strengthened it. And even British capitalists, and their political spokesmen, were not in most cases sufficiently blinkered not to see something of this, or even all of it.

But it is also important to understand that this result of nationalisation was not something unwelcome to the Labour leaders. On the contrary, the modernisation of capitalist enterprise was one of their main purposes. Given this purpose, conservative forces had little to fear from marginal nationalisation or from the system of controls through which the government, having inherited that system from war time, sought, not very effectively, to regulate and direct economic life.[1]

Even so, and for all its inadequacies, the nationalisation programme of the Labour government might have assumed a very different perspective had it been intended as the foundation of a continuing and extended programme of nationalisation, destined to capture the 'commanding heights' of the 'private sector'. But there had been no such intention in 1945 and there certainly was none by 1948. On the contrary, the government resolutely set its face against any such further 'experiment', save for iron and steel, and embarked on a programme, if such it might be called, of 'consolidation', which amounted in effect to the Labour Party's explicit and permanent installation in the 'mixed economy'.[2] From then onwards, and with the exception of the nationalisation of the steel industry, the Labour leaders turned into the stubborn opponents of any significant extension of public ownership, and have remained opposed to it until the present day.

It was also in 1948 that the Labour government brought into being a National Health Service and a comprehensive system of social insurance. These measures, which were the pillars of the 'Welfare State', represented of course a major, it could even be said a dramatic, extension of the system of welfare which was part of the 'ransom' the working classes had been able to exact

[1] See, e.g. A. A. Rogow, with the assistance of P. Shore, *The Labour Government and British Industry 1945–1951*, 1955.
[2] Miliband, *Parliamentary Socialism*, pp. 298ff.

from their rulers in the course of a hundred years. But it did not, for all its importance, constitute any threat to the existing system of power or privilege. What it did constitute was a certain humanisation of the *existing* social order. As such, it was obviously significant to the working classes. But it was nothing which conservative forces, for all their opposition to it, need have viewed with any degree of genuine alarm or fear – as indeed even its strongest opponents did not.

In any case, reassurance, if it was required, was amply provided by the general retreat which the turn to 'consolidation' entailed. From 1948 onwards the government rapidly shed whatever propensities to reform it had had. The economic and financial crisis it faced, which had much to do with its own foreign policy and defence commitments, provided it with the excuse to move into steadily more orthodox directions in home policy, notably in the adoption of an early version of an 'incomes policy' whose main purpose was to foist upon wage-earners severe restrictions and indeed a freeze on wage increases. Nevertheless, the government retained a high measure of electoral support. But in parliamentary terms it saw its triumphant majority of 1945 melt, in the election of February 1950, to a mere six seats. Within eighteen further months, which only confirmed its decline and loss of purpose, the Conservatives were back in office.

Let it be said again that much that the Government had done during its tenure of office was certainly unwelcome to the conservative forces and interests. But let it also be repeated that the latter had good cause to be grateful that the Labour government had not sought to do more; and they had even more cause for gratitude in that what it had done had in no serious sense been injurious to them. From a conservative point of view, it was no small thing that the price which the dominant classes knew they would have to pay, because of the radicalism of war, for the maintenance of the existing social order should have been so relatively low. For this they had to thank the Labour leaders – and a Labour movement which accepted without too much demur the 'moderation' of its leaders.

This 'moderation' was not something which came as a happy but unexpected surprise to the leaders of British conservatism.

They were well aware of it even in the dark days of July 1945, at the time the Labour government took office.

In the case of Léon Blum in 1936, and of some of his ministers, French conservatism might well feel that these men were temperamentally, ideologically and politically unpredictable; and that they might be tempted, notwithstanding their earlier reassurances, to move further to the Left under the pressure of their Communist allies, their own rank and file, and popular demands.

No such apprehension could be seriously entertained about the men who assumed executive power in Britain in 1945. The Conservatives, and notably Churchill, had sought to suggest in the election campaign that Britain was faced with the urgent danger of totalitarianism, a police state, and red socialism generally. But this was clearly intended for popular consumption, as it turned out unavailingly; and it is extremely unlikely that most of those who raised the scare seriously believed a word of it. For they knew the men who were to lead a Labour government not only as moderate and 'responsible' opponents before the war, one of whose main endeavours had been to subdue and repel the demands of the Left for more radical policies, but as trusted wartime colleagues, from whom they were separated on major issues of policy by differences of degree rather than of kind. That men like Attlee, Bevin, Dalton and Morrison, or for that matter Cripps, the erstwhile champion of the Left, would suddenly be fired by revolutionary urges on assuming office (or rather on resuming office) was not a notion which could greatly trouble experienced men of affairs.

One clear indication, among many others, of how much continuity could be hoped for in the coming period of change, was the fact that the new government accepted without any kind of question that it should be served by precisely the same civil servants who had served its predecessors. Attlee later recalled that when he returned to the Potsdam Conference after the elections, this time as prime minister, 'our American friends were surprised to find that there was no change in our official advisers and that I had even taken over, as my Principal Private Secretary, Leslie Rowan, who had been serving Churchill in the same capacity'.[1] The same pattern

[1] Attlee, *As It Happened*, p. 149.

prevailed throughout the government, and throughout its life. What made this reassuring to the conservative forces was not only that ministers would be advised by men in whose 'good sense' these forces could have every confidence; even more important was the indication it gave that the new men had no purposes which required them to surround themselves with different, less orthodox advisers.

In no field was the congruity of views between Labour and Conservative leaders more pronounced than in foreign affairs. The Labour ministers in the Churchill Coalition had already shown that they did not much depart from Conservative views and attitudes on the broad lines of postwar policy, and Attlee had indeed assured Churchill before the Potsdam Conference that he did not anticipate 'that we shall differ on the main lines of policy, which we have discussed together so often'.[1] Nor was this any less the case when Attlee assumed the premiership and returned to Potsdam, accompanied by Ernest Bevin as his new Foreign Secretary. The then American Secretary of State later noted that 'Britain's stand on the issues before the Conference was not altered in the slightest, so far as we could discern, by the replacement of Mr Churchill and Mr Eden by Mr Attlee and Mr Bevin. This continuity of Britain's foreign policy impressed me.'[2] In fact, Byrnes noted that Bevin's manner towards the Russians was 'so aggressive' that 'both the president and I wondered how we would get along with this new Foreign Minister'.[3] Well might Churchill write in March 1946 to James Forrestal, the American Secretary of Defence, that 'there was considerable consolation in the victory of Bevin because Bevin was able to talk more firmly and clearly to Russia than he could have, by virtue of being a Labour Government'.[4] And the following retrospective comment of a later Conservative prime minister may equally serve as an accurate indication of the closeness of views which prevailed over foreign policy between the Labour Government and the Conservative opposition 'Though my handling of some events would have been different from his' (i.e. Bevin's), Sir Anthony Eden (as he

---

[1] K. Martin, *Harold Laski, 1893–1950*, 1953, p. 169. A notable example of this agreement on 'the main lines of policy' was the Labour ministers' support for the Coalition government's military intervention in Greece against the Left.

[2] J. Byrnes, *Speaking Frankly*, 1947, p. 79. [3] *Ibid.*, p. 79.

[4] W. Millis (ed.), *The Forrestal Diaries*, 1951, p. 144.

was then) wrote in 1960, 'I was in agreement with the aims of his foreign policy and with most of what he did, and we met quite frequently. He would invite me to his room in the House of Commons where we discussed events informally. In Parliament I usually followed him in debate and I would publicly have agreed with him more, if I had not been anxious to embarrass him less'.[1] It need hardly be said that this agreement did not stem from some miraculous conversion of the Conservative opposition to distinctive Labour, let alone socialist, policies. There were no such policies: only, as Eden rightly noted, differences of views on the 'handling' of a number of issues. Thus, it may well be that a Conservative government would not have found it so easy to commit itself, as the Labour government did in 1947, to the acceptance of political independence for India, Burma and Ceylon. Whether a Conservative government, in the circumstances of the period, could or would have long opposed independence, is a matter for speculation. But what is more relevant here is that by accepting it the Labour government could in no sense be said to have injured or outraged conservative interests. And it is also very much to the point that both in foreign and colonial affairs these interests, whether they knew it or not, had in the Labour government a resolute and dependable ally. All in all, the same judgment may reasonably be passed about the government's whole conduct of affairs between 1945 and 1951.

Mention must also be made of a third case, that of France at the time of its liberation in 1944, when traditional elites, massively discredited by their wartime record of collaboration with the enemy, were, for a brief moment which must have seemed interminable, effectively bereft not only of any degree of political influence over their own destiny and that of their country but also of the protection of the state, since the state on which they could rely had ceased to exist – and this at a time when a resurgent and armed Left seemed about to come into its own.[2]

[1] Sir A. Eden, *Memoirs. Full Circle*, 1960, p.5.
[2] See, e.g. P. M. de la Gorce, *De Gaulle entre deux Mondes*, 1964, pp. 339ff.; for the political collapse of the 'classical Right' after Liberation, see, e.g. René Rémond, *La Droite en France*, 1963, pp. 243ff.

But here too the reality was very much less dramatic. There were two main (and related) reasons why appearance so belied reality. The first was the fact that de Gaulle had managed, during the war, to gain recognition from all Resistance movements, including the Communists, as the leader of the Resistance and therefore as the leader of the government that would rule France once it was liberated. But de Gaulle's purpose throughout the war was not simply to liberate France; it was also to prevent that liberation from assuming a revolutionary character and from providing the Left, particularly the Communists, with an important, let alone a predominant voice in the post-liberation settlement.[1] In this, the general was extraordinarily successful.

But that success was made a great deal easier by a second factor in the political situation of France at the time of the Liberation, namely that the French Communist Party, though bent upon major economic and social reforms, was in no sense committed to anything resembling a revolutionary bid for power,[2] and accepted, with little difficulty, a minor place in the reconstructed Provisional Government which de Gaulle appointed on 9 September 1944. That government included two Communists, one as minister of air and the other of public health. It also included four members of the Socialist Party; but no suspicion of socialist leanings could possibly be attached to the rest of the government, some of whose members, for instance René Pléven and George Bidault, subsequently became leading

[1] See, e.g. Charles de Gaulle, *Mémoires de Guerre*, vol. 2, *L'Unité, 1942–1944* 1956.

[2] In November 1944 an amnesty made possible the return to France from Russia of Maurice Thorez, the general secretary of the Communist Party. In explaining why he agreed to this, de Gaulle notes that: 'compte tenu des circonstances d'antan, des évènements survenus depuis, des nécessités d'aujourd'hui, je considère que le retour de Maurice Thorez à la tête du Parti communiste peut comporter, actuellement, plus d'avantages que d'inconvénients . . . Dès le lendemain de son retour en France, il aide à mettre fin aux dernières séquelles des "Milices patriotiques" que certains, parmi les siens, s'obstinent à maintenir dans une nouvelle clandestinité. Dans la mesure où le lui permet la sombre et dure rigidité de son parti, il s'oppose aux tentatives d'empiétement des comités de libération et aux actes de violence auxquels cherchent à se livrer des équipes surexcitées. A ceux, – nombreux – des ouvriers, en particulier des mineurs, qui écoutent ses harangues, il ne cesse de donner pour consigne de travailler autant que possible et de produire coûte que coûte' (Charles de Gaulle, *Mémoires de Guerre*, vol. 3, *Le Salut, 1944–1946*, 1959, p. 100–1). See also J. Fauvet, *Histoire du Parti Communiste Français*, 1965, vol. 2, part 3.

conservative politicians in the Fourth Republic. In any case the government was dominated by the general himself, who could always be relied on to opt, in the economic and social fields, for orthodox rather than radical policies.

Nevertheless, even so essentially 'moderate' a government could not avoid, and had indeed no great wish to avoid, commitment to a substantial, if limited and unsystematic, programme of nationalisation, which encompassed the northern coalfields, the Renault works, gas, electricity, the Bank of France and the four major credit institutions. Even less than in the English case were these measures intended to serve as the first step in the wholesale transformation of the French social and economic order. Their purpose, in the eyes of most members of the Provisional Government, and certainly in those of de Gaulle, was to strengthen the role of the state in an economic situation which urgently required its intervention; and the same purpose was also to be served by the planning mechanisms which were then set in place. But intervention was intended to occur in the context of a predominantly private enterprise economy, whose continuing private and capitalist character was taken for granted both by de Gaulle and by most of his ministers. As the Socialist minister of production put it at the time, 'a wide free sector remains the fundamental condition of French activity and economic recovery'.[1]

Just over a year after the Liberation, on 21 October 1945, general elections gave the Communist and Socialist parties an absolute majority in the new Constituent Assembly, and also in the country. 'La France', Jacques Fauvet notes, 'semble alors mûre pour le Front Populaire, peut-être même pour la démocratie populaire'. But, he adds, 'la seule présence d'un homme – de Gaulle – et avec lui, et après lui, celle d'un parti – le M.R.P. – vont l'en préserver'.[2] The 'classical Right' had been utterly defeated at the polls. But a new, heterogeneous, Christian Democratic party, the Mouvement Républican Populaire, had polled some 4,780,000 votes and obtained 141 seats, against 148 for the Communists and 134 for the Socialists. There was much 'radicalism' in the M.R.P., but that party

---

[1] Quoted in B.D. Graham, *The French Socialists and Tri-partisme 1944–1947*, 1965, p. 48.

[2] J. Fauvet, *La IVe République*, 1959, p. 53.

soon, and inevitably, became a precious political substitute for explicitly conservative parties and served, *faute de mieux*, as a crucially important instrument of conservative purposes. Or rather, it was able to play that role because of the Socialist Party's determination not to participate in a government which would not include the M.R.P., who in turn wanted no one but de Gaulle as president of the new provisional government. The Communist Party, which would have preferred a Socialist-Communist government without de Gaulle, readily subdued its own demands for the sake of governmental participation; and its leaders also agreed to their exclusion by de Gaulle from any 'strategic' ministry, such as defence, interior, or foreign affairs.[1] Instead, they got four 'economic' ministries, economic affairs, industrial production, labour and armaments; and Maurice Thorez became one of four ministers of state, or super-ministers, who had, however, more rank than power.

In accepting so many rebuffs and compromises the Communist leaders were no doubt giving concrete expression to the 'national' image they were then ardently concerned to project; and they may well have believed that their participation in what was a clearly non-socialist and even anti-socialist government was a necessary stage in a process of advance which must ultimately lead to a socialist conquest of power, with their own party at the head of affairs.

If this is what they did believe, it turned out to be a very bad miscalculation. Communist participation, far from notably 'radicalising' the government, helped, on the contrary, to 'de-radicalise', or at least to subdue, the most militant part of the working-class movement. This was what de Gaulle had hoped for when he took Communists into his government: 'At least for a certain time', he wrote later, 'their participation under my leadership would help to assure social peace, of which the country had such great need'.[2]

The situation was not much transformed by de Gaulle's abrupt resignation on 20 Janurary 1946. The ministry which was then formed by the Socialist Félix Gouin included an additional Communist, who became head of a department concerned with ex-servicemen and war victims; and Maurice Thorez became vice-premier. The French Communist Party,

[1] De Gaulle, *Mémoires de Guerre*, vol. 3, pp. 274ff.   [2] *Ibid.*, p. 276.

penetrated as its leadership was by 'the spirit of Yalta', proudly continued to call itself 'le Parti de la Reconstruction Française', and it may well have deserved the appellation. But the 're-construction' in which it played so notable a part was that of a predominantly capitalist economy, and the renovation which occurred was that of a regime whose main beneficiaries were not the working classes but those capitalist and other traditional elites whose situation had at the time of liberation seemed so parlous. Here too, it is a matter for argument whether a different strategy would, in the circumstances of the time and from the point of view of the Communist Party and the working classes, have yielded better results. But it can at any rate hardly be doubted that the Communist presence in the government between 1944 and 1947, when the Communist ministers were forced out, entailed no threat to the French dominant class, and was in fact of quite considerable advantage to it.

The same conclusion is also applicable to the Italian experi-ence of Communist participation in government after the war. Even more than in France, liberation appeared to present the Left with unparalleled opportunities for a revolutionary bid for power. But while Italian conservatism had no de Gaulle to protect it, it had the Allied forces, whose governments, it has been noted, 'could not have permitted the establishment of a Communist or para-Communist government in a country which, according to the wartime inter-Allied agreements, was stated to be within the Western sphere of influence'.[1] Nor in any case had the Communist and Socialist leaders any revolutionary ambitions. What they sought, as in France, was ministerial participation in a governmental coalition which was not of the Left. This they got. But they did not get much else. 'Revival of the economy', as has also been noted, 'was left essentially to the operations of a system of laissez-faire'.[2] In this case too, a battered but unbowed dominant class had to pay a remarkably small price for the perpetuation of its predominance.

I have argued in this chapter that the business and propertied interests of advanced capitalist countries have generally been able to rely on the positive and active good will of their governments;

[1] G. Mammarella, *Italy After Fascism*, 1966, p. 92.
[2] N. Kogan, *A Political History of Postwar Italy*, 1966, p. 42.

and also that where, occasionally, governments have come into being whose members, or some of whose members, could not, in terms of the ultimate purpose and official rhetoric of their parties, be so relied on, their *actual* approach to affairs has greatly reduced or altogether nullified the dangers which these interests were deemed to face.

But there are other elements of the state system whose ideological dispositions and practical activities are of crucial importance in the determination of the state's relationship to society and to the different classes and interests within it. An adequate picture of the role of the state must therefore take into account the contribution of these other elements. This is what I propose to do in the next chapter, which is devoted to the part played by administrative, coercive and judicial elites in the political configuration of advanced capitalism.

5

Servants of the State

I

While political leaders in the countries of advanced capitalism generally wear specific political and party labels, top civil servants generally do not. No doubt, governments in some of these countries bring into the administrative apparatus men of their own party and political coloration, or promote such men in preference to others. But for the most part, administrative elites in these political systems are not expected to be party men. On the contrary, the claim is insistently made, not least by civil servants themselves, that they are politically 'neutral', in the sense that their overriding, indeed their exclusive concern, is to advance the business of the state under the direction of their political masters.

It has already been suggested that to view higher civil servants as the mere executants of policies in whose determination they have had little or no share is quite unrealistic. This is not to say that 'bureaucrats' are necessarily 'hungry for power', that they 'run the country' and that ministers only provide a convenient façade for bureaucratic rule. That picture does not correspond to reality either. The true position lies somewhere in between these extremes: the general pattern must be taken to be one in which these men do play an important part in the process of governmental decision-making, and therefore constitute a considerable force in the configuration of political power in their societies.

As for the manner in which this power is exercised, the notion of 'neutrality' which is often attached to it is surely in the highest degree misleading; indeed, a moment's reflection must suggest that it is absurd: men who are deeply immersed in public affairs and who play a major role not only in the application but in the determination of policy, as these men undoubtedly do, are not likely to be free of certain definite ideological inclinations, however little they may themselves be conscious of them; and these inclinations cannot but affect the whole character and orientation of the advice they proffer, and the way in which they approach their administrative tasks.[1]

Nor can there be much doubt as to where these ideological inclinations lie: higher civil servants in the countries of advanced capitalism may generally be expected to play a conservative role in the councils of the state, to reinforce the conservative propensities of governments in which these propensities are already well developed, and to serve as an inhibiting element in regard to governments in which they are less pronounced.

As in the case of conservative political leaders, these inclinations may admit a liberal and progressive-minded interest in this or that item of reform, and a sceptical, even a cynical view of many aspects of the social order. In every capitalist country, individual civil servants have occasionally played a notable part in social, economic, administrative and military reform. But this has on the whole been the exception rather than the rule; and where it has occurred, this propensity to reform has also been perfectly compatible and consistent with a strong disposition and determination to strengthen the existing social order.

Given their ideological inclinations, there is obviously no reason why top civil servants should not be more or less 'neutral' as between different conservative parties and groupings whose representatives succeed each other in office; and there is every reason for them to serve with equal zeal whatever government, within this narrow spectrum, may be swept in by the tide of universal suffrage.

Nor even need there be any major departure from such 'neutrality' when that spectrum is somewhat widened, as when

---

[1] As one former American top official puts it: 'Officialdom, whether civil or military, is hardly neutral. It speaks, and inevitably it speaks as an advocate' (R. Hillsman, *To Move a Nation: The Politics of Foreign Policy in the Administration of John F. Kennedy*, 1967, p. 8).

social democratic governments accede to office. The latter, as has already been argued, have never attempted to implement a coherent set of policies so much at variance with conservative interests and modes of thought as to be utterly intolerable to them; and civil servants confronted with such governments have not therefore been forced to make a clear choice between serving what they viewed as the 'national interest' and serving the government of the day.

This, incidentally, is why the fulsome tributes which social-democratic ministers have often paid to the loyalty, dedication and zeal of 'their' civil servants must appear somewhat naïve, even pathetic. For the loyalty they praise is much less an expression of the infinite ideological and political adaptability of civil servants as of the infinite adaptability of social-democratic leaders to conservative purposes.

It may plausibly be argued that, since the scenario has never been written in an advanced capitalist country, the precise role which high civil servants would choose or be able to play if a government bent on revolutionary change came to power must remain a matter of speculation. In any case, such a government would presumably seek to make far-reaching changes in the administrative apparatus, and to bring in men upon whose zeal and support it could count. In fact, the determination to achieve major administrative changes would be one important criterion of the seriousness of its purpose. For if it did not, it would inherit a set of officials one of whose main concerns, indeed whose overriding concern would be, it must be assumed, to limit the 'damage' such a government would do; and to do everything in their power to interpose administrative inhibitions on policies they found utterly abhorrent and in their honest belief detrimental to the 'national interest'. Whether this would amount to the kind of 'administrative sabotage' which the Left has often predicted and feared is largely a matter of definition. The important point is that, no doubt depending on place and circumstance, governments bent on revolutionary change cannot reasonably expect the vaunted 'neutrality' of traditional administrative elites to apply to them, let alone count on the dedicated and enthusiastic support for their policies which they would require.

Nor even, for that matter, is it only this kind of government which must expect difficulties at the hands of these traditional elites. *Any* government bent on reforms which have a 'radical' connotation is most likely to find many if not most of its career advisers much less than enthusiastic and quite possibly hostile. A strong and determined political leader who knows his mind and has the support of his colleagues may well be able to negotiate the obstacles in his way. But this is not the same as saying that the obstacles will not be there, not least, as Professor Neustadt puts it in regard to the United States, because 'specialists at upper levels of established career services may have almost unlimited preserves of the enormous power which consists of sitting still'.[1] For Britain, Mr Sisson has argued that the task of the top civil servant, 'like that of the Crown, is to maintain continuity', and that 'his profession requires him to care more for the continuity of the realm than for the success of party'.[2] This is a very odd argument: for, very far from involving the kind of 'neutrality' which Mr Sisson proclaims as the distinguishing characteristic of the top administrator, it commits the latter to a very un-neutral attitude towards *policies* which, in his view, ensure 'the continuity of the realm', and towards innovations which, in his view, do not, or appear to him to threaten it. Even so, the administrator may well yield to his political masters and serve them in the execution of policies which he deems mistaken. But he will do so, and cannot but do so, in ways which seek to 'limit the damage'. This is a stance more likely to stultify radical innovation than to improve its chances of success. In short, top civil servants are, inside the state system, the voice of caution and moderation, and their permanent motto is 'Pas trop de zèle', at least for radical reform. Insulated as they have generally been from popular pressures which politicians in search of votes have, at least partially, been forced to heed, they have mostly played the role of advocates of the *status quo*, of conservative precedent, of hallowed routines. This

[1] R. E. Neustadt, *Presidential Power*, 1960, p. 42. Note also the comment of a French writer: 'Il y a dans chaque administration une résistance plus ou moins ouverte aux directions des ministres, conflit dans lequel l'administration a le double atout de la compétence technique et de la stabilité. Les ministres passent, mais les services demeurent et l'on dit souvent que si la France n'est plus gouvernée, elle est administrée, et que c'est à cela qu'elle doit sa survie', (M. Waline, 'Les Résistances Techniques de l'Administration au Pouvoir Politique', in *Politique et Technique*, 1958, p. 168).

[2] C. H. Sisson, *The Spirit of Administration*, 1959, p. 124.

may or may not be reckoned to be an admirable and necessary function. But it is incompatible with the notion of 'neutrality' which is generally attached to the Civil Services of advanced capitalist countries.

The conservatism of top civil servants in advanced capitalist countries needs to be seen not in general terms but in specific ones, related to the class configurations and hierarchies of these particular societies, and to have as its major purpose not simply the defence of *a* social order but of *the* particular social order typical of these societies in all its major manifestations. In other words, top civil servants in these countries are not simply conservative in general; they are conservative in the sense that they are, within their allotted sphere, the conscious or unconscious allies of existing economic and social elites.

There is more than one reason for this. The most obvious one, which has already been touched on, is that the social provenance, and the education and class situation of top civil servants makes them part of a specific milieu whose ideas, prejudices and outlook they are most likely to share, and which is bound to influence, in fact to define, their view of the 'national interest'.

But this is by no means all. There is also the fact – which is often overlooked in this context – that the ideological 'soundness' of top civil servants (and of many others as well) is not a matter which, in these countries, is now left to chance. Recruitment and promotion are no longer in the main determined on the basis of social provenance or religious affiliation.[1] Nor are civil servants in these systems expected to subscribe to a specific political doctrine or ideology. But they are nevertheless expected to dwell within a spectrum of thought of which strong conservatism forms one extreme and weak 'reformism' the other. Outside that spectrum, there lurks the grave danger, and in some countries the absolute certainty, of a blighted administrative career or of no administrative career at all.

In all capitalist countries, though with different degrees of

---

[1] Though the *absence* of religious affiliations, let alone an explicit profession of free thought can, in some countries, be distinctly unpropitious to an administrative career (see, e.g. A. Grosser, *La Démocratie de Bonn*, 1958, p. 180).

thoroughness (the United States easily leading the field) candidates to the civil service and members of it are subjected to screening procedures and security checks which have become a familiar and permanent feature of Western administrative life.[1] The official reason given for these procedures is that they are required to exclude 'security risks' from employment by the state, particularly in important and 'sensitive' posts. But the notion of what constitutes a 'security risk' is an elastic one and can easily be stretched to encompass anyone whose opinions and ideas on important issues depart from a framework of 'soundness' defined in terms of the prevailing conservative consensus.[2] Moreover, the knowledge which civil servants have of what is expected, indeed required, of them in ideological and political terms is likely to be more than sufficient to ensure that those of them who might be tempted to stray from the narrow path they are expected to tread will subdue and suppress the temptation. Their number is in any case not likely to be large.

But perhaps more important than these factors in reinforcing the conservative outlook of higher civil servants, and in giving to that outlook a specific direction, of a kind to turn them into the positive supporters of the world of corporate capitalism, is their ever-greater closeness to that world.

---

[1] For the grotesque lengths to which these screening procedures have gone in the United States, see e.g. R. G. Sherill, 'Washington's Bland Bondage', in *The Nation*, 20 and 27 February 1967.

Nor is the process confined to administrative life. In the United States, one writer notes, 'about 25,000 privately owned industrial facilities across the nation operate under security regulations devised by the Pentagon and carefully checked by visiting military teams .. security officers, operating under guidance from military authorities and often to the displeasure of company officers, have taken over substantial portions of the functions of personnel divisions. In theory, they are not supposed to hire and fire. In practice, their word often is law' (J. Raymond, *Power at the Pentagon*, 1964, pp. 154–5). In 1956, another writer observed that 'within a very brief period probably a fifth of all persons employed in the United States (plus many of their families) have been subjected to inquiry concerning their associations, politics and beliefs in order to weed out a tiny group about whom some suspicion might arise' (W. Gellhorn, *Individual Freedom and Governmental Restraints*, 1956, p. 41).

[2] On the other hand, two French authors point, legitimately, to the entry in the Ecole Nationale d'Administration in 1962 of two highly deviant students, one on the Left and the other on the Right (the latter having been interned for 'activisme d'extrême droite'); and they suggest that this symbolises 'un libéralisme dont on ne trouve guère d'équivalent dans d'autres pays, même dans ceux qui passent pour les plus démocratiques' (F. Goguel and A. Grosser, *La Politique en France*, 1964, p. 224).

There, is, to begin with, the fact that state intervention in economic life entails a constant relationship between business-men and civil servants, not as antagonists or even as repre-sentatives of different and divergent interests, but as partners in the service of a 'national interest' which civil servants, like politicians, are most likely to define in terms congruent with the long-term interests of private capitalism.

Furthermore, the world of administration and the world of large-scale enterprise are now increasingly linked in terms of an almost interchanging personnel. We have already seen that more and more businessmen find their way into one part or other of the state system at both political and administrative levels. But so do high civil servants ever more regularly find their way into corporate enterprise. As early as 1946, a French writer was arguing that 'for the elite making up the *grands corps* of the state, the administration is now but the anti-chamber to a business position'.[1] Since then, the pattern has become much more pronounced. 'For a good many years', another French writer notes, 'the Finance Inspection Service, the Conseil d'Etat ... the Préfets and *Sous-Préfets* who head French regional and local administration have supplied major French industries with a growing number of higher executives, vice-presidents and presidents'; indeed, this writer speaks of the likely 'construction of one single oligarchy of managers or technocrats working in business, public industries or govern-ments'.[2] Precisely the same conclusion is applicable to all other capitalist countries.

This interchangeability between government service of one kind or another and business is particularly characteristic of the new breed of 'technocrats' who have been spawned by the economic interventionism of the 'neo-capitalist' state, and who wield considerable influence and power in a variety of depart-ments, planning organisms, regulatory boards, financial and credit institutions, nationalised industries and services; and it also applies to the even newer breed of international 'technocrats' who man the supranational institutions which have come into being as a result of the internationalisation of advanced capitalism.

[1] P. Dieterlen, *Au Delà du Capitalisme*, 1946, p. 359.
[2] G. M. Sauvage, 'The French Businessman in his Milieu', in Cheit, *The Business Establishment*, p. 235.

These men belong exclusively neither to the world of government nor to the world of business. They belong and are part of both, and move easily between them, the more easily in that the boundaries between these worlds are increasingly blurred and indistinct. 'It is not rare,' one writer notes in relation to France, 'to see managers of the public or nationalised sector hold posts on the board of mixed companies or technical bodies; similarly, *Inspecteurs des Finances* are often detached to managing posts in private enterprise or in banks or nationalised enterprises. In turn, the managers of the private sector are more and more called upon to participate in the elaboration of the state's economic policy'.[1]

The difficulty which technocrats have in distinguishing between the interests of the 'private sector' and the public one is well exemplified by the following comment of one of the 'grands commis', who became the chairman of Schneider, one of the largest industrial complexes in France, after having been the chairman of *Electricité de France*:

Ce qui me frappe le plus [he notes], c'est qu'il n'y a pas grande différence entre ces fonctions dans l'Etat, dans le semi-public et dans le privé ... les fonctions de dirigeant dans les trois domaines ne sont pas entièrement différentes. Et ce n'est pas particulièrement extraordinaire car, lorsqu'on est à un certain niveau dans la direction, au fond l'intérêt public rejoint l'intérêt général ou, tout au moins, est une forme de l'intérêt general, ou encore l'intérêt général devient l'intérêt privé, dans une certaine mesure.[2]

Other 'technocrats', however, have less difficulty in articulating a quite precise ideological stance. Thus M. Lalumière, on the basis of an analysis of the writings and pronouncements of *Inspecteurs des Finances*, notes among them a very pronounced belief in state intervention in economic life; but he also finds that:

[1] J. Billy, *Les Techniciens et le Pouvoir*, 1960, p. 55. See also J. Brindillac, 'Les Hauts Fonctionnaires', in *Esprit*, June 1953, p. 837. It is worth noting that, of 240 *Inspecteurs des Finances* or former such members of the French state's economic super-elite who were alive in 1953, seventy or nearly 30 per cent belonged to the private sector of the economy after having resigned from the service or obtained leave ('La France et les Trusts', in *Economie et Politique* no. 5–6, 1954, p. 194). A detailed survey of this elite corps also notes that these men went into the most dynamic and powerful sectors of French large-scale enterprise. (See P. Lalumière, *L'Inspection des Finances*, 1959, p. 88).

[2] Baumier, *Les Grandes Affaires Françaises*, p. 193.

... among none of the authors analysed do we find views advocating the collective appropriation of the means of production. *L'Inspection* is not a corps of professional revolutionaries working inside the state for the establishment of a socialist regime ... Its members remain attached to the capitalist system. They are the agents of a capitalist state. They must serve it, not overthrow it.[1]

And Jean Meynaud, in a study devoted to French technocrats, writes pertinently:

As for the will, so often affirmed, to treat problems without reference to ideology – which is one of the constant themes of the technocratic argument – it simply means the acceptance of dominant ideologies and, consequently, of the relations of forces which they express or justify.[2]

And he also notes about French planning that:

... at the start one might have thought of the Plan as a system which would make possible an improvement in economic efficiency and in the quality of the regime. But in practice, planning has revealed itself as a simple means of consolidation of capitalism, with the planners in the Commissariat never losing an opportunity to exalt the merits of private initiative and free enterprise.[3]

These conclusions are applicable to 'technocrats' in all capitalist countries. And the same is also true, in the United States, for the independent regulatory agencies which one writer has described as 'not so much hostile organisms in a war for survival as a functional unit in a self-perpetuating industrial system. Each complementary part of the unit learns to respond to the system's needs. Seen in this light, an agency is not so much captured and enslaved as it is integrated; it adjusts to a system whose status quo it helps to protect'.[4] These regulatory agencies of advanced capitalism may be independent of the political executive; but their members are not independent of ideological and political dispositions which make of the regulatory process more of a help than a hindrance to the interests regulated.

Nor is it to be forgotten that the opportunities which business now offers to members of the administrative elites cannot, in

[1] Lalumière, *L'Inspection des Finances*, p. 191.
[2] Meynaud, *La Technocratie*, p. 222.   [3] *Ibid.*, p. 122.
[4] Kariel, *The Decline of American Pluralism*, p. 91.

many cases, but help shape the latter's attitudes to business requirements. These opportunities are only likely to be offered to men who have, while in office, shown a proper understanding for the needs and purposes of capitalist enterprise. 'Rare are the able regulatory officials,' one American writer notes, 'who cannot report discussions with the regulated interests concerning the greener pastures that could lie ahead if they behave more cooperatively while in office.'[1] Such siren calls may have no immediate bearing on the actual conduct of civil servants; and they may not even be made at all. All the same, there is a great difference, particularly in an age of inflation, between two retired civil servants, one of whom has entered the world of big business and the other who has not.

Moreover, to anticipate on the next chapter, where the attractions of business fail to act there remains the vast weight of pressure which organised business is able to apply upon recalcitrant or hostile officials. Civil servants concerned with economic decision-making, intervention and regulation can ill afford to ignore the fact that attitudes and actions which are capable of being construed as 'anti-business' are bound to antagonise powerful and influential people and are not likely to be particularly popular with political office-holders either. Here is no path to a successful administrative career, and even less to a post-administrative business career.

None of these advantages, it need hardly be stressed, operates in favour of labour, or of other 'interests' and classes. Labour has little to offer to administrative elites – there are not many instances of top civil servants entering the service of trade unions upon retirement. Nor is labour generally able to exercise anything remotely approaching the kind of pressure or influence which business can apply to administrative elites and to governments.[2] As between contending classes and interests in advanced capitalist societies, civil servants are not 'neutral': they are the allies, whether they are aware of it or not, of capital against labour. The state bureaucracy, in all its parts, is not an impersonal, un-ideological, a-political element in society, above the conflicts in which classes, interests and groups engage. By virtue of its ideological dispositions, reinforced by its own interests, that bureaucracy, on the

[1] R. Engler, *The Politics of Oil*, 1961, p. 318.   [2] See chapter 6.

contrary, is a crucially important and committed element in the maintenance and defence of the structure of power and privilege inherent in advanced capitalism. The point applies at least as much to economic 'technocrats': for all their vast pretensions, these men, in the work they do, are not engaged in purely technical and un-ideological exercises. Their whole purpose is the strengthening and consolidation of the prevailing economic structures and the latter's rationalisation and adaptation to the needs of capitalist enterprise. In this light, contemporary capitalism has no more devoted and more useful servants than the men who help administer the state's intervention in economic life.

II

Perhaps even more than the members of the administrative elites, top military men tend to see themselves, and are often seen by others, as altogether free from the ideological and political partisanship which affects (and afflicts) other men. This image of exclusive dedication to a 'national interest' and to 'military virtues' – honour, courage, discipline, etc. – free from 'partisan' connotations, has been nourished and reinforced by the fact that military men in advanced capitalist countries have, on the whole, kept out of 'politics', in the sense that they have not generally been directly involved in the open, visible part of the political process of these countries.

Here too however, the notion of the military as ideologically uncommitted and uninvolved is manifestly false; and so is the view that its influence in the conduct of affairs is not, at the least, considerable.

It does not seem worth labouring the point that high-ranking officers in these countries have constituted a deeply conservative and even reactionary element in the state system and in society generally, and that their social origin, class situation and professional interest have led them to view the character and content of 'democratic' politics with distaste, suspicion and often hostility. There are societies in which certain parts of the officer corps have been moved by radical, 'modernising' impulses, and where military men have led movements designed to overthrow or at least to reform archaic social, economic and political structures. In advanced capitalist countries, on the other hand, the military elites have always stood for a 'national interest' conceived in acutely conservative terms, which might not exclude a generally qualified and contingent acceptance of 'democratic' processes, but which has entailed an unswerving hostility to radical ideas, movements, and parties. One writer, describing the values of the French officer corps, speaks of its 'stress on the role of force and on nationalism, and preference for unity, self-sacrifice, hierarchy, and order over individualism and democratic politics'.[1] The same themes regularly reappear in all descriptions of the 'military mind' in the countries of advanced capitalism.

But here also, as in the case of civil servants, it is not sufficient to speak of military conservatism in general terms. For that conservatism has long assumed a much more specific character, in the sense that it encompasses an often explicit acceptance, not simply of 'existing institutions', or of particular 'values', but of a quite specific existing economic and social system and a corresponding opposition to any meaningful alternative to that system. In an earlier epoch in the history of capitalism, military elites tended to look with aristocratic disdain upon money-grabbing entrepreneurs, and to hold values, derived from a pre-capitalist age, which set them at odds with the industrial, bourgeois, civilian-oriented regimes of which they found themselves the servants. Attitudes proceeding from these values may still persist, but just as the civilian aristocrat has long come to achieve a happy reconciliation with capitalist values and purposes, so have military elites – which have in any case undergone a definite if limited process of social dilution – come to make their peace, in ideological and political terms, with their capitalist regimes. As Professor Huntington writes for the United States:

Few developments more dramatically symbolised the new status of the military in the postwar decade than the close association which they developed with the business elite of American society ...

---

[1] J. F. Ambler, *The French Army in Politics 1945–1962*, 1966, p. 278.

Professional officers and businessmen revealed a new mutual respect. Retired generals and admirals in unprecedented numbers went into the executive staffs of American corporations; new organisations arose bridging the gap between corporate management and military leadership. *For the military officers, business represented the epitome of the American way of life.*[1]

This may not be quite as true in other advanced capitalist countries but the military everywhere has nevertheless come to have a particularly close relationship to large-scale enterprise, simply because the vast military requirements of the state have fostered an association between them more intimate than at any time in the past.[2] From this point of view, the 'industrial-military' complex, not only in the United States, is not a figure of speech but a solid fact, cemented by a genuine community of interests.

The question which remains, however, is that of the precise role of the military inside the state system and in society. For while the conservatism of military elites may be taken as a fact, the degree to which this finds expression in the process of decision-making requires further consideration. This is the more true in that the political regimes of advanced capitalism have been characterised by a high measure of civilian predominance over the military. In these countries, the military elites, with very partial exceptions, as in Japan in the 1930s, have never spoken as masters to their mainly civilian governments. Nor have they seriously attempted to *replace* the civil power. The dictatorships which some of these countries have occasionally known have not in fact been army ones: Hitler was a very civilian ex-corporal and Mussolini was an equally civilian figure. Both came to power with the help, *inter alia*, of regular officers; but both also subdued their military elites as they had

---

[1] Huntington, *The Soldier and the State*, 1957, pp. 361–2 (my italics). 'In the middle fifties', Professor Huntington also notes, 'over two thousand regular officers each year were leaving the services for the more lucrative positions in business' (*ibid.*, p. 366). For a well-documented analysis of this process, see also F.J.Cook, *The Warfare State*, 1963, and L.Reissman, 'Life Careers, Power and the Professions: The Retired Army General', in *American Sociological Review*, 1956, vol. 21, no. 2.

For Britain, see P.Abrams, 'Democracy, Technology, and the Retired British Officer', in S.P.Huntington (ed.), *Changing Patterns of Military Politics*, 1962, pp. 166ff.

[2] For the United States, see, e.g., C.R.Mollenhof, *The Pentagon. Politics, Profit and Plunder* (1967).

never been subdued before or have been subdued since – it is quite likely that British generals in Baldwin's England had more influence on policy-making than had their counterparts with Hitler in Germany and with Mussolini in Italy.

It is in fact very remarkable that the officer corps in advanced capitalist countries has very seldom played an independent political role, and that it has even more seldom sought to substitute itself for civilian governments by way of military *putsch* or *coup d'état*. The classical example of this inhibition is that of the German officer corps after the military collapse of 1918, and indeed throughout the life of the Weimar republic, when army officers played an important, even a crucial role in political life, yet resolutely refused for the most part to countenance the overthrow of weak and irresolute governments.[1] Even in Japan in the late 1930s, it has been noted, 'there were limits to its [the army's] power. It could not rule the country directly and, indeed, preferred the traditional Japanese method of indirect rule. It could not dispense with the politicians, the Foreign Office officials, the bureaucrats and the industrialists.'[2] Nor does the experience of France in recent years offer more than a very partial and even doubtful exception to the general pattern. The French army, never the most democratic and republican-minded institution in the state, was utterly disaffected because of the defeats and humiliations it had suffered in Indo-China and Algeria, and for which it blamed the weak and vacillating governments of the Fourth Republic.[3] Yet it showed until the late 1950s a significant lack of predilection for any kind of open challenge to the civilian power, despite the steady political degradation of the regime and the ever more acute military crisis in the field. The revolt which broke out in Algeria in May 1958 was a remarkably half-baked affair, not least because of the anxiety of senior army men on the spot to cling to the appearance of 'constitutionality':[4] that the revolt did topple the Fourth Republic owed much less to the deter-

[1] See, e.g. Carsten, *The Reichswehr and Politics, 1917 to 1933* and Wheeler-Bennett, *The Nemesis of Power*.

[2] F. C. Jones, 'Japan', in M. Howard (ed.), *Soldiers and Governments*, 1957, p. 94.

[3] See R. Girardet et al., *Le Crise Militaire Française 1945–1962*, 1964, part 3, and Ambler, *The French Army in Politics*.

[4] R. Girardet, 'Pouvoir Civil et Pouvoir Militaire dans la France Contemporaine', *Revue Française de Science Politique*, 1960, vol. 10, no. 1, pp. 31–2.

mination of military men in Algeria than to the weakness and demoralisation of the politicians in Paris. And having made possible de Gaulle's accession to power, the rebels very soon found that de Gaulle could not be relied on to serve their purposes, either in relation to Algeria or to much else either. It was this which three years later caused the further rebellion of a few generals in Algeria. This was an authentic example of an attempt at a military coup: the ease with which it was put down shows the essential limitations and difficulties of such enterprises in advanced capitalist societies.

The most important of these difficulties, in such countries, is that no overt 'unconstitutional' challenge from the Right can have any serious chance of success without a substantial degree of support from one part or other of the subordinate classes, preferably from a substantial part of the working class, disillusioned with its own economic and political defence organisations. Moreover, this popular support needs to be integrated and mobilised into a party with its own ancillary mass organisations. In short, a challenge from the Right requires something like a Fascist movement with a wide popular basis. But the organisation of such a movement also requires a kind of leadership – popular, demagogic, charismatic, politically adroit – which high-ranking officers, given their whole tradition, are unlikely to possess. And even if a man or men with such qualities were to be found inside the military elite, the attempt to put these qualities to use must very soon lead to exclusion from the army: it is very difficult, if not impossible, at least in the countries concerned, to lead a Fascist-type political movement from *within* an army. This helps to explain why high-ranking army officers have sometimes, as in Germany and Italy, played an important role as *allies* of counter-revolutionary movements of the Right, but have been neither the initiators nor the leaders of such movements.

As for a military attempt to usurp power *without* a fair measure of popular support, the danger of failure must appear overwhelming. For one thing, the army, from this point of view, is not a monolithic bloc, and differences of rank crucially affect the propensity to adventurism, the most senior officers being much less likely to show such propensities than more junior ones. As Mr Ambler notes 'colonels, who have more to

gain and less to lose, have figured heavily in the history of
military revolt in both Western and non-Western countries'.[1] In
any case, officers, of whatever rank, have to reckon with
conscripts, of whose automatic obedience to their orders
in conditions of unconstitutionality they cannot be certain. This
was one of the factors which precipitated the collapse of the
military rebellion in Algeria in 1961, and it has often helped to
defeat similar military attempts in other countries, for instance
in the German case of the Kapp putsch in 1920.

But this unreliability of the lower ranks is only a specific expression of a more general and ultimately decisive handicap
which would-be military putschists in advanced capitalist
countries are most likely to face, namely the hostility and
potential resistance of the organised labour movement.
Practically any civilian government in these countries, however
weak, can, *if it is so minded*, deal effectively with rebellious
military men by calling upon the help of organised labour. Thus
even Noske, who had presided over the liquidation of the
Spartakus rising and who bore at least indirect responsibility
for the assassination of Rosa Luxemburg and Karl Liebknecht,[2]
was able to tell the German military conspirators of 1920: 'If
you use force, we shall proclaim a general strike';[3] and when
the Kapp putsch did occur, the government of which Noske
was a member did proclaim a general strike, which greatly
helped to unnerve and defeat the putschists.[4] It is only where
the labour movement is exceptionally weak, or paralysed, that
military men bent on seizing power can afford to ignore its
hostility or hope to overcome it. Where it is neither weak nor
paralysed, straightforward Bonapartism in these countries is an
exceedingly perilous venture. To have any chance of success,
subversion from the Right, in the conditions of advanced capitalism, needs to assume different, more 'popular' forms. But on those
occasions where it has assumed such forms, military men, as noted
earlier, have provided it with a precious measure of assistance.

The risks and difficulties which must attend military *putschism* in
advanced capitalist societies are not, however, a sufficient

---

[1] Ambler, *The French Army in Politics*, p. 342.
[2] See J. P. Nettl, *Rosa Luxemburg*, 1966, vol. 2, p. 774.
[3] Wheeler-Bennett, *The Nemesis of Power*, p. 74.   [4] *Ibid.*, p. 78.

explanation of its rarity. Where circumstances appear to them to require it, men do take risks, however long the odds. That military men in these societies have not sought more frequently to challenge and defy the civilian power may be attributed to a variety of other causes than the risks and difficulties of doing so; the most important of these is that, like civil servants, military men have mostly had to deal with politicians and governments whose outlook and purposes have not been *radically* different from their own. Even when 'left-wing' governments have been in office, the military, however poor their opinion of such governments has been, have very seldom had occasion to feel a sense of total political and ideological alienation. After all, these governments have generally pursued foreign and defence policies which were not of a kind to suggest to the military that collaboration with such governments was utterly impossible. The German military leaders collaborated with the Social-Democrats Ebert and Noske in 1918 and after, in order to ensure a 'social stability' which they knew the latter wanted as much as they did themselves. Had the new men appeared less 'moderate', it is unlikely that the same high-ranking officers, despite what Mr Carsten describes as their tradition of not 'directly entering the field of party politics',[1] would have accepted quietly their inevitable dismissal and gone into peaceful retirement.

There have, it is true, been many instances where army men *have* been at odds, even very seriously at odds, with their civilian masters over this or that aspect of policy, and where a tension which is in any case inherent in military-civilian relations has reached a dangerously high level – with the military always well to the Right. Yet, given the essential ideological and political 'moderation' of the governments which have held office in advanced capitalist countries, and the basic conservatism which most of them have had in common with their military elites, the differences between them, however genuine and serious, have generally been susceptible to compromise and accommodation. Here, it may be said, lies the essential clue to the general pattern of military subordination which has characterised civilian-military relations in the countries of advanced capitalism.

[1] F. L. Carsten, 'Germany', in Howard (ed.), *Soldiers and Governments*, p. 94.

'Subordination', however, is a somewhat misleading description
of the position and role of the military in present-day capitalist
regimes. It has, indeed, been forcefully argued, notably by C.
Wright Mills,[1] that, in the United States at least, the steady
militarisation of life and the extraordinary growth of the
'military domain' had produced a situation in which the military must be viewed as a power group coequal with the civilian
government and the corporate elite.

This would appear to be something of an exaggeration. For
there is no really good evidence to suggest, either for the
United States or anywhere else, that the military, in terms of
major policy decisions, has achieved an independent and equal
position *vis-à-vis* the political executive – and what element of
doubt there may persist about this proposition in regard to the
United States certainly cannot apply to countries like France,
or Britain, or Germany or Japan. Nor is it at all clear that
despite its control of phenomenally vast resources, economic as
well as military,[2] the military elite in the United States has been
able to establish anything resembling an independent power
base, on a par with the power base of the economic elite, from
which it could deal with the presidency and the civilian government from a position of equality, let alone of superiority. The
point is well symbolised by the fact that it was a former president
of General Motors who ruled the Pentagon for seven years and
asserted a degree of control over the military which, though by
no means unqualified, was yet substantial. Nor is it to be ignored
that, by all repute, the men who have exercised the greatest
influence with such presidents as Kennedy and Johnson were
not military men but civilians. Thus, so far as is known, no
military man has had a greater influence over the conduct of
the war in Vietnam than various civilian advisers inside the
White House. The exaggeration of the role of the military in the
counsels of capitalist governments has its dangers, for it tends to
deflect attention from the responsibility of civilian power-
holders for the state's policies and actions. That these power-
holders, particularly in the United States, have accepted what

[1] See *The Power Elite*, ch. 9.
[2] For which see, e.g. F. J. Cook, who notes that the American military establishment is 'by any yardstick of measurement the world's largest organisation' (*The
Warfare State*, p. 21).

Mills called a 'military definition of reality' may well be true. But there is no reason to believe that it is military men who have, anywhere, *imposed* it on their civilian masters.

This said, the fact remains that military elites in advanced capitalist countries do play an important role in the determination of many crucial aspects of national policy. Nor is their influence confined to the area of policy which is their special concern. Decisions about defence are necessarily decisions about much else as well, from diplomacy to economic policy and from social welfare to education. As Professor Meynaud puts it, 'il n'est aucun problème, économique ou financier qui dés le temps de paix ne soit, directement ou indirectement, rattachable à la défense extérieure'.[1] Moreover, that influence is not confined to the state system itself; in a variety of ways it also extends to political life in society at large.

In the perspective of this study, the important point is not so much that the military do wield a great deal of influence inside the state system. This may be taken for granted, and scarcely warrants emphasis. More important is the fact that this influence is most likely to be exercised in highly conservative directions and that the military elites may always be expected to reinforce the conservative bias of their governments and to do their best, in whatever domain they have influence, to act as an additional voice of caution, restraint and admonition against whatever policies do not correspond to their own conservative view of 'the national interest'. Furthermore, and given their whole ideological orientation, military and police elites may always be expected to support with particular zeal the determination of the civil power to combat 'internal subversion', at least from the Left,[2] and to act, wherever required, as the coercive agents of the existing social order, particularly in periods of social strife and open class conflict. These are the managers of that coercive function which is the state's unique prerogative; and in whatever other regards the civil power may at one time or another have entertained doubts as to their

[1] Meynaud, *La Technocratie*, p. 38. Professor Finer goes even further and suggests that 'nowadays, deference to the military in the fields of foreign policy and even domestic policies is a commonplace' (S. E. Finer, *The Man on Horseback*, 1962, p. 74).

[2] This, on the other hand, cannot quite so readily be taken for granted in the case of dissenting activists at the other end of the political spectrum.

reliability, loyalty and subordination, it has hardly ever had occasion to have any serious doubts as to their readiness to take the field, so to speak, against striking workmen, left-wing political activists, and other such disturbers of the *status quo*.

III

Judges, in Western-type political systems, are independent. But independent of what? The answer usually given is that they are independent of the government of the day, that they have no obligation to it, and need not do its bidding or be concerned either with its convenience or pleasure or wrath. Wherever else it may not apply, the concept of the separation of powers, it is claimed, at least applies here. And in this specific sense, the notion of judicial independence has indeed undoubted merit, and the fact which it enshrines has been of very considerable importance in the life of the political systems in which it holds sway.

Yet, the notion of judicial independence requires to be considered rather more broadly, for it tends in its restricted sense to obscure some major aspects of the judicial role in these systems.

One such aspect is that judges of the superior courts (and of the inferior courts as well for that matter) are by no means, and cannot be, independent of the multitude of influences, notably of class origin, education, class situation and professional tendency, which contribute as much to the formation of their view of the world as they do in the case of other men.

We have, in this respect, already noted that the judicial elites, like other elites of the state system, are mainly drawn from the upper and middle layers of society: and those judges who are not have clearly come to belong to these layers by the time they reach the bench. Moreover, the conservative bias which their class situation is thus likely to create is here strongly reinforced by the fact that judges are, in many of these systems, also recruited from the legal profession, whose ideological dispositions are traditionally cast in a highly conservative mould. In the words of A. V. Dicey, 'the judges are the heads of the legal profession. They have acquired the intellectual and moral tone of English lawyers. They are men advanced in life. They are for the most part men of a conservative disposition'.[1] This was written at the beginning of the twentieth century, but it has remained true until the present day, and is certainly as true for other countries as it is for England; judges in advanced capitalist countries *are* men of a conservative disposition, in regard to all the major economic, social and political arrangements of their society.

Moreover, governments which are generally in charge of the appointment and promotion of judges are most likely to favour men of precisely such conservative dispositions. Notwithstanding the general ideological bias of the legal profession, there have been radical lawyers eminently qualified, on every other criterion but this one, to hold high judicial office. But they have seldom found much favour in the eyes of the appointing power; nor have the judges of the inferior courts who have given rise to the belief that they were moved by strongly reforming impulses. Notably liberal judges have on occasion adorned the judicial system of their countries, for instance in the United States. But they have always constituted a tiny minority. Nor for that matter should their liberalism, however admirable, be mistaken for anything like hostility to the basic economic and social institutions of capitalist society. Holmes, Brandeis, and Cardozo were, in the American context, great liberal judges. But only antediluvian reactionaries have believed that their liberalism was not well contained within the framework of American capitalism; and they themselves, the evidence clearly shows, would have found grotesque the idea that they had any predilection for any alternative system. Precisely the same may be said for liberal judges in other capitalist countries.

The reason why these ideological dispositions are important is obvious – they greatly affect the manner in which the judicial function is discharged. Judges, it is generally accepted, are not 'law-vending machines', or the helpless prisoners of a set legal framework or the mere exponents of the law as they find it. In the legal system of all these countries there is room, inevitably, for judicial discretion in the application of the law and for

[1] A. V. Dicey, *Law and Opinion in England during the 19th Century*, 1963, p. 364.

judicial creativity in actually making law; as one writer puts it,
'the infinite variety of social problems and legal situations
makes discretion an inevitable element in the judicial process'.[1]
That element is much larger in some systems than in others, for
instance in the United States, where the Supreme Court has at
times assumed the role of a 'third Chamber'. But in no Western-
type system is this element of judicial discretion negligible. This
is not to say that judges necessarily seek to expand the area of
discretion, and many of them have in fact agreed with the view
enunciated by one judge in 1824 that 'public policy is an unruly
horse and dangerous to ride'. But many of them have nevertheless also found themselves, for good reasons or bad, compelled to
ride that horse.[2]

In thus interpreting and making law, judges cannot fail to be
deeply affected by their view of the world, which in turn
determines their attitude to the conflicts which occur in it.[3]
They may well see themselves as guided exclusively by values and
concepts which soar far above mundane considerations of class
and special interest. But in their concrete application, these
concepts will nevertheless often exhibit a distinct and identifiable ideological position and bias, most commonly of a strongly
conservative kind. An eminent English judge eloquently
asserted some years ago that judges in Britain and the United
States should 'see themselves ... as committed for good to the
principle that the purpose of society and all its institutions is
to nourish and enrich the growth of each individual human
spirit'.[4] Unfortunately, these words are subject to diverse and
contradictory interpretations; as they stand, they are not a
guarantee against any kind of bias, merely a cloak for it.

Judges themselves have sometimes been quite conscious of
their particular bias. Thus a highly conservative judge, Lord
Justice Scrutton, noted in 1922 that:

---

[1] W. Friedmann, *Law in a Changing Society*, 1959, p. 60.

[2] 'The law is not a static but a dynamic and developing body of doctrine, and
many of its developments are produced by judges who are consciously or sub-
consciously reaching decisions on the basis of what they think the law ought to be'
(D. Lloyd, *The Idea of Law*, 1964, p. 111).

[3] Thus Mr Justice Holmes: 'The very considerations which judges most rarely
mention, and always with an apology, are the secret root from which the law draws
all the juices of life. I mean, of course, considerations of what is expedient for the
community' (O. W. Holmes, *The Common Law*, 1881, p. 35).

[4] Lord Radcliffe, *The Law and its Compass*, 1960, p. 65.

... the habits you are trained in, the people with whom you mix, lead to your having a certain class of ideas of such a nature that, when you have to deal with other ideas, you do not give as round and accurate judgments as you would wish. This is one of the great difficulties at present with Labour. Labour says: 'Where are your impartial judges? They all move in the same circle as the employers, and they are all educated and nursed in the same ideas as the employers. How can a Labour man or a trade unionist get impartial justice?' It is very difficult sometimes to be sure that you have put yourself into a thoroughly impartial position between two disputants, one of your own class and one not of your class.[1]

Or, in the words of Mr Justice Cardozo, 'the spirit of the age, as it is revealed to each of us, is too often the spirit of the group to which the accidents of birth or education or occupation or fellowship have given us a place'.[2] This kind of awareness is no doubt coupled with a genuine desire to overcome blatant partisanship. Nor is it to be denied that so far as its more obvious forms are concerned the attempt may not infrequently be successful.

As a general rule, however, success in this field is the more likely to be achieved the less crucial to the social fabric the issues at stake appear to be, the less they affect the basic pattern of relationships between capital and labour, the less they involve what is taken to be the security of the state and the safety of the social order; and relatedly, the avoidance of outrageous bias is also much more likely in periods of relative social calm than in periods of acute social conflict and stress.

Where, on the other hand, the issues do have, or appear to have, a direct or even an indirect bearing on the constitution of the social order or on important parts of it, particularly in periods of crisis, judges are much less likely to recognise their partiality, nor in any case would they wish to avoid a partiality

[1] Quoted in B. Abel-Smith and R. Stevens, *Lawyers and the Courts*, 1967, p. 117.

[2] B. N. Cardozo, *The Nature of the Judicial Process*, 1921, p. 175. Note in contrast Lord Evershed's much more complacent view: 'It also may well be that the law, and the judges and the members of the legal profession in administering the law, tend to conservatism. Having regard to its long traditions and history it would be surprising were it otherwise; and I would not think in this regard the legal profession different from other professions. Nor, in effect, is such conservatism a bad thing; for it must tend to promote a sense of stability in a rapidly changing world' (Lord Evershed, 'The Judicial Process in Twentieth Century England', in *Columbia Law Review*, 1961, vol. 61, pp. 773–4, in Abel-Smith and Stevens, *Lawyers and the Courts*, pp. 300–1).

which their every instinct and mental process would suggest to them to be a duty.

In sentencing two journalists for contempt of court because they refused to disclose their sources of information to the Vassall tribunal, the Lord Chief Justice of England appeared to commit himself to the interesting proposition that 'the citizen's highest duty is to the state'.[1] More important in this context than the philosophical questions this requirement raises is the fairly high probability that Lord Parker did not wish to exclude the judiciary from it. And whether this be so or not, it is certain that judicial elites everywhere have often been moved by such sentiments. One of the most extreme examples of judicial partiality in any Western-type political system in this century was the blatant bias displayed by German judges under the Weimar republic in favour of murderers and hooligans of the far Right on the one hand, and against the extreme Left, or the Left *tout court*, on the other.[2] Yet it may be doubted whether these judges felt they were betraying their judicial duty; on the contrary, it is more likely that they believed they were fulfilling it by showing extreme leniency to men who were, even though perhaps somewhat over-enthusiastically, fighting 'Communist subversion', and by showing extreme severity against those who were in these judges' eyes the agents of that subversion.

This is of course an extreme case. But the fact remains that judges in advanced capitalist countries have generally taken a rather poor view of radical dissent, and the more radical the dissent, the greater has been judicial hostility to it; and judicial discretion has, in this respect, tended to be used to support rather than to curb the attempts which governments and legislatures have made at one time or another to contain, subdue or suppress dissident views and activities. True, the courts have on occasion helped to restrain the intolerant zeal of other elements of the state system, and the importance of this fact ought certainly not to be under-estimated.[3] But more generally, and particu-

---

[1] B.N. Cardozo, *The Nature of the Judicial Process*, p. 306.

[2] For which see, e.g. Neumann, *Behemoth*, pp. 27–9.

[3] The United States Supreme Court provides an obvious example. But note also the comment of one informed (and by no means unsympathetic) writer: 'It seems clear that the [Supreme] Court in recent terms has approved a relatively conservative policy permitting suppression of political dissent' (G. Schubert, *Judicial Policy-Making*, 1965, p. 129).

larly in times of social crisis and challenge, and in the circumstances of a permanent 'Cold War', judges have often shown a disposition to share the zeal of repressive authority and to view the erosion of civil liberties which was its result as a lesser evil or as no evil at all.

It may be argued that there are forms of repressive legislation or executive action which leave very little or even no room for judicial discretion and where the judge, if he is to apply the law at all, must apply it with the harshness intended by those who promulgated it. But the judicial application of the law and judicial acceptance of the repressive efforts of governments and legislatures do not simply constitute a 'neutral' discharge of the judicial function; they constitute a *political* act of considerable significance and provide these governments and legislatures with a precious element of additional legitimation. Where no discretion exists, the only option left to judges in the face of state repression is resignation from the bench. It is not an option which many judges have found it necessary to take up. In any case, some degree of judicial discretion normally does exist in this area as in others; and while the courts have at times used it in favour of dissenters, they have more commonly been willing to strengthen the arm of the state in its encounter with dissent.

This, however, is only part of a more general bias which the courts, in their concern to protect 'society' (i.e. unequal class societies) have consistently displayed in favour of privilege, property and capital. Thus, the history of trade unionism in capitalist countries is also the history of an unending struggle against the courts' attempts to curb and erode the unions' ability to defend their members' interests; and here, moreover, the judicial arm has not simply been content to second the curbing endeavours of governments and legislatures; the courts have often themselves taken the initiative and sought, through the exercise of judicial creativeness in the interpretation of statutes, to reduce or annul trade union and working-class rights which even quite conservative governments and legislatures had, under pressure, come to endorse and promulgate.

No doubt, judges, like governments and capitalist interests themselves, have come to recognise that trade unions, far from constituting a menace to 'society', could in fact greatly contribute to its stability and help to limit rather than to exacerbate social conflict; and judicial attitudes to trade-union rights have consequently ceased to be defined in terms of an unremitting hostility which would, in any case, have been difficult to sustain without exposing the judges to massive and damaging criticism.[1]

Even so, wage earners and their defence organisations are never finally safe from judicial attacks even upon rights which they have long come to regard as beyond further challenge;[2] perhaps less blatantly than in former days, yet quite unmistakably, judicial discretion remains a permanent threat to such 'countervailing power' as labour has been able to develop over the years, and particularly to the militant assertion of that power.

More generally, the courts have always conceived it as one of their main duties to 'society' to protect the rights of property against such attempts as the state has been compelled to make to reduce their scope. The judiciary has not been able to prevent the state's 'interference' with the freedom of property-owners to do what they willed with their own; and judges have slowly come to accept what Dicey called the movement from 'individualistic liberalism' to 'unsystematic collectivism'. But they have generally done their best to limit and retard that

---

[1] It could in this sense be said that, according to a consecrated formula, the judges have 'followed the election returns'. But it is a formula which is rather misleading. It suggests that judges are not indifferent to popular sentiment and extra-legal currents of thought. But what this can also mean, and not infrequently does, is that judges are not indifferent to the pressures of *preponderant* and *special* interests. This is particularly likely to be the case with inferior courts, whose members may well be acutely responsive to the prejudices and claims of dominant elites of which they are in any case a part, or to the prejudices and passions of a particular section of the community, for instance a racially dominant section. This has certainly been the case with many state courts in the United States, notably in the southern states; and inferior courts, it needs to be stressed, form a part of the judicial process whose crucial importance is often underestimated because of the concentration of attention upon the superior courts.

[2] See, e.g. the Law Lords' decision in 1964 in *Rookes v Barnard and Others*, which 'knocked the bottom out of the certainty of the right to strike and take other industrial action' (K. W. Wedderburn, *The Worker and the Law*, 1965, p. 273). Note also the comment of one of the Law Lords that 'the injury and suffering caused by strike action is very often widespread as well as devastating and *a threat to strike would be expected to be certainly no less serious than a threat of violence*' (ibid., p. 266, my italics). Note also the following comment from a distinguished labour lawyer: 'One is under the impression that the repressive tendencies of the courts, which in the nineteenth and twentieth centuries had to be repeatedly counteracted by Parliament, are on the point of being revived' (O. Kahn-Freund, cited in Wedderburn, *The Worker and the Law*, p. 274).

movement; in no field have they been more vigilant guardians of the 'citizen' against the state than in this one.

The judiciary, in short, has no more been 'above' the conflicts of capitalist society than any other part of the state system. Judges have been deeply involved in these conflicts; and of all classes it is certainly the dominant class which has had least to complain about the nature and direction of that involvement.

It has been argued in this chapter and the previous one that the dominant economic interests in capitalist society can normally count on the active good-will and support of those in whose hands state power lies. This is an enormous advantage. But these interests cannot, all the same, rely on governments and their advisers to act in perfect congruity with their purposes. As was noted earlier, governments may wish to pursue certain policies which *they* deem altogether beneficial to capitalist enterprise but which powerful economic interests may, for their part, find profoundly objectionable; or these governments may be subjected to strong pressure from other classes which they cannot altogether ignore. This situation is particularly likely to arise in Western-type political regimes. In other words, the initial good-will and general support which capitalist interests may expect to find inside the state system does not remove the need for them to exert their own pressure for the achievement of their immediate and specific goals. As will now be seen, however, these interests bring to the task resources far greater, in a variety of ways, than those of any other interest in capitalist society.

6

Imperfect Competition

Democratic and pluralist theory could not have gained the degree of ascendency which it enjoys in advanced capitalist societies if it had not at least been based on one plainly accurate observation about them, namely that they permit and even encourage a multitude of groups and associations to organise openly and freely and to compete with each other for the advancement of such purposes as their members may wish. With exceptions which mainly affect the Left, this is indeed the case.

What is wrong with pluralist-democratic theory is not its insistence on the fact of competition but its claim (very often its implicit assumption) that the major organised 'interests' in these societies, and notably capital and labour, compete on more or less equal terms, and that none of them is therefore able to achieve a decisive and permanent advantage in the process of competition. This is where ideology enters, and turns observation into myth. In previous chapters, it was shown that business, particularly large-scale business, did enjoy such an advantage *inside* the state system, by virtue of the composition and ideological inclinations of the state elite. In this chapter, we shall see that business enjoys a massive superiority *outside* the state system as well, in terms of the immensely stronger pressures which, as compared with labour and any other interest, it is able to exercise in the pursuit of its purposes.

I

One such form of pressure, which pluralist 'group theorists' tend to ignore, is more important and effective than any other, and business is uniquely placed to exercise it, without the need of organisation, campaigns and lobbying. This is the pervasive and permanent pressure upon governments and the state generated by the private control of concentrated industrial, commercial and financial resources. The existence of this major area of independent economic power is a fact which no government, whatever its inclinations, can ignore in the determination of its policies, not only in regard to economic matters, but to most other matters as well. The chairman of the editorial board of *Fortune* magazine said in 1952 that 'any president who wants to seek a prosperous country depends on the corporation at least as much – probably more than – the corporation depends on him. His dependence is not unlike that of King John on the landed barons at Runnymede, where Magna Carta was born'.[1] The parallel may not be perfect but the stress on the independent power of business, and on the dependence of government upon it, is altogether justified, not only for the United States but for all other advanced capitalist countries.

Of course, governments do have the formal power to impose their will upon business, to prevent it, by the exercise of legitimate authority, from doing certain things and to compel it to do certain other things. And this is in fact what governments have often done. But this, though true and important, is not at all the point at issue. Quite obviously, governments are not *completely* helpless in the face of business power, nor is it the case that businessmen, however large the concerns which they run, can openly defy the state's command, disregard its rules and flout the law. The point is rather that the control by business of large and crucially important areas of economic life makes it extremely *difficult* for governments to impose upon it policies to which it is firmly opposed. Other interests, it may well be said,

---

[1] Mills, *The Power Elite*, p. 169. Or, as Alfred de Grazia puts it, 'whoever controls the great industries will have awful political power' (*Politics and Government*, 1962, vol. 2, p. 56).

are by no means helpless *vis-à-vis* their government either; they too may oppose, sometimes successfully, the purposes and policies of the state. But business, in the very nature of a capitalist system of economic organisation, is immeasurably better placed than any other interest to do so effectively, and to cause governments to pay much greater attention to its wishes and susceptibilities than to anybody else.

Writing about the United States, Professor Hacker has noted in this connection that:

> ... what Parsons and other liberals like to think of as business regulation is, despite the predictable complaints of businessmen, more a paper tiger than an effective system of economic controls in the public interest ... [and, he goes on] a few questions may be asked about these supposed powers of the national government. Can any public agency determine the level of wages, of prices, of profits? Can it perhaps, more important, specify the level and direction of capital investment? Can any government bureau allocate raw materials or control plant location? Can it in any way guarantee full employment or the rate of economic growth? Has any writ of the Anti-Trust Division actually broken up one of our larger corporations in any appreciable way? The simple answer is that measures such as these are neither possible under the laws nor do we know what the reaction to them would be.[1]

Even for the United States this may well underestimate the influence which governments do have, by direct and indirect intervention, on economic life; and in many other capitalist countries, where a more positive philosophy of intervention has generally come to prevail, governments have been able to do rather more than what is here suggested as possible.

Nevertheless, the *limits* of intervention, at least in relation to business, and particularly *against* it, are everywhere much more narrow and specific than insistence on the formal powers of government would tend to suggest; and the area of decision-making which is left to private enterprise is correspondingly greater than is usually conveyed by the assiduously propagated image of a 'business community' cribbed and confined by bureaucratically meddlesome governments and their agents.

Even governments which *are* determined to 'control' private

---

[1] A. Hacker, 'Sociology and Ideology', in M. Black (ed.), *The Social Theories of Talcott Parsons*, 1961, p. 302.

enterprise soon find that the mechanisms of intervention which they seek to superimpose upon business are extremely cumbersome and almost impossible to operate without the collaboration and help of business itself. But that collaboration and help is unlikely to be forthcoming unless a price is paid for it – the price being that governments should not be too determined in the pursuit of policies which business itself deems detrimental to it, and of course to the 'national interest'.

What is involved here is not necessarily or at all the active resistance of the controllers of economic power to the law, or the deliberate evasion of duly promulgated regulations, though there may be that as well. More important than such defiance, which may be politically damaging and even dangerous, is the *inert* power of business, the failure to do such things as are not positively commanded by the state but merely asked for, and the doing of other things which are not strictly illegal. Much is possible on this basis, and would be sufficient to present a reforming government with formidable problems, so long as it chose to operate within the framework of a capitalist regime. As Professor Meynaud notes, in a reference to Italy which is of more general application, private ownership and control

... makes it very difficult to undertake a policy of reform within the framework of established economic structures. Any government concerned to engineer a certain redistribution of economic power and of the social product without bringing into question the foundations of the system rapidly comes up, in the medical sense of the word, against a kind of intolerance of the regime to such changes.[1]

This 'intolerance', it must be stressed, is not such as to prevent *any* kind of economic policy of which business disapproves. The veto power of business, in other words, is not absolute. But it is very large, and certainly larger than that of any other interest in capitalist society.

It has sometimes been argued that governments have now come to possess one extremely effective weapon in relation to business, namely the fact that they are now by far the largest customer of private enterprise and have thus 'an important and speedy instrument for influencing the decisions of private industry and commerce in such a way as to enable the government

---

[1] Meynaud, *Rapport sur la Classe Dirigeante Italienne*, p. 191.

to achieve *on time* its major national industrial objectives'.[1]

Yet it was only a few months before this was written that a Labour Government White Paper on state purchasing had elicited from *The Times* the comment that 'it is quite clear that any idea of wielding the big stick of the Government's purchasing power to compel individual firms or industries radically to change their methods as an instrument of long-term economic policy has been completely rejected'.[2] Nor is there much evidence that other governments have been notably effective in the use of this power in their relations with private enterprise.

In the abstract, governments do indeed have vast resources and powers at their command to 'wield the big stick' against business. In practice, governments which are minded to use these powers and resources – and most of them are not – soon find, given the economic and political context in which they operate, that the task is fraught with innumerable difficulties and perils.

These difficulties and perils are perhaps best epitomised in the dreaded phrase 'loss of confidence'. It is an implicit testimony to the power of business that all governments, not least reforming ones, have always been profoundly concerned to gain and retain its 'confidence'. Nor certainly is there any other interest whose 'confidence' is deemed so precious, or whose 'loss of confidence' is so feared.

The presidency of John F. Kennedy provides some illuminating instances of this concern. Soon after he came to office, President Kennedy found himself engaged in a 'spectacular power struggle' with the Business Advisory Council, 'an exclusive and self-perpetuating club of top corporate executives that had enjoyed a private and special relationship with the government since 1933' and which 'from Administration to Administration ... had a continuous privilege to participate in government decisions with no public record or review'.[3] The

---

[1] R. Maxwell, 'How to Buy a New Industrial Efficiency', in *The Times*, 3 October 1967 (Italics in text).

[2] *The Times*, 25 May 1967.

[3] Rowen, *The Free Enterprisers. Kennedy, Johnson and the Business Establishment* pp. 61–2. Another writer has described the Council as follows: 'Although nominally a private organisation, the BAC is publicly influential in a way in which pressure groups without the same ease of access to the federal government can never be. It is apparent, for instance, that it serves as a recruiting and placement agency for personnel in many of the federal agencies. More significantly, it prepares elaborate

Secretary of Commerce, Luther Hartwell Hodges, though hardly a fiery radical, entertained the odd notion that the manner of appointment of BAC members, and its procedures, ought to be modified. In the event, the difficulties this produced led the BAC itself to sever its official connections and to rename itself the Business Council. 'Hodges drew plans for a new BAC, one that would include a broad cross-section of American business – big, medium and small-sized. It would include representatives as well of labor, agriculture and education'.[1]

But these plans never materialised: faced with many problems which appeared to him to require business support, 'and sensitive to the growing insistence that he was "anti-business", the President turned full circle from his earlier, firm and bold posture toward the Business Advisory Council'.[2] A rapprochement was engineered and arrangements were made for 'small committees of the BC to be assigned to each of several government departments and agencies – and to the White House itself'.[3] For their part, 'labor leaders complained about the Kennedy campaign against "inflationary wage increases", itself part of Kennedy's assurance to business that he was playing no favorites. But the President wanted to restore a good working relationship with the Business Council *regardless of labor's concerns*'.[4]

It was only a few months later that the President found himself 'at war' with no less a member of the business establishment than Roger Blough, the chairman of U.S. Steel, who announced a substantial increase in the price of steel produced by his company and who was soon followed by other steel giants. On this occasion, the mobilisation of various forms of presidential pressure,[5] including a spectacular display of presidential anger on television, succeeded in causing the rescinding of the increases – though only for a year However, the episode was no loss to business in general, since it merely enhanced the

---

"studies" and "reports". Although the specific import of such advisory reports is often hard to gauge, the Justice Department has found it necessary to inform the Secretary of the Interior that "fundamental questions of basic policy" are being initially settled by industry advisory committees, with the result that government action amounts to no more than giving effect to decisions already made by such committees' (Kariel, *The Decline of American Pluralism*, p. 99).

[1] Rowen, op cit., p. 70.   [2] *Ibid.*, p. 71.   [3] *Ibid.*, p. 71.
[4] *Ibid.*, p. 73 (my italics).   [5] For which see *ibid.*, chapter 6.

President's almost obsessional concern to earn and enjoy its 'confidence'. Indeed, Governor Connally, who was riding in the President's car at the time of the assassination, has recalled that part at least of Kennedy's purpose in undertaking the trip to Texas was to reassure its 'business community' as to his intentions; 'I think it galled him', Governor Connally writes, 'that conservative business people would suspect that he, a wealthy product himself of our capitalistic system, would do anything to damage that system'.[1]

The 'confidence' of business is also that elusive prize which the Labour government of Mr Wilson has pursued with unflagging zeal ever since it first came to office – though to no great avail. Thus, *The Times* reported in the autumn of 1967 that:

> ... leading industrialists are likely to be called on by the Prime Minister during the coming months for private talks aimed at convincing the business community that its views will be of central importance in the Government's planning of its economic policies ... Labour came to power with a large fund of good-will among the business community.[2] It is perhaps a recognition of its subsequent disillusion that the Prime Minister is now ready to intervene in the constant Whitehall-industry dialogue to restore confidence necessary for promoting higher investments and changing practice.[3]

The zeal is not a matter for surprise. Given the degree of economic power which rests in the 'business community' and the decisive importance of its actions (or of its non-actions) for major aspects of economic policy, any government with serious pretensions to radical reform must either seek to appropriate that power or find its room for radical action rigidly circumscribed by the requirements of business 'confidence'. So far, no government in any Western-type political system, whatever its rhetoric before assuming office, has taken up the first of these options. Instead, reform-minded governments have, sometimes reluctantly, sometimes not, curbed their reforming propensities (though never enough for the men they sought to appease) or adapted their reforms to the purposes of business (as happened in the case of the nationalisation proposals of the 1945 Labour government), and turned themselves into the allies of the very

[1] J. Connally, 'Why Kennedy went to Texas', *Life*, 24 November 1967, p. 100.
[2] This may well be doubted.
[3] *The Times*, 3 October 1967.

forces they had promised, while in opposition, to counter and subdue. Politics, in this context, is indeed the art of the possible. But what is possible is above all determined by what the 'business community' finds acceptable.

Nowadays, however, it is not only with the power of their own business class that reform-minded and 'left-wing' governments have to reckon, or whose 'confidence' they must try and earn. Such governments must also reckon, now more than ever before, with the power and pressure of outside capitalist interests and forces – large foreign firms, powerful and conservative foreign governments, central banks, private international finance, official international credit organisations like the International Monetary Fund and the World Bank, or a formidable combination of all these. Economic and financial orthodoxy, and a proper regard for the prerogatives and needs of the free enterprise system, is not only what internal business interests expect and require from their office-holders; these internal interests are now powerfully seconded by outside ones, which may easily be of greater importance.

Capitalism, we have already noted, is now more than ever an international system, whose constituent economies are closely related and interlinked. As a result, even the most powerful capitalist countries depend, to a greater or lesser extent, upon the good will and cooperation of the rest, and of what has become, notwithstanding enduring and profound national capitalist rivalries, an interdependent international capitalist 'community'. The disapproval by that 'community' of the policies of one of its members, and the withdrawal of good will and cooperation which may follow from it, are obviously fraught with major difficulties for the country concerned. And so long as a country chooses to remain part of the 'community', so long must the wish *not* to incur its disapproval weigh very heavily upon its policy decisions and further reduce the impulses of reform-minded governments to stray far from the path of orthodoxy. Central bankers, enjoying a high degree of autonomy from their governments, have come to assume extraordinary importance as the guardians of that orthodoxy, and as the representatives *par excellence* of 'sound finance'. A *conservative* government in a relatively strong economic and financial position, such as the government of President de Gaulle long enjoyed, may play rogue elephant without undue risk of retribution. A radical government, on the other hand, would be unlikely to be given much shrift by these representatives of international capitalism.

Moreover, radical governments, as was also noted earlier, normally come to office in circumstances of severe economic and financial crisis, and find that credits, loans and general financial support are only available on condition that they pursue economic and foreign policies which are acceptable to their creditors and bankers and which are only marginally distinguishable, if at all, from the conservative policies they had previously denounced.

A case in point is that of the Labour government which was elected in October 1964 and re-elected in March 1966. It was Mr Wilson himself who, in an often-quoted phrase, warned the Trades Union Congress before the election of 1964 that 'you can get into pawn but don't then talk about an independent foreign policy or an independent defence policy'.[1] This was well spoken, and applies at least as much to an 'independent' economic policy. But Mr Wilson did, all the same 'get into pawn' soon after he came to office, and went deeper into pawn in subsequent years. His government duly pursued policies of a sufficiently conservative character to ensure the continued, unenthusiastic, support of capitalist governments, central banks and international financial agencies. But that support was naturally conditional upon the strict observance of economic and financial orthodoxy, of which an 'incomes policy' mainly designed to keep down wages was a central element; and the creditors had to be given the right to assure themselves, by a process of continuous surveillance, that the Labour government did pursue the required policies.

This kind of dependence and surveillance has always been characteristic of the relations between the world of advanced capitalism and those governments of the 'Third World' which have sought aid and credits from it; and the price of such aid and credits has always been the pursuit by the governments concerned of policies designed to favour, or at least not to hinder, foreign capitalist enterprise, and the adoption in

[1] *T.U.C. Annual Report*, 1964, p. 383.

international affairs of policies and attitudes not likely, at the least, to give offence to the creditors and donors.

But these external pressures do not only now affect the under-developed countries of the 'Third World'. They can also be directed, with considerable effect, upon the governments of advanced capitalist countries; and here, obviously, is a great source of additional strength to national capitalist interests faced with governments bent on policies unacceptable to these interests. Class conflict, in these countries, has always had an international dimension, but this is now even more directly and specifically true than in the past.

II

In the light of the strategic position which capitalist enterprise enjoys in its dealings with governments, simply by virtue of its control of economic resources, the notion, which is basic to pluralist theory, that here is but one of the many 'veto groups' in capitalist society, on a par with other 'veto groups', must appear as a resolute escape from reality.

Of these other groups, it is labour, as an 'interest' in society, whose power is most often assumed to equal (when it is not claimed to surpass) the power of capital. But this is to treat as an accomplished fact what is only an unrealised potentiality, whose realisation is beset with immense difficulties.

For labour has nothing of the power of capital in the day-to-day economic decision-making of capitalist enterprise. What a firm produces; whether it exports or does not export; whether it invests, in what, and for what purpose; whether it absorbs or is absorbed by other firms – these and many other such decisions are matters over which labour has at best an indirect degree of influence and more generally no influence at all. In this sense, labour lacks a firm basis of economic power, and has conse-quently that much less pressure potential *vis-à-vis* the state. This is also one reason why governments are so much less concerned to obtain the 'confidence' of labour than of business.

Moreover, labour does not have anything, by way of exer-cising pressure, which corresponds to the foreign influences

which are readily marshalled on behalf of capital. There are no
labour 'gnomes' of Zurich, no labour equivalent of the World
Bank, the International Monetary Fund, or the OECD, to
ensure that governments desist from taking measures detrimental to wage-earners and favourable to business, or to press
for policies which are of advantage to 'lower income groups'
and which are opposed to the interests of economic elites. For
wage-earners in the capitalist world, international solidarity is
part of a hallowed rhetoric which seldom manifests itself concretely and effectively; for business, it is a permanent reality.

The one important weapon which labour, as an 'interest',
does have is the strike; and where it has been used with real
determination its effectiveness as a means of pressure has often
been clearly demonstrated. Again and again, employers and
governments have been forced to make concessions to labour
because of the latter's resolute use of the strike weapon, or even
because of the credible threat of its use. On innumerable
occasions, demands which, the unions and the workers were told,
could not conceivably be granted since they must inevitably
mean ruin for a firm or industry or inflict irreparable damage to
the national economy, have somehow become acceptable when
organised labour has shown in practice that it would not desist.

Determination, however, is the problem. For labour, as a
pressure group, is extremely vulnerable to many internal and
external influences calculated to erode its will and persistence.
Because of the effectiveness of these influences, governments
have generally found it unnecessary to treat labour with anything like the deference which they have accorded to business.
They have sometimes trod on the latter's toes, but never as
heavily as they have trod on the toes of labour – as Mr Wilson's
Labour government, for instance, has done in pursuit of an
'incomes policy'.

One important weakness which affects labour as a pressure
group, as compared to business, is that the latter's national
organisations are able to speak with considerably more
authority than can their labour counterparts.

There are a number of reasons for this. One of them is that
business organisations can truly claim to 'speak for business',
either because they include a very high percentage of individual
business units or because the firms which they do represent are

responsible for a crucial part of economic activity. The equivalent labour organisations on the other hand nowhere include a majority of wage-earners, and mostly include far less. Business associations, in this sense, are much more representative than trade unions.

Secondly, and more important, business is nowhere as divided as labour. The point has been made before that business is neither an economic nor an ideological monolith, speaking always or even normally with one single voice on all issues. Indeed, its separate interests find everywhere expression in the different national associations which represent different sectors of the 'business community'. These divisions, notably the division between large-scale enterprise and medium or small business, are by no means negligible, either in specific or in general terms. But they do not prevent a basic ideological consensus, which is of fundamental importance in the representation and impact of business. Thus the policies advocated by the Diet of German Industry and Commerce may well be more 'moderate and liberal' than those of the Federation of German Industry;[1] and similar shades of difference may also be found among national business associations in other countries. But these differences obviously occur within a fairly narrow *conservative* spectrum of agreement which precludes major conflict. Business, it could be said, is tactically divided but strategically cohesive; over most of the larger issues of economic policy, and over other large national issues as well, it may be expected to present a reasonably united front.

This is certainly not the case for trade union movements anywhere. *Their* outstanding characteristic, in fact, is division, not unity; and the divisions from which they suffer, far from being tactical and superficial, are more often than not deep and fundamental.

Trade unions have of course always been divided from each other (and often, indeed, within themselves) in terms of the particular functions and skills of their members, sometimes by geography, often by religious, ethnic or racial factors. But, whether because of these factors or for other reasons, they are above all divided by ideology and attitudes from each other and within themselves.

[1] Braunthal, *The Federation of German Industry in Politics*, p. 27.

In some countries, for instance France and Italy, these divisions find institutional expression in the existence of separate, distinct and often bitterly antagonistic federations – Communist, social-democratic and Christian, whose conflicts are a profoundly inhibiting factor in their encounter both with employers and with the state, and in their effectiveness as pressure groups. Nowhere does business suffer anything remotely comparable to these divisions.

Moreover, even in countries where ideological cleavages have not found institutional expression, trade union movements have still been subject to profound divisions, which may be contained within one organisation, but which are scarcely less debilitating.

This, for instance, has always been the case for the trade union movement in Britain, where the divisions have often been based on functional differences between the unions, upon which have also, often coincidentally, been superimposed differences and conflicts between more militant and less militant unions; and this latter difference has also regularly occurred inside individual unions, with a more militant and left-wing element at odds with a generally more 'moderate' and 'responsible' leadership and following.

This division between leaders and members is also one which has not usually affected business associations. The basic cause of that division, from which Communist unions have by no means been immune, lies in the profoundly ambiguous role which trade union leaders tend to assume in capitalist societies. For on the one hand, these leaders are expected to defend the 'sectional' interests of their members with the utmost determination, both against employers and, where occasion arises, as it often does, against the state; but on the other hand, they are also expected by 'public opinion', and often required by the state, to act 'responsibly', in the 'national interest', which generally means that they should curb and subdue their members' demands rather than defend and advance them.

This is particularly true in regard to strike action. As Dr V. L. Allen has noted,

Strikes take place within a hostile environment even though they are a common every-day phenomenon. They are conventionally described as industrially subversive, irresponsible, unfair, against the interests of the community, contrary to the workers' best interests, wasteful of resources, crudely aggressive, inconsistent with democracy and, in any event, unnecessary.[1]

But what is important about this is that trade union leaders, particularly 'reformist' ones, are themselves deeply influenced by these notions. As Dr Allen also notes,

Union officials are particularly prone to the anti-strike environmental influences because they are frequently made out to be responsible for the behaviour of their members ... Once they are committed to a strike call, union officials tend to become defensive, apologetic and concerned about taking avoiding action. When they are actually engaged in a strike, they are frequently motivated by a desire to end it quickly irrespective of the merits of the issue.[2]

These 'environmental influences' are indeed formidable. They include not only the mass media, which may be relied on, almost unanimously, to blast the 'irresponsibility' of any major (or even minor) strike, whatever the merits of the case, and similarly to condemn those who lead it; they also include the government which may equally be expected, whatever its political label, to use every available means of influence and power at its command to erode the will and purpose of the strikers, and particularly of their trade union leaders.[3] This may not always be successful; but it is at least always tried.

Nor is it only 'environmental influences' of this sort which tend to cause union leaders to be chary of sustained militant action for the advancement of their members' interests. Such action is likely to involve a serious drain of union resources. It is also likely to strengthen the hand of militant elements inside the unions whose challenge to their authority trade union leaders are naturally concerned to resist. Moreover, the fear of failure, despite great sacrifices, always looms large, and is enhanced by an unnerving awareness of the strength of the forces arrayed against labour. And while the success of militant action must often depend upon the solidarity and support of other unions, this is seldom easy to obtain; even when it is obtained, it is not at all guaranteed to last the necessary length of time.

[1] V. L. Allen, *Militant Trade Unionism*, 1966, p. 27.   [2] *Ibid.*, p. 27.
[3] For a notable recent example, involving the Labour government, see P. Foot, 'The Seamen's Struggle', in Blackburn and Cockburn (eds.), *The Incompatibles*.

Some of these weaknesses are inherent in the position of trade unions in capitalist society. But in this instance too, structural constraints may be more compelling, or less; and this is at least in part determined by the ideology and outlook which trade union leaders bring to their task.

With the exception of France and Italy where the largest trade union movements are run by Communists and other Marxist socialists, the trade union movements in the countries of advanced capitalism are led and dominated by men who call themselves socialists, or social-democrats, or Christian democrats, or, as in the case of the United States, mainly plain Democrats. These different labels obviously betoken substantial differences in attitudes towards the capitalist system. Where some trade union leaders, notably in the United States, accept that system as given, and do so very gladly, others tend to subscribe to a belief in the ultimate achievement of an altogether different social order. And where American trade union leaders generally believe and proclaim that there exists a fundamental identity of interests between capitalist management and labour,[1] most trade union leaders in other capitalist countries are on the whole less apt to believe this, or at least to proclaim it.

On the other hand, the practical importance of the ideological differences between American and the vast majority of non-Communist trade union leaders and officials in other capitalist countries can easily be exaggerated.[2] For while American trade union leaders explicitly accept capitalist structures as beyond challenge, their counterparts in other countries have tended, *in practice*, to act on the same view, and to treat as irrelevant to trade union strategy whatever commitment they may have to another social order.

This has greatly eased the relations of trade union leaders with employers and governments and provided a firm basis for a

---

[1] Thus, even a trade union leader like Walther Reuther, who is often thought of as being to 'the left' of most other American trade union leaders, is apt to proclaim that 'we must shape policies in the knowledge that free labor and free management are less antagonistic than partners, that they have more in common than in conflict. We need to broaden areas of understanding and minimise areas of conflict' (Quoted in Kariel, *The Decline of American Pluralism*, p. 63).

[2] Indeed, it can easily be exaggerated, as far as their trade union activities are concerned, in regard to many Communist trade union leaders as well.

process of collaboration between them which has turned these leaders into junior partners of capitalist enterprise. That process has now assumed a much more official character than in the past: trade unions are now regularly 'consulted' by their governments, and their representatives are also to be found in various organisms of the state system. Trade union leaders have found it easy to believe that, because they have been recognised as a necessary element in the operation of capitalism, they have also achieved parity with business in the determination of policy. In fact, their incorporation into the official life of their countries has mainly served to saddle them with responsibilities which have further weakened their bargaining position, and which has helped to reduce their effectiveness.

There are, however, other and more specific reasons for dismissing as altogether unrealistic the view of labour as an interest group comparable in strength to business.

Serious pressure group activity, it is generally agreed, now occurs much more at executive and administrative, rather than at legislative, level. As the state has increasingly come to assume greater powers in all fields of economic and social activity, so have the major 'interests' in society also naturally come to direct their pressure activities towards government and administration. This, as will be seen presently, does not mean that legislatures are of no consequence in this respect. But it does mean that the most significant part of pressure group activity must now bear on the executive power; it is now only the weakest groups which seek to wield influence primarily through legislatures, precisely because they have little or no hold over the executive. The major 'interests' use both means, with the greater emphasis on the government and the administration.

But as has already been argued at length, business enters this competition on extremely favourable terms in comparison with labour or any other 'interest'. For businessmen and their representatives normally have a *rapport* with ministers, civil servants and other members of the state elite which is very different from that of labour and *its* representatives. Given the influences which affect political office-holders and administrators, and which were noted in previous chapters – social provenance, personal ties and connections,[1] class situation, self-interest, ideological inclinations, conceptions of the 'national interest' – business pressure groups may reasonably expect that their views and demands will meet with an *initial* degree of comprehension, sympathy or at least respect of a kind entirely different from that accorded to their labour equivalents; and this is just as likely to be the case when 'left-wing' governments are in office as when labour has to deal with conservative administration.

An additional and important reason for this difference is that labour, as a pressure group, always *appears* as a very much more 'sectional' interest than business. Its demands, however worthy in themselves, are easily capable of being construed as detrimental to economic and financial viability, as inflationary, as inimical to the efficient conduct of industrial or other affairs, as dangerous to the maintenance of 'confidence', not least abroad, as certain to imperil the competitiveness of home enterprise, as 'selfish' or 'unrealistic' or 'unsound' – in short, as clearly against the 'national interest'.

The demands of business, in contrast, are *always* claimed to be in the 'national interest'. For one thing, business opposition to labour demands which can be, and are, characterised in the terms just noted is, by definition, congruent with that interest. For another, business demands which are designed to strengthen the position of individual firms or of particular industries, or of capitalist enterprise at large, can always be presented, with a high degree of plausibility, given the capitalist context in which they are made, as congruent with the 'national interest'.

This may not always achieve the desired results, and it is obviously not the case that all business pressure is always successful and labour pressure always in vain. It is rather that governments and civil servants are very likely to feel that in endorsing the former, they are in all conscience furthering the 'national interest'; and equally likely to feel that this is not the case, or is very much less likely to be the case, in relation to labour's demands.[2]

---

[1] One Japanese writer recalls the rather charming fact that 'shortly after he took office late in 1954, Prime Minister Hatoyama Ichiro issued an order to all government agencies forbidding civil servants to play golf and mahjong with businessmen' (N. Ike, *Japanese Politics*, 1958, p. 160). For the closeness of the relations of civil servants to business in Japan, see *ibid.*, pp. 161ff.

[2] A French writer notes, in this connection, that 'top civil servants prefer to deal

This likelihood is further increased by the vast resources which business interests are able to marshall in the advancement of their cause. Government departments and regulatory agencies which are concerned with matters and policies affecting the major interests are strongly influenced by the information and evidence presented to them by these interests, and indeed often rely, in the determination of their policies, upon it. Moreover, they are highly susceptible to the weight and intensity of the pressures which interests are able to generate. From this point of view, business is infinitely better placed than labour, or any other interest, given its vastly superior resources. Moreover, the largest and most powerful firms do not need to rely on any intermediate body to speak to governments and present their case on their behalf – they do so for themselves, with the confidence born of their power. As Professor Meynaud also notes, 'Siemens, Rhône-Poulenc, Montecatini, Courtaulds, General Motors, need no intermediary to deal with the authorities'.[1] But these intermediaries are all the same of no mean importance in the presentation of industry's demands, in the pressures they are able to generate, and in the degree to which they are able, by the deployment of their resources, to help shape the official mind, and also 'public opinion'.[2] As Professor Ehrmann has observed for France, 'the large, well-organised economic interests in the nation, especially when they are represented by competently staffed peak associations, such as the National Employers' Council, are in almost constant consultation with the Ministry's tax section' (i.e. the Ministry of

---

with the top men of industry and finance rather than with the representatives of small or medium enterprises, or vine or beet growers. To the failings of the former, the latter add a complete lack of understanding of economic life and an all too evidently exclusive concern for their particular interests. Moreover, the interests of large employers are interlinked with the national interest. This creates a community of language between these employers and officials; and though officials are aware of a certain ambiguity in the situation, they appreciate the knowledge these men have, and the fact that they are able to give to their demands the polish of general ideas' (Brindillac, 'Les Hauts Fonctionnaires', p. 871).

[1] Meynaud, *Nouvelles Etudes sur les Groupes de Pression en France*, p. 27. An American study also notes that among the 200 largest manufacturing concerns in the United States, 'Washington representatives are the rule rather than the exception, particularly among companies making "hard goods" for the government' (P.W. Cherrington and R. L. Gillen, *The Business Representative in Washington*, 1962, p. 1).

[2] For which see chapter 7.

Finance).[1] No interest other than business, anywhere, has the same ease of access to the most important organs of executive power, and none enjoys the same familarity with its agents. Nor is any other interest able to wage, when required, the kind of pressure campaign which business interests can undertake. Thus, the Labour-Management Relations Act of 1947, better known as the Taft-Hartley Act, was profoundly detrimental to American trade union interests, and they fought hard against it; but their struggle was as nothing to the campaign which the National Association of Manufacturers was able to wage for its promulgation. In a different context, it is very difficult to think that any interest other than business could muster the kind of resources and sympathies which were mobilised in Britain to persuade the government to establish commercial television;[2] and it is equally difficult to believe that a trade union, or any other interest, would be able to command the resources required to wage for their own purposes the anti-nationalisation campaigns which British firms have waged at one time or another since the war.[3] One American writer has said, in regard to the United States, that 'the flaw in the pluralist heaven is that the heavenly chorus sings with a strong upper-class accent ... the system is skewed, loaded and unbalanced in favour of a fraction of a minority'.[4] This is also true for other capitalist countries.

The argument, it may be worth stressing yet again, is not that this imbalance automatically ensures that business interests always achieve their purposes and necessarily impose their will upon the state in regard to their every demand. Nor is it to suggest that other organised groups of every sort have not often waged highly successful campaigns, sometimes even against

[1] H. W. Ehrmann, 'French Bureaucracy and Organised Interests', in *Administrative Science Quarterly*, 1961, vol. 5, no. 4, p. 541.

[2] For which see H. H. Wilson, *Pressure Group: The Campaign for Commercial Television in England*, 1960.

[3] See, e.g. H. H. Wilson, 'Techniques of Pressure', in *The Public Opinion Quarterly*, 1951, vol. 15.

[4] E. E. Schattschneider, *The Semi-Sovereign People*, 1960, p. 31. Some thirty years ago Professor Schattschneider made the point in terms which remain singularly apposite: 'Business men collectively constitute the most class-conscious group in American society. As a class they are more highly organised, more easily mobilised, have more facilities for communication, are more like-minded, and are more accustomed to stand together in defence of their privileges than any other group' (E E. Schattschneider, *Politics, Pressures and the Tariff*, 1935, p. 287).

strong business opposition. Had business predominance been absolute, it would be absurd to speak of competition at all. There *is* competition, and defeats for powerful capitalist interests as well as victories. After all, David did overcome Goliath. But the point of the story is that David *was* smaller than Goliath and that the odds *were* heavily against him.

This imbalance between business and labour as pressure groups manifests itself also in the workings of two other elements of the state system, namely legislatures and the organs of sub-central government, which must now be considered.

III

Legislative assemblies in advanced capitalist countries now tend to play a subsidiary role in the decision-making process. Though solemn tributes continue to be paid to them as the ultimate repositories of the 'popular will', governments seek increasingly to insulate themselves from effective parliamentary pressure.

Nevertheless, legislatures do retain a certain degree of influence; and while major 'interests' now tend to consider them as auxiliary instruments in the advancement of their purposes, they still find it worth while to exert what pressure they can through representative assemblies. In this instance too, however, business interests are much better placed than their competitors.

For one thing, it is conservative parties of one denomination or another which have continued, throughout this century, to dominate legislative assemblies. There have been exceptions to this pattern, but the general situation has, in simple terms of majorities, been one of conservative predominance. The conservative majorities in these assemblies have for the most part been made up of men drawn from the upper and middle classes; and whatever their social origin, the members of these majorities have in any case been strongly disposed to take a favourable view of capitalist activity and a correspondingly unfavourable view of proposals and policies which appeared to them detrimental to it. The extreme case is obviously that of the United States, where men with a strong bias in favour of private enterprise have always formed the overwhelming majority of the House of Representatives and the Senate. American labour has always had to depend upon such legislators as it could enlist to defend its interests and advance its claims, with no great guarantee that these men could be relied on to be its consistent advocates, let alone effective ones. But even in the legislative assemblies of other countries it is normally interests associated with business and property which have had the big parliamentary battalions on their side.

Moreover, it would not do to forget that the parliamentary groups of social-democratic parties, like social-democratic trade union leaders and officials, have often acted, at the behest of their leaders, on a view of the 'national interest' which required them, not to *advance* working class interests but to help *subdue* them. Most members of these groups have easily succumbed to a parliamentary embrace which markedly affected such political virility as they possessed and caused them to see the world through a parliamentary haze not at all conducive to the militant assertion of a class consciousness which many of them in any case never had in the first place. And those of them who did have it and who sought to act upon it have always found that they had to contend with a variety of procedural and other obstacles precisely designed to curb that assertion. Even more important, they have also regularly found themselves at odds, often very sharply, with their parliamentary and party leaders and with their 'loyal' and 'responsible' colleagues: of all the forces which have contained socialist parliamentarians in social-democratic parties, none has been more effective than their own leaders and fellow parliamentarians.[1]

For their part, Communist parliamentarians, protected by a thicker ideological carapace, have been rather less vulnerable to the debilitating effects of what Marx called 'parliamentary cretinism'; but they have not by any means been immune to the disease. It is not necessarily true that 'there is more in common between two parliamentarians one of whom is a Communist than between two Communists one of whom is a parliamentarian'. Nor is it inevitable that the parliamentary groups of revolutionary parties should assume the characteristics of their bourgeois counterparts. Yet, parliamentary participation,

[1] The Parliamentary Labour Party is a classic example of this phenomenon.

which parties pledged to revolutionary change cannot reasonably shun in the political conditions of Western-type regimes, does greatly enhance opportunistic tendencies, and provides much encouragement for the view that politics is above all a matter of parliamentary strategy, tactics and manœuvre, for the sake of which much in terms of principle and purpose may be sacrificed.

Conservative majorities work to the advantage of business and related interests. But for many of their purposes, these interests rely not on numerical legislative superiority but on other favourable factors.

One of these has to do with the important fact that powerful and established interests often need do no more, in order to remain, as it were, in possession, than to prevent the passage of legislation and the promulgation of measures which adversely affect their privileges. As Professor Ehrmann has noted, 'this negative effect of parliamentary action is frequently all that matters, since to defeat competing claims is for organised business generally more decisive than to secure new laws for which there is little need as long as business can count on a sympathetic administration'.[1]

Legislative assemblies lend themselves admirably to this negative inhibiting and blocking purpose, which an American writer has characterised in an apt phrase as 'policy-making by default'.[2] The House of Lords, in the days when it enjoyed substantial powers, fulfilled this role to perfection, and its history has in fact been a saga of struggle against the erosion of privilege of every kind. The United States Senate is another body exceptionally well adapted to wage this struggle. 'Even one senator', one writer notes, 'can make a nuisance of himself; a handful of them in a wrecking mood can bring the executive branch into a cowering state of contemptible paralysis.'[3] This is perhaps a little strong and tends to underestimate the means of pressure upon recalcitrant legislators

[1] Ehrmann, *Organised Business in France*, p. 218.

[2] Blaisdell, *American Democracy Under Pressure*, p. 39. Professor Blaisdell also notes that 'the failure of Congress to deal resolutely with the issues involved in the control of property through the corporate form of business organisation amounts to a tacit acceptance of the situation as in the public interest' (*ibid.*, p. 39).

[3] V. O. Key, *Politics, Parties and Pressure Groups*, 1958, p. 476.

which the executive branch itself possesses, if it is minded to use them, which is admittedly a large qualification. The important point, however, is that the 'wrecking mood' of senators or of members of the House of Representatives is most likely to be directed against measures of which the 'business community' also disapproves, including many measures of welfare which may affect property rights and which can conveniently be denounced as 'creeping socialism', or some such.[1]

Similarly, it is no small advantage to German business interests to have as chairman of an important financial sub-committee of the Bundestag a man who 'frankly asserted that he himself would favour no bill that was regarded by important segments of industry as too heavy a burden'.[2] It is not very likely that any other group in German society could find so staunch and explicit a defender of *its* interests in a position of equivalent power.[3]

This kind of pro-business bias, which is encountered in all the legislatures of the capitalist world, stems in part from the *unprompted* inclinations of legislators. As in the case of governments and civil servants, it would be naïve to think that members of legislatures are the unwilling instruments of powerful business and other propertied interests. If they defend these interests, it is because they find it easy to equate that defence with the 'national interest'.

[1] At the end of 1967, the Washington correspondant of *The Times* was moved to write that 'the fact that there are some 35 million poor people in this, the richest country in history, is sufficient evidence of the middle-class interests of Congress and its devotion to business needs .. A medical report of the southern regional council spoke of children lucky to eat one meal a day, of children afflicted with chronic diarrhoea, chronic sores and deformities, and of shacks without running water or electricity.

Many families have a diet of cornmeal, flour, rice and non-fat dried milk. In California, the richest state in the union, migrant workers earn as little as $1,000 (just over £400) a.year. These are the so-called "invisible poor", and to these material wants must be added the oppression of Negroes, and unpunished violence and murder. This is an old story for the United States, but Watts, Newark and Detroit are ominous warnings that the poor are no longer invisible or quiescent. Yet Congress managed to spend 340 days in session doing remarkably little about it' ('Cloud Cuckoo Land of American Congress', *The Times* 19 December 1967).

[2] Braunthal, *The Federation of German Industry in Politics*, p. 172.

[3] Professor Braunthal also notes that 'the BDI [*Bundesverband der Deutschen Industrie*] is primarily interested in the work of the Economic Affairs, Foreign Trade and Finance Committee [of the Bundestag]. By and large, it has been successful in "colonising" these committees with chairmen and members who tend to be responsive to its aims' (*ibid.*, p. 169).

On the other hand, pressure helps and may often be required, in regard to specific policies and demands.

That pressure may be very diffuse. One American study notes that 'most lobbyists believe that the best argument for most senators most of the time is advantage to the senator's state'.[1] But it is also very likely that a Senator will believe that measures which are of advantage to business and which are pressed for by business interests will be of advantage to his state; and he will find far fewer reasons for thinking so in regard to measures which are of advantage to, and advocated by, labour.

However, a personal element also enters. For the same senator also knows that election campaigns are expensive: '... perhaps the "normal" expenditures, to strike a rough average of the varying reports of experts, is in the neighbourhood of $500,000 and closely contested battles in large two party states often cost over a million dollars'.[2] The same writer adds that 'the bulk of his campaign fund ... is likely to be made up of a few large contributions from individuals and groups with a vital interest in his behaviour in office'.[3] These contributions will obviously mainly come from business and will at least make their recipients attentive to the requirements of the contributors.

But even where the relationship between pressure and parliamentary behaviour is not quite so obvious, business and other propertied interests have immeasurably greater resources than any other interest to shape the legislative mind and will, and to influence the legislative process. The pressure may be direct and personal, and take a multitude of forms; or it may be exercised via 'public opinion', by means of 'grassroots' campaigns, which are vastly expensive, and which on this and other grounds (for instance the control of mass media) business interests are far better placed to undertake effectively than anyone else. Mr Rowen, for the United States, notes in regard to President Kennedy's tax reform proposals in 1961, particularly the proposal for tax withholding on dividend and interest income, that 'although the Ways and Means Committee approved withholding, the mail campaign inspired by businessmen, bankers, and savings and loan associations, ultimately defeated the proposal. Congress's susceptibility to this kind of

---

[1] D. R. Matthews, *U.S. Senators and Their World*, 1960, p. 182.
[2] *Ibid.*, p. 72. [3] *Ibid.*

pressure is a sad commentary on the American legislative process.'[1] Such campaigns may not always succeed; and other interests are often able to exercise considerable pressure upon legislatures. But the fact remains that business groups are infinitely better equipped than other economic groups to exercise effective pressure upon these bodies.

Professor Almond has written that what is 'striking' about

> ... the structure of business influence in German politics and government is not the mere [!] fact that the business community has a degree of influence disproportionate to its size. *This is a pattern which is familiar in the United States, England, and indeed in any country with a capitalist economy and a democratic government.* What is unusual in the German pattern, as compared to the American, is the direct and massive involvement of business pressure-groups in representation in the Bundestag and in the financing of the parties. By virtue of their penetration of the middle-class parties and their delegations in the Bundestag, these pressure group organisations acquire a crucial political importance, influencing in important ways both the spirit and content of German politics.[2]

This is a curious emphasis. For what *is* really striking is precisely what Professor Almond dismisses so casually as a 'mere' fact, namely the 'disproportionate' influence which the 'business community' exercises upon the parliamentary assemblies of advanced capitalist countries: the *forms* this assumes are no doubt matters of genuine importance; but, it might be thought, rather less so than the *fact* of predominance, however achieved.

What that fact indicates is that the legislative element of the state system, like all the other elements which have been considered previously, has normally remained, notwithstanding universal suffrage and competitive politics, much more the instrument of the dominant classes than of the subordinate ones, even though it is now rather less exclusively their instrument than in former days. Legislatures may help to attenuate

---

[1] Rowen, *The Free Enterprisers*, p. 54.

[2] G.A. Almond, 'The Politics of German Business', in H. Speier and W.P. Davidson (eds.), *West German Leadership and Foreign Policy*, 1957, p. 211 (my italics). Note also, in confirmation of this pattern, that in 1958, 52 per cent of the Liberal-Democratic Party's members of the Japanese Diet had associations of one kind or other with business (R.A. Scalapino and J. Masumi, *Parties and Politics in Contemporary Japan*, 1962, p. 63).

the pattern of class domination; but they also remain one of its means.

IV

Just as legislative assemblies have lost power to the executive, so have local and regional units of government in advanced capitalist countries become ever more markedly dependent on central power and subordinate to it. Even in the United States, with its powerful tradition of decentralised power, what Harold Laski called in 1940 the 'obsolescence of federalism' had steadily increased in the succeeding years.

Yet, while the trend towards the nationalisation of public power has been very marked, the process is very far from complete. Not only have local and regional units of government retained many powers as agents of the centre; in many cases they have also, even though contingently, retained a substantial degree of independent initiative and decision, most obviously in the United States. Even as agents of the central government, these units often have had a certain amount of freedom as to the manner in which they have discharged their functions, and this has been of considerable importance to those who have come under their authority.

These are reasons enough for a brief consideration of the character and distribution of sub-central power in advanced capitalist societies, particularly in the United States, where much of pluralist theory has used 'local community power' as its context and sought to rebut 'ruling class' and 'power elite' concepts by reference to it.[1]

The main lines of the pluralist argument in regard to 'local community power' are essentially similar to those employed for the more general contention that power in the United States is dispersed, not concentrated, democratic and not pluto-oligarchic.

The claim, it must be noted, is not that 'everybody' in local

---

[1] For a bibliography of relevant material up to 1962, see C. Press, *Main Street Politics: Policy Making at the Local Level*, 1962; for more recent references, see, e.g. A. Rose, *The Power Structure. Political Process in American Society*, 1966.

communities has an equal share of power. Thus Professor Dahl, the leading theorist of pluralist local community power, notes that in New Haven, 'a wage earner is rarely appointed or elected to any of the city's leading offices'.[1] The claim is rather that power is distributed between *different* elites who are influential in *different* 'issue areas', and whose power is 'non-cumulative'. Nor, Professor Dahl suggests, is there any specific evidence, in regard to major decisions, that economic power is a decisive element in the determination of policy. As one critic of the thesis summarises it: 'There are elites but there is no elite'.[2]

Moreover, and equally important in terms of pluralist claims, Professor Dahl, while admitting that blue-collar workers are almost totally excluded from decision-making groups,[3] also argues that:

> None the less it would be wrong to conclude that the activities and attitudes of people in these strata have no influence on the decision of government officials ... Though wage earners lack social standing, they are not without other resources, including the ballot, and what they lack as individuals *they more than make up* in collective resources. In short, although their direct influence is low, their indirect collective influence is high.[4]

With minor variations, these are the basic contentions of pluralist theoreticians.

The most important flaw in the argument stems from what C. Wright Mills called 'abstracted empiricism', which signifies in this instance the accumulation and usage of relevant data without proper regard to the total socio-economic context in which it alone has meaning.

Thus, it is perfectly true that members of the upper classes and the holders of economic power do not necessarily or even very often take a direct part in local and state government. But this does not mean that they do not form the crucial reference point for those who do actually run these units of government.[5] Professor Kaysen has written that:

[1] R. A. Dahl, *Who Governs? Democracy and Power in an American City*, 1961, p. 230.

[2] T. Gitlin, 'Local Pluralism as Theory and Ideology', in *Studies on the Left*, 1965, vol. 5, no. 3, p. 25. This is an excellent critique of pluralist theory in regard to local community power.

[3] Dahl, *Who Governs?*, p. 230.   [4] *Ibid.*, p. 233 (my italics).

[5] For the predominantly middle-class character of American state legislatures, see B. Zeller, *American State Legislatures*, 1954.

The branch manager of the company whose plant is the largest employer in a town or the vice-president of the firm proposing to build a plant which will become the largest employer in a small state treats with local government not as a citizen but as a quasi-sovereign power ... Even large industrial states and metropolitan cities face similar problems: the largest three employers in Michigan account for probably a quarter of the state's industrial employment; in Detroit the proportion is more nearly a third. At this level, the corporation's scope of choice, its financial staying power, its independence of significant local forces are all sources of strength in dealing with the characteristically weak governments at the local and often at the state levels.[1]

In the light of the real economic power which business enjoys, and of the prevailing culture which legitimates this power, the question whether top executives or middle ones actually run for election and serve in local or state government appears grotesquely irrelevant. One study, concerned with 'Cibola', duly notes that 'the overt direction of the political and civil life of Cibola has passed almost wholly into the hands of a group of middle-class business and professional men, almost none of whom occupies a position of economic dominance in the community .[2] But there is every reason to assume that these 'middle-class business and professional men' are acutely conscious of the importance to their communities of those who do occupy 'a position of economic dominance', that they themselves are not moved by ideas and purposes which are likely to clash greatly with the views of these power-holders, and that they also know full well how large are the resources the latter have at their disposal, should conflict arise. Indeed, Professor Dahl himself aptly notes that 'notables' are influential on decisions which touch upon business because 'politicians are wary of their potential influence and avoid policies that might incite the Notables in bitter opposition'.[3]

[1] C. Kaysen, 'The Modern Corporation: How Much Power? What Scope?', in Mason (ed.), *The Modern Corporation*, pp. 100–1. See also H. Zeigler, 'Interest Groups in the States', in K. Vines (ed.), *Politics in the American States*, 1965: 'No matter what kind of economy enjoyed by the state, the businesses dominate the structure of lobbying' (p. 109). For an illuminating account of this power as wielded at local level by oil interests, see Engler, *The Politics of Oil*.

[2] R. O. Schulze, 'The Role of Economic Determinants in Community Power Structure', in *American Sociological Review*, 1958, vol. 23, no. 1, p. 6.

[3] Dahl, *Who Governs?*, p. 84.

Other people than businessmen are of course consulted and deferred to by politicians and officials; and other interests than business are taken into the reckoning. As in national terms, power and influence at local and state level are not a zero-sum affair. But what is important here is that given the incidence of economic, social and cultural power in the United States, those who hold political power and office, whoever they may be, are at all times much more likely to defer to powerful business interests than to any other.[1] In any case, most other such interests are also likely to defer to business. Those people who do not and who put forward policies to which business is opposed, *may*, on occasion and in particular places, find politicians and officials on their side in the conflict: B movies are full of such heroes. Actual life is likely to be different, and has fewer happy endings. As Professor Dahl says, it would indeed be wrong to conclude that wage-earners and others have *no* influence. But it is profoundly misleading to claim that 'their indirect collective influence is high'. For, taken in conjunction with the systematic underestimation of the power of business and property, what this implies is that 'ordinary voters' compete in a pluralist political market situation on more or less equal terms (indeed on *advantageous* terms) with organised interests whose resources are immensely greater than their own. The notion is absurd, and is rendered the more absurd, in the American context, by the fact that the 'ordinary voter' is influenced by a variety of communications agencies which are overwhelmingly on the side of business interests, with few, if any, ideological 'countervailing forces'. Nor, it should be added, does this complacent pluralist view take account of the active discouragement which those who hold 'radical' opinions must expect to encounter in many 'communities', particularly smaller ones.

In this connection, community power theorists of the pluralist persuasion take little account of what has been called 'the second face' of power, or 'the fact that the power may be, and often is, exercised by confining the scope of decision-making to relatively "safe" issues' and by 'creating or reinforcing social and political values and institutional practices that limit the

---

[1] 'The price of survival of a state regulatory agency ... is accommodation within its field of regulation, whether the field is insurance, milk or oil' (Kariel, *The Decline of American Pluralism*, p. 103).

scope of the political process to public consideration of only those issues which are comparatively innocuous'.[1] Innocuous, that is, to privileged interests. Given the political and ideological weakness of the American labour movement, it is of course above all in the United States that these interests are able to avail themselves of this power. For nowhere else is their political and ideological hegemony so marked. As in national terms, business at local and state level is not only at an enormous competitive advantage in getting those things it wants; it is also uniquely well placed to prevent those things from being done, or even seriously discussed and considered, which it does *not* want.[2]

Ultimately, the proof of the pudding is in the eating: had not privileged interests exercised so potent a hold on local power, the 'shame of the cities' would not now be as crying as it was when Lincoln Steffens, writing at the turn of the century, made his name by denouncing it: the answer to pluralist theories of local power is provided by the cities themselves.

One difference between the United States and other capitalist countries is immediately obvious in relation to local community power, namely that in many of the latter, a number of cities and even regions have in this century passed under the control of labour, socialist and communist authorities, thus sometimes forming veritable 'red enclaves'.

Here is one instance where working-class movements have made a distinct inroad in the political hegemony of the dominant classes, and supplanted hitherto entrenched traditional elites. As a result, many such authorities have been able to boast of substantial achievements in housing, welfare, civic amenities, etc.; and their own example has often established criteria of local administration which have served an important purpose.

---

[1] P. Bachrach and M. Baratz, 'Two Faces of Power', in *American Political Science Review*, 1962, vol. 56, no. 4, p. 948.

[2] 'On some questions that are considered settled, there is a constant pressure for conformity. It is only on the unsettled issues that discussion is permissible. Such questions as land policy, private enterprise, and other matters dealing with the established interests are considered settled, and no discussion of the change of the rules is deemed desirable' (F. Hunter, *Community Power Structure: A Study of Decision Makers*, 1953, p. 182).

The power of these authorities has, however, been severely circumscribed, both by the general context in which they have operated and by central governments.

Thus, it has been noted, for Germany, that 'although the SPD is in control of a majority of the cities and some of the Länder, it must be cautious in its economic and financial policies because it cannot afford to alienate the local businessmen of whose tax support it would be deprived if they were to move to a more hospitable area'.[1] This may well exaggerate the economic constrictions under which these particular authorities need to have laboured, but it is obviously true that even progressive local authorities, not only in Germany, have been much concerned to placate propertied interests, and have suited their behaviour and policies to the purpose.

More important than this 'local community power', however, has been the control of central government and the powers it has been able to exercise to curb the radical tendencies of even the reddest of red enclaves. For that purpose, central governments have not least been able to rely on their own agents. Thus the powers of the *préfet* in France are sufficiently large to constitute a powerful additional check upon the radicalism of local authorities; as one student of the French prefectorial system has noted, 'the possibility of a Prefect in high office holding extreme views or marked prejudices is as unprobable as an extreme Minister of the Interior in a normal French cabinet'.[2] 'Extreme' may here safely be read as 'extreme left'. These representatives of the central power are, like their colleagues in central government, most likely to be men of very 'moderate' views; and they are also more likely to count many more industrialists, landowners and other notabilities among their friends and acquaintances than left-wing trade unionists and 'extreme' socialists. They are, in fact, an intrinsic part of the bourgeois establishment of their alloted areas. Nor in any case are they likely to be unmindful of the fact that the most prominent members of that establishment are likely to have good contacts in governmental circles, upon whose favourable opinion a successful prefectoral career depends.

Also, it should not be overlooked that while more or less

---

[1] Braunthal, *The Federation of German Industry in Politics*, p. 186.
[2] B. Chapman, *The Prefects in Provincial France*, 1955, p. 161.

radical authorities have long been a familiar feature of all advanced capitalist countries save the United States, conservative elites everywhere have maintained a remarkably strong hold on vast areas of administration, notably in the countryside but by no means only there. As in national politics but rather more slowly, these conservative elites have undergone notable changes in their social composition, in the sense that 'feudal' and aristocratic local leaders have increasingly been replaced by, or have at least had to make some room for, middle-class professional and managerial or entrepreneurial ones.[1] This kind of change in the nature of local leadership may have a variety of important consequences for local government; but it does not, of course, negate the fact of middle- and upper-class predominance.

Neither for that matter is that predominance necessarily negated by the election of radical or socialist authorities. As Mr Guttsman has noted for England:

> The local political oligarchs who hold positions of power, honour and trust as councillors, magistrates, governors of schools and hospitals, reach their eminence largely through the party organisation. They, like the national political leaders are recruited mainly from the middle class. This is clearly so in the Conservative Party, but even the representation of the Labour Party on local elected bodies contains a considerably larger proportion of men and women from groups above the manual working class than we find with the population as a whole, let alone in the group of labour voters.[2]

Middle-class radical councils may well do much *for* their working-class electorates: the point, however, is that at this level as at national level not much is done *by* the working

---

[1] 'Traditionally in rural Japan', one writer notes, 'the *yuryokusha* (i.e. the men of influence) almost always sprang from the larger landowning families, because landownership and power were related. This is to some extent still the case; but it is also true that new sources of influence have appeared in recent decades as a result of economic and social change' (Ike, *Japanese Politics*, p. 75). These new sources of influence, the same writer suggests, are 'wealth and capability'. The same pattern of 'de-feudalisation' and 'bourgeoisification' has been characteristic of all advanced capitalist countries. For Britain, see, e.g. A. H. Birch, *Small-Town Politics*, 1959, chapter 3.

[2] Guttsman, *The British Political Elite*, p. 27. See also L. J. Sharpe, 'Elected Representatives in Local Government', in *The British Journal of Sociology*, 1962, vol. 13, no. 3; for specific cases, see, e.g. F. Bealey, J. Blondel and W. P. McCann, *Constituency Politics. A Study of Newcastle-under-Lyme*, 1961, and Birch, *Small-Town Politics*.

classes. Here too the largest part by far of the population remains for ever ruled by others who may or may not have welfare and radical orientations, who may or may not combine these orientations with bureaucratic propensities, but who are, in any case, *them*.

At the end of the previous chapter it was said that the economic elites of capitalist society cannot rest content with the general support of governments and other parts of the state system. But neither can these elites be content with the massive advantage which they enjoy in the pursuit of their specific purposes. For the whole structure of economic and political domination which has been analysed here depends, in Western-type political regimes, on the support or at least on the acquiescence of those who are subjected to it. The subordinate classes in these regimes, and 'intermediary' classes as well, have to be persuaded to accept the existing social order and to confine their demands and aspirations within its limits. For dominant classes there can be no enterprise of greater importance, and there is none which requires greater exertion on a continuous basis, since the battle, in the nature of a system of domination, is never finally won. It is with this process of legitimation of capitalist society that the next two chapters are concerned.

7

The Process of Legitimation-I

In many regimes the men who control the state have found it necessary to rely on the continuous and systematic repression of all or most manifestations of opposition for the maintenance of their power and for the preservation of the existing social order.

With some notable exceptions in this century, this has not been the case for the political systems of advanced capitalism. Communist parties and other organisations of the Left have been suppressed or drastically inhibited in some countries and variously discriminated against everywhere; and the law also circumscribes or prohibits certain forms of political expression and activity. But even so, it is obviously the case that these regimes have admitted, though no doubt with different degrees of tolerance, a very large amount of opposition, including opposition whose explicit purpose was the wholesale recasting of capitalist society and even its overthrow. Where that purpose has assumed dangerous forms or has been construed as having assumed such forms (not at all the same thing), the state has deployed its coercive forces in order to meet the threat, real or imagined. But it has usually done this without resort to massive repression.

In any case, the Left, in advanced capitalist countries, has hardly ever, since the first world war, seriously nourished any insurrectionary intention. Some elements of it have certainly believed that a revolutionary trial of strength must ultimately occur or that such a trial was at least very likely. But even those parties and groups which have thought so have also acted on the assumption that a revolutionary confrontation with the bourgeois state could not occur for a long time and must be preceded by an extended period of political activity within the constitutional framework provided by these regimes. And inside that framework, the socialist forces, though no doubt with various more or less serious impediments, have been able to organise and to compete for popular support.

The outstanding fact about that competition for popular support has of course been that all parties of the Left, whether social-democratic or communist, have only achieved a relatively moderate degree of success in it. Under conditions of relative but nevertheless considerable political freedom, the parties of the working classes, the parties explicitly pledged to the defence and the liberation of the subordinate classes have generally done much less well politically than their more or less conservative rivals, whose own purpose has preeminently included the maintenance of the capitalist system. The most obvious token of that fact is that these latter parties have regularly achieved much better results in elections than the working-class parties, and have obviously done so because they have attracted very substantial sections of the subordinate classes, in addition to the largest part by far of the middle and upper classes.

The obvious question this suggests is why this has been so; why the anti-socialist parties have so regularly been legitimated by popular support in elections; why the dominant classes in these societies have been able, in conditions of open political competition, to ensure the continuance of the kind of economic and political predominance which has been outlined in the previous chapters. This was the question which Gramsci implicitly posed when he spoke of the 'hegemony' of the dominant classes in civil society, by which he meant their ideological predominance over the subordinate classes.[1]

The answer which Marx gave to that question was, in a famous formulation, that 'the ideas of the ruling class are in

---

[1] Professor Gwynn Williams has usefully defined the concept of hegemony as 'an order in which a certain way of life and thought is dominant, in which one concept of reality is diffused throughout society in all its institutional and private manifestations, informing with its spirit all taste, morality, customs, religious and political principles, and all social relations, particularly in their intellectual and moral connotations' (G. A. Williams, 'Gramsci's Concept of *Egemonia*', in *Journal of the History of Ideas*, 1960, vol. 21, no. 4, p. 587).

every epoch the ruling ideas' and that the reason for this was that 'the class, which is the ruling material force in society, is at the same time its ruling intellectual force. The class which has the means of material production at its disposal, has control at the same time over the means of mental production, so that thereby, generally speaking, the ideas of those who lack the means of mental production are subject to it'.[1]

Much has happened in the world of capitalism since this was written in 1845, and it was not even then a sufficient answer to the question. But it remains, as will be seen in the following pages, the basic element of an answer to it. Much also has happened since Gramsci wrote, not least in Italy itself, to erode the hegemony which dominant classes exercise in their societies. But that erosion has obviously nowhere proceeded far enough, up to the present, to constitute a major political threat to the existing social order. With various qualifications, the problem remains. To deal with it in all its many complexities would require more than a couple of chapters: what is proposed here is to outline some of the main components of an answer.

Two preliminary remarks, however, are necessary. First, it needs to be stressed that 'hegemony' is not simply something which happens, as a mere superstructural derivative of economic and social predominance. It is, in very large part, the result of a permanent and pervasive *effort*, conducted through a multitude of agencies, and deliberately intended to create what Talcott Parsons calls a 'national supra party consensus' based on 'higher order solidarity'.[2] Nor is this only a matter of 'agencies'. The latter are part of the world of macro-politics. But there is also a world of micro-politics, in which members of the dominant classes are able, by virtue of their position, for instance as employers, to dissuade members of the subordinate classes, if not from holding, at least from voicing unorthodox views. Nor of course does this only affect members of the working classes or of the lower middle classes: many middle-class employees are similarly vulnerable to pressure from 'above'. This process of dissuasion need not be explicit in order to

[1] Karl Marx, *The German Ideology*, 1939, p. 39.
[2] T. Parsons, ' "Voting" and the Equilibrium of the American Political System', in E. Burdick and A. J. Brodbeck, *American Political Behaviour*, 1959, p. 101.

be effective. In civil life as well as in the state service, there are criteria of 'soundness', particularly in regard to politics, whose disregard may be highly disadvantageous in a number of important respects. This applies in all walks of life, and forms a definite though often subterranean part of the political process.

It is the notion of process and activity which is present in the concept of 'political socialisation', meaning, to take one definition of it, 'the processes through which values, cognitions and symbols are learned and internalised, through which operative social norms regarding politics are implanted, political roles institutionalised and political consensus created, either effectively or ineffectively'.[1] The weakness of this formulation, and of much of the discussion of 'political socialisation' in relation to Western political systems, is that it tends to be rather coy about the specific ideological content of that socialisation, and about the fact that much of the process is intended, in these regimes, to foster acceptance of a *capitalist* social order and of its values, an adaptation to its requirements, a rejection of alternatives to it; in short, that what is involved here is very largely a process of massive *indoctrination*.

The reason why this needs to be stressed is quite simply that it is so often obscured by the cultural, ideological and political competition which obtains in these countries. Indoctrination is an ugly word, and brain-washing an even uglier combination of words. It describes an activity which is assumed to be unique to totalitarian, dictatorial, one-party regimes; and it is also assumed to be incompatible with, indeed impossible in, more-than-one party systems, conditions of pluralistic competition, freedom of opposition, the absence of monopolistic control over the mass media, etc.

This is a mistake. For indoctrination to occur it is not necessary that there should be monopolistic control and the prohibition of opposition: it is only necessary that ideological competition should be so unequal as to give a crushing advantage to one side against the other. And this is precisely the position which obtains in advanced capitalist societies. Raymond Williams has described the purpose of an authoritarian system of control over culture, i.e. a system in which a monopoly of the means of communication by the ruling group is a neces-

[1] H. Eckstein and D. Apter (eds.), *Comparative Politics*, 1963, p. 26.

sary part of the whole political system, as 'to protect, maintain or advance a social order based on minority power'.[1] But this is an excellent description of the purpose of those who control the economic and political systems of advanced capitalism, and its successful implementation does not require a monopoly of the means of communication, or the prohibition of expression of all alternative views and opinions. Indeed, that purpose may well be *better* served without such a monopoly.

The second preliminary point that needs to be made concerns the role of the state in this process of 'political socialisation'. Gramsci, it may be recalled, saw the establishment and perpetuation of ideological hegemony as primarily the task of the dominant classes and of the cultural institutions they controlled; hegemony in this sense was the artefact of 'civil society', with the state mainly providing the required balance between coercion and consent.[2] For the most part, this has indeed remained the position up to the present: the 'engineering of consent' in capitalist society is still largely an unofficial private enterprise, in fact largely the business *of* private enterprise. This, incidentally, also helps to account for the belief that indoctrination and brain-washing happen *elsewhere*, since these are believed to be the peculiar prerogatives of the state, particularly of the monopolistic state. It has to be noted however that the liberal and constitutional state has, since Gramsci wrote, come to play a *much* more important part than previously in this process of 'political socialisation', and that just as it now intervenes massively in economic life so does it also intervene very notably, and in a multitude of different ways, in ideological competition, and has in fact become one of the main architects of the conservative consensus. Nor certainly has this state intervention by any means reached its furthest limits. On the contrary, it may be said to be in its early days yet, and is likely to grow much more intense as the need for systematic indoctrination in capitalist society intensifies.

One form of intervention in ideological and political competition which the state alone can undertake has already been referred to, namely the actual suppression or near-suppression

---

[1] R. Williams, *Britain in the Sixties: Communications*, 1962, p. 125.
[2] For a discussion of the point, see J. Merrington, 'Theory and Practice in Gramsci's Marxism', in *The Socialist Register, 1968*.

in some capitalist countries of certain parties and organisations; and, in other countries, various less drastic forms of harassment and discrimination. These are obviously directly relevant not only to political competition but to ideological competition as well, since they tend to weaken the impact which these parties and organisations may hope to achieve. But there are many other and less obvious forms of intervention in favour of the conservative consensus in which the state now engages, as will be shown at different points in the course of the discussion, to which we may now turn, of the main agencies of 'political socialisation' in capitalist society.

II

In all advanced capitalist countries there are certain parties which are the favoured, chosen vehicles or instruments of the business classes and of the dominant classes generally. In most countries, one major party fulfils that role, though a second or a third party often enjoys a certain amount of the same kind of support. Thus, the Republican Party in the United States is pre-eminently the 'party of business' and of businessmen, but the Democratic Party is not, therefore, bereft of business support.[1] The same is true of the Christian Democratic Union and the Free Democratic Party in Germany, and of different political formations in other countries.

Still, there is usually one party in each country which is *the* conservative party, which commands the greatest degree of support among members of the dominant classes, and which is pre-eminently 'their' party.

In most of these countries, moreover, this is also one of the largest, if not the largest and best implanted of all parties, the 'party of government' *par excellence*, with other political formations, particularly of the Left, only occasionally achieving office and remaining what Professor La Palombara aptly calls 'guests in power'.[2]

In some countries the main party of business is not necessarily

[1] See, e.g., H. E. Alexander, *Financing the 1964 Election*, 1966.
[2] J. La Palombara, *Organised Groups in Italian Politics*, 1964, p. 316.

the one which is electorally most consistently successful. Thus, for instance, the Republican Party in the United States has, on the whole, fared rather less well, electorally, than the Democratic Party, though this has been much less than catastrophic for business interests since that party could always be expected to respond generously to business expectations. And in one capitalist country at least, France, business interests and the dominant classes generally have not even been able to create and rely on one solid conservative formation of a durable kind; they have instead had to make do with a fragmentation of parties of the Right, or have had to depend on a variety of parties of the Centre, though again with no particularly dire consequences.[1]

What these examples suggest is that dominant interests do not necessarily manage to create dominant parties; but also that this need not, given other means of influence and pressure, be particularly crippling. It is perfectly possible, for these interests at least, to achieve their purposes through parties which are not properly speaking their own, and through many other agencies.

But while this is possible, it is not particularly desirable; it is obviously much better for dominant classes to be able to rely on a major 'party of government'; and such parties do indeed exist in most advanced capitalist countries.

This is surely a remarkable achievement, which has greatly surpassed even the most optimistic conservative hopes of pre-universal suffrage days.

A major reason for that achievement has precisely been that the large conservative parties have not *only* been the parties of the dominant classes, of business and property, either in terms of their membership or in their policies. In fact, one of the most remarkable things about them is how successfully they have adapted themselves to the requirements of 'popular politics'. Thus old, aristocratic, pre-industrial political formations like the

---

[1] This dependence on parties not truly of the Right was particularly notable after 1945, when the political forces of the Right had altogether collapsed and had to make do with a party, the M.R.P., many of whose leaders professed radical, reformist and even anti-capitalist views. 'In 1946', it has been noted, 'in most cases, the great majority of the M.R.P. electorate came from areas, and almost certainly from groups which formerly supported the right' (F. Goguel and M. Einaudi, *Christian Democracy in Italy and France*, 1952, p. 123). It was only subsequently that the M.R.P. became, though never exclusively, a properly conservative party.

Conservative and Liberal parties in Britain first adapted themselves to the new industrialism and made room in their councils
for its representatives; and then consciously set out, after the
Second Reform Act of 1867 (and even before), to create something of a popular base and mass membership in the country.[1]
Nor has the Conservative Party at least ever ceased to retain
that popular base. In Germany, on the other hand, a mass
conservative party had to be created in 1945 on the political
ruins of war and defeat. 'In 1945', Mr Kitzinger has noted,
'the CDU set out to integrate into a single all-embracing
popular party both Protestant employers and Protestant
workers, Catholic employers and Catholic workers, the pen-
sioners, civil servants, and professional classes, whose interests
in a modern economy so often conflict with those common to
employers and workers alike – and in addition the farmers
whose interests very often are all their own'.[2]

With endless variations in timing and character, the process
has been everywhere the same: parties whose primary purpose
is the maintenance of the existing social order, and whose
programme therefore includes as a central feature the defence of
capitalist enterprise, are solidly implanted (with the possible
exception of France) in all capitalist countries, and include
among their members and activists large numbers of people
who belong to the lower-middle and even to the working classes.
In many cases, these parties, together with their associated
organisations – youth movements, women's organisations, etc. –
have at least as wide a popular base in terms of membership as
the working-class parties of the Left. In this sense and also in the
nature of their cross-class electoral support, it is perfectly true
that these are 'national' parties.[3]

Nor is it to be denied that they fulfil an 'aggregative' function
and that they do 'articulate' (to use consecrated language)
many aspirations, demands and interests of groups and classes
other than those of the dominant classes. They could not serve
the latter efficiently if they did not also concern themselves with
the former. The point has already been made but is worth

---

[1] See, e.g. R.T.McKenzie, *British Political Parties*, 1963, chapter 4; and I.
Bulmer-Thomas, *The Growth of the British Party System*, 1965, vol. I, chapters 10–12.

[2] U.W.Kitzinger, *German Electoral Politics*, 1960, p. 103.

[3] For Britain, see R.T.McKenzie and A.Silver, *Angels in Marble. Working Class
Conservatives in Urban England* (1968).

stressing: conservatism, however pronounced, does not entail the rejection of all measures of reform, but lives on the contrary by the endorsement and promulgation of reform at the least possible cost to the existing structure of power and privilege.[1]

Nevertheless, the conservative parties, for all their acceptance of piecemeal reform and their rhetoric of classlessness, remain primarily the defence organisations, in the political field, of business and property. What they really 'aggregate' are the different interests of the dominant classes. Precisely because the latter are not solid, congealed economic and social blocs, they require political formations which reconcile, coordinate and fuse their interests, and which express their common purposes as well as their separate interests. These purposes and interests also require ideological clothing suitable for political competition in the age of 'mass politics'; one of the special functions of conservative political parties is to provide that necessary clothing.

The membership of these parties, and many of their activists, may be drawn from a wide cross-section of the population. But their leading figures are nevertheless overwhelmingly drawn from the upper and middle classes and generally include a substantial proportion of businessmen. Moreover, major conservative politicians, as already noted, are closely associated with the world of business by ties of kinship, friendship, common outlook and mutual interest. Nor of course are the leading lights of conservative parties unfamiliar figures in the boardrooms of large corporations: it would be truer to say that, out of office, this is their natural habitat. By contrast, people engaged in occupations associated with the subordinate classes are not, on the whole, familiar figures in the directing councils of conservative parties.

Nor, for that matter, are they familiar figures in the parliamentary representation of these parties, or even, generally speaking, in the leadership of their grassroots organisations. The lower the income group, the less likely is it to be well represented on the leading organs of the local conservative parties.

---

[1] As Mr J. Halliday aptly puts it, the main problem for conservative parties is 'how to conciliate the interests of the social forces *it represents* with those of the social forces which *support it*' ('Japan–Asian Capitalism', in *New Left Review*, no. 44, July – August 1967, p. 21 (italics in text).

As was suggested earlier, the trend towards middle- or at least lower-middle-class preponderance in local party leadership is often also pronounced in the working-class parties, most of all in the social-democratic parties. But the contrast in social composition between them and the conservative parties nevertheless remains very marked, and is often extreme. 'National', in terms of membership and electoral support, these parties may well be; but in terms of national and local leadership they are clearly class parties and much less 'representative' than the working-class parties.

Secondly, and quite apart from all other sources of influence, business is assured of a most attentive hearing on the part of the leaders of conservative parties because it constitutes an important, even an essential source of financial support, both for electoral and for general propaganda purposes. Sustained electoral and political activity requires vast and ever-increasing expenditure; and while conservative parties do rely for part of their finances on membership subscriptions and small donations, they also rely heavily on business contributions. This may not ensure that the piper plays the right tune without any discordant notes; but it at least ensures that there are fewer such notes. Professor Harrison in 1965 noted that

... publicly the Conservatives now play down the importance of big contributors. Privately they court them as assiduously as ever. The Central Board of Finance, set up in 1946 and comprising the party and area treasurers and a few coopted members, raises funds primarily from wealthy individuals and industry ... In recent years organisations have developed to collect political contributions from industry. These share the party's discretion. One of them, United Industrialists' Association, canvassed managing directors of selected firms by circulars for 'very large' contributions which were to be distributed 90 per cent to the Conservatives, 5 per cent to the National Liberal Party, and 5 per cent to Aims of Industry for conducting public relations on behalf of free enterprise.[1]

For Germany, it has been said that

[1] M. Harrison, 'Britain', in R. Rose and A. J. Heidenheimer (eds.), Comparative Studies in Political Finance, *The Journal of Politics*, 1963, vol. 25, no. 4, pp. 666–7. Professor Rose has also noted that the average annual expenditure of the Conservative Central Office for the years 1960–4 was around £1,250,000 of which £800,000 was raised between some 250 and 400 large business firms (R. Rose, *Influencing Voters*, 1967, p. 264).

... through considerable financial donations and personal contact with their leaders, the BDI assures itself of an influence on the economic policies and ... to a lesser extent on their selection of parliamentary candidates.[1]

Similarly, Professor Scalapino notes for Japan that

... the larger industrial and commercial elements remain, of course, strongly committed to the conservative parties, provide the overwhelming proportion of their funds, and have great influence in determining their policies and personnel.[2]

The story is in fact monotonously the same everywhere. Nor is it in the least surprising that it should be.

A further reason for describing these parties as pre-eminently the parties of their dominant classes and business elites, and as their defence organisations, stems from the particular and crucially important ideological function which they fulfil in their society. For these parties are obviously among the most important forces in the dissemination, at national and local level, of conservative and anti-socialist ideas. Like other parties, conservative parties are also propaganda agencies, however much their leaders may pride themselves on their absence of doctrine, ideology and theory, all of which these leaders normally tend to view as diseases to which only parties of the Left are prone. This is of course nonsense. Conservative ideology and propaganda, as put forward by conservative parties, assumes many different forms from country to country, and has also undergone substantial transformations over time inside each country. But its essential content, in the conditions

---

[1] Braunthal, *The Federation of German Industry in Politics*, p. 88. Professor Almond also noted in 1955 that 'the political parties of the centre and the right are dependent almost entirely on the business community for their financing' (G. A. Almond, *The Politics of German Business*, 1955, p. 29).

[2] R. A. Scalapino, 'Japan: Between Traditionalism and Democracy', in S. Neumann (ed.), *Modern Political Parties*, 1956, p. 235. See also J. R. Soukup, 'Japan', in Rose and Heidenheimer, *The Journal of Politics*, pp. 742ff. A Japanese writer also states that 'personal and corporate wealth, access to cabinet posts, an intimate working relationship with the conservative parties that have dominated the government, close relations with the government itself, and identification with all Japanese economic activities combine to make business extremely influential in Japanese democracy' (J. M. Maki, *Government and Politics in Japan*, 1962, p. 138). It is worth noting, since it is so typical of works about the politics of advanced capitalist countries, how easily the assumption is made that such preponderance is compatible with 'democracy'.

of advanced capitalism, is much the same everywhere, with the defence of the free enterprise system as its very kernel. Surrounding that kernel, and often serving to conceal it, there stand guard many different ideological sentinels, called freedom, democracy, constitutional government, patriotism, religion, tradition, the national interest, the sanctity of property, financial stability, social reform, law and order, and whatever else may be part of the pot-pourri of conservative ideology at any given time and place.

In the dissemination of these themes, and in their anti-left-wing propaganda generally, party leaders and activists may well seek to fulfil a large variety of purposes, personal as well as public, which far transcend the advancement of specific economic interests. But however this may be, it can hardly be doubted that this ideological activity is of immense value to those interests associated with private enterprise.

The ideological and political activities of conservative parties occur, of course, under conditions of competition; in these systems, neither the Right nor the Left has it all its own way, either at election time or in between. But as in the case of pressure group politics, the conditions in which the competition occurs greatly affects its nature and character, and in some cases even its reality.

The first and most obvious point which needs to be noted in this connection is that bourgeois parties have always a lot more money to spend for election and general propaganda purposes than their working-class counterparts. The point is often made that just as money cannot buy happiness neither can it buy electoral success. This is quite true. Superior financial resources are not sufficient for such success. But whatever may be the relationship of money to happiness, its relationship to ideological and political work in this particular context cannot be thought of as other than highly beneficial. To have a lot more money to spend than one's opponents for electioneering and general propaganda purposes is not a final guarantee of success but it is very helpful all the same; and the all but universal rule in advanced capitalist countries is that the parties of the Right do have a lot more money to spend at election time and in between elections than the parties of the Left.

The main reason for this is obviously that the latter cannot rely on the financial contributions of large firms or (no doubt with some exceptions) of wealthy people which are available to the former. But to this must be added the fact that the parties of the Right are much more assured of the financial support of their backers than the parties of the Left are of their own 'natural' allies, the trade unions. For one thing, legal restrictions upon the financial contributions of both business and unions to party funds are much more easily circumvented by businessmen than by wage-earners, for instance by way of personal contributions.[1] For another, trade unions are often fairly distant, politically and even more so financially, from the working-class parties, and, indeed, as in the case of German trade unions, may be officially 'neutral' in politics. In this particular case, it has been noted:

> ... whatever help labour may have given the SPD was in the form of indirect activity, engaged in by the unions themselves, rather than in contributions to the party for campaign purposes. This at best half-hearted and indirect effort, always undertaken with a furtive glance at the neutrality pledge, put both the unions and the SPD at a distinct disadvantage as compared to the CDU and right-wing parties that were liberally financed by industry.[2]

And even where trade unions are closely linked to a particular party, as in the case of Britain, their financial contribution to its funds, though substantial, has never matched the contribution of business to the Conservative Party.

Money does not only ensure that conservative parties are able to run much more 'professional' electoral campaigns than their rivals. It also helps to ensure better organisation, nationally and at local level, for the pursuit of those all-the-year-round political and propaganda activities which are an essential element of electoral effectiveness. For Britain, Professor Rose has also noted, 'even today it is only the Conservative Party which has a fully developed and comprehensive party organisation with specialist staffs';[3] and part of that comprehensive

[1] For the operation of the law in the United States, see, e.g. Key, *Politics, Parties and Pressure Groups*, p. 556.

[2] O. Kirchheimer, 'West German Trade Unions: Their Domestic and Foreign Policies', in H. Speier and W. P. Davison (eds.), *West German Leadership and Foreign Policy*, p. 160.

[3] Rose, *Influencing Voters*, p. 22.

organisation is made up of the corps of full-time and relatively well-paid agents which are to be found in almost every constituency, as compared with the far fewer numbers of full-time (and ill-paid) agents of the Labour Party.[1] There are countries, for instance Italy, where the working-class parties are much better matched, organisationally and financially, with the conservative formations. But even here the total resources of these formations remain superior to those of the parties of the Left, particularly if account is taken of the support which the former enjoy (and the point applies to all these countries) from other well-financed organisations.[2]

It is also relevant to note that the social composition of the conservative parties at grassroots level affords them certain advantages of an often very substantial kind. These parties, as already suggested, are generally run by middle-class activists. This may also be the case in some local parties of the Left. But *their* activists are obviously much more likely to include people who belong to the 'lower income groups'.[3] And this means that they are also people who have much less time for propaganda activities, fewer facilities of every kind, fewer means of influence, fewer contacts with influential people in their communities, and so forth. No more than money are these advantages necessarily decisive. But neither can they be left out of the reckoning in an assessment of the respective ideological and political impact of bourgeois and working-class parties.

Nor can the fact that, in every capitalist country, parties of the Left are still in many areas, notably in the countryside, not much more than political interlopers whose challenge to the traditional predominance of the local upper classes has at best only eroded the latter's power. It is after all only in this century,

[1] Rose, *Influencing Voters*, pp. 256, 264. One American observer has recently noted that 'there were many divisions which had no party offices, and their secretary-agents worked without even the rudimentary time-saving devices. In one appalling case, a secretary in a weak marginal division had no office, no typewriter, no telephone and no private transport, even though the constituency was composed of a few small villages and an extensive agricultural area' (E. G. Janosik, *Constituency Labour Parties in Britain*, 1968, p. 15).

[2] See below, pp. 211 ff.

[3] A stratified random sample of thirty-six constituency Labour parties recently found that their party leaders included, on average, 20 per cent professional people, 12 per cent business, 17 per cent white collar, 12 per cent skilled workers, 14 per cent semi-skilled, 16 per cent trade union and party officials, and 9 per cent housewives (Janosik, *Constituency Labour Parties in Britain*, p. 17).

even in the last few decades, that working-class parties have achieved a genuinely national implantation and penetrated into many areas which had until then been closed to them. Even today in the United States it is only in a number of major cities that Labour, as a distinct entity, may be said to have achieved a notable degree of specific political influence; and even that influence can hardly, in this case, be said to bear genuinely counter-ideological connotations.

The voting process itself has from the conservative point of view certain advantages which illustrate well the contradictory nature, in capitalist societies, of institutions which appear at first to present an unqualified advantage to the working classes.

The extension of the suffrage was of course a natural and inevitable demand of working-class movements; and its achievement did indeed make available to the hitherto disenfranchised subordinate classes an extremely useful element of additional pressure upon the rulers of society.

But, as far-sighted conservative leaders like Disraeli and Bismarck well understood, the suffrage also brought into the political process a mass of new voters who could be relied on to give their electoral support to traditional elites. Engels once said that 'universal suffrage is a gauge of the maturity of the working class',[1] by which he meant that the greater the vote for working-class parties, the more mature the workers could be reckoned to be. However, since a substantial part of the working class was, in this sense, immature, its access to the suffrage was clearly calculated to reinforce conservative electoral strength. And this, to a greater or lesser extent, has remained the case to the present day.

Moreover, the achievement of another demand closely associated with the demand for the extended suffrage, namely the secret ballot, also turned out to be something of a double-edged weapon. Professor Rokkan has noted that

... the primary motive for the introduction of the ballot system was to make it possible to escape sanction from superiors; this was the essence of the Chartists' early demands and has always been a basic concern of working-class movements ...[2] [But, he adds],

[1] F. Engels, *The Origins of the Family, Property and the State*, in *Selected Works*, vol. 2, p. 29.
[2] S. Rokkan, 'Mass Suffrage, Secret Voting and Political Participation', in *Archives Européennes de Sociologie*, 1961, vol. 2, no. 1, p. 143.

what has been less emphasised in histories of electoral institutions is that provisions for secrecy could cut off the voter from his *peers* as well as his *superiors* ... by ensuring the complete anonymity of the ballots it became possible not only to reduce bribery of the economically dependent by their superiors[1] *but also to reduce the pressures towards conformity and solidarity within the working class.*[2]

Leaving aside the question of principle itself, the argument, obviously, cannot be taken to mean that working-class movements were mistaken in pressing for the secret ballot, if only because the pressures from 'superiors' are normally far stronger than the pressure of 'peers'. The point is rather that, given the 'immaturity' of large parts of the working classes, the secret ballot, by helping to protect that immaturity, could hardly be said to have been *wholly* disadvantageous to conservative parties.

Similarly, and even more important, universal suffrage appears to enshrine what Professor Rokkan also calls 'the equality of influence – each vote cast counts as one anonymous unit of influence and is completely divorced from the person and the roles of the participating citizen'.[3] But while this is formally the case, 'equality of influence' is in actual fact an illusion. The act of voting is part of a much larger political process, characterised, as I have argued, by marked *inequality* of influence. Concentration on the act of voting itself, in which formal equality does prevail, helps to obscure that inequality, and serves a crucially important legitimating function.

The political parties of the Left have always, in comparison with the parties of the Right, also suffered from certain marked disabilities which have profoundly affected their capacity as political weapons and as agencies of ideological dissemination. Some of these have already been touched on in previous chapters but need to be set inside the framework of the present one.

To begin with, there is the fact that some of the most important parties of the Left, namely social-democratic ones, have

[1] But not only bribery – disfavour, threats and retribution as well, and rather more important.

[2] *Ibid.*, p. 143 (my italics). See also R. Bendix: 'The provision for secret voting puts the individual before a personal choice and makes him at least temporarily independent of his immediate environment: in the voting booth he can be a national citizen' (*Nation-Building and Citizenship*, p. 100).

[3] Rokkan, 'Mass Suffrage, Secret Voting and Political Participation', p. 133.

mainly been led by men who, in opposition but particularly in office, have always been far more ambiguous about their purpose, to put it mildly, than their conservative rivals. After all, however aggregation-minded and reform-oriented conservative leaders have been, they have never actually pursued *revolutionary* policies. But social-democratic leaders have quite often supported and pursued reactionary ones, at home and abroad, and acted, as in the clear case of Germany in 1918, as the saviours of a social order in a state of collapse.

An extreme example, in the framework of parliamentary politics, of the kind of service which such leaders have been willing to perform for conservatism is that of Ramsay MacDonald who, from being the leader of the Labour Party and a Labour prime minister, ended up by leading a Conservative-dominated coalition and by appealing to the voters in 1931 to return to office 'National Government' candidates, which meant in effect an appeal that they should vote Conservative. In the process the Labour Party found its parliamentary representation reduced from 289 seats to 52 and the Conservative forces in command of 556 seats out of 615.[1] There is no instance of a Conservative leader rendering the same kind of service to labour and socialist movements. Many other labour leaders have very commonly supported and adopted policies far more in tune with the philosophy of their opponents than with the philosophy of their own movements. Nothing of the same sort can be said of conservative leaders in respect of their own parties and movements. There are, in this respect, no conservative equivalents of Harold Wilson, or Guy Mollet, or Paul-Henri Spaak, or Willi Brandt, or any of the leading or not so leading figures of European social-democracy, past and present.

This, it need hardly be said, has nothing to do with the personal attributes of social-democratic leaders as compared with those of conservative ones. The question cannot be tackled in these terms. It needs rather to be seen in terms of the tremendous weight of conservative pressure upon labour leaders; but also in terms of the fact that the ideological defences of these leaders have not generally been of nearly sufficient strength to enable them to resist with any great measure of success conservative pressure, intimidation and enticement.

[1] For details of that episode, see Miliband, *Parliamentary Socialism*, pp. 181ff.

This ideological weakness, and the political failures and derelictions associated with it, have had as one inevitable consequence a situation of more or less constant tension and often open warfare inside social-democratic parties between their leaders and various more radical-minded minorities. By comparison, conservative parties have been models of harmony and unity. They have of course known endless stresses and strains, and divisions of every sort. This is inevitable in any political formation, however united it may claim to be. But conservative parties have never been so fundamentally divided as to what they were *ultimately* about, as has regularly and increasingly been the case for social-democratic ones.

Relatedly, and of even greater importance in the present context, is the fact that these large and powerful political formations have been singularly weak agencies of mass education in socialist principles and purposes. The abolition of capitalism in Western societies obviously requires an enormous transformation in popular consciousness, at least part of the responsibility for which must rest on party organisations. It is a responsibility which social-democratic parties have not (particularly in recent decades) been at all keen to discharge – not very surprisingly since their leaders have not included anything remotely resembling the abolition of capitalism as part of their purpose. In fact, it is no exaggeration to say that these leaders and their parties have not seldom turned themselves into agencies of determined propaganda *against* socialist ideas and purposes, and used their considerable audience with large parts of the working classes to cast discredit on any concept of socialism other than, at best, their own blurred and exceedingly anaemic version of it. It is surely remarkable that those analysts who seek to account for the attunement of large parts of the working classes in advanced capitalist countries to conservative ideology should not have stressed more the contribution to political demobilisation which has regularly been made by social-democratic leaders, both because of what they have said, and also because of what they have done, particularly when given a chance of office.

Reference has also been made in previous chapters to the crippling impact of the divisions which have afflicted the parties and movements of the Left, most notably of course the division between social-democratic and communist parties throughout the world. Here too, it is easy to point to divisions between the parties which make up the conservative camp. But again, the point needs to be made that nowhere have these divisions been as fundamental and bitter as those which have affected the parties of the Left. It is not proposed here to try to apportion 'blame' for a situation which had been made inevitable by the whole evolution of the working-class movements in advanced capitalist countries, and to which the Bolshevik victory in Russia only gave an added, though critically important, dimension. More relevant in the present context is to note the fact of division, its debilitating effects upon the working-class movements, and the corresponding advantages which the conservative parties have derived from it.

What does, however, require further mention are some of the specific characteristics of the Communist parties which came into being in the aftermath of the Russian Revolution. It was to be expected that these parties should make solidarity with the fledgling Soviet State, threatened and attacked from all sides, a prime element of their being; and it was also to be expected that this legitimate attitude of solidarity would provide all conservative forces with a convenient excuse for denouncing them as 'foreign agents'. This was a price which, in the circumstances, had to be paid, and which need not have been crippling. What did make it crippling was the exceedingly negative features which soon came to mar the Soviet regime, combined with the fierce insistence of the Communist parties that these features were of no account, or that they were a pure invention of bourgeois reaction. Legitimate solidarity thus turned into slavish apologetics of every aspect of what came, much later, to be known as Stalinism, and the automatic endorsement, not only of every twist and turn of internal Soviet policy, but of Soviet policies concerning the international Communist movement in general and specific countries in particular – very often, as in the case of Germany, with quite disastrous results.

The Communist parties in advanced capitalist countries would in any case have faced major difficulties and obstacles in their ideological and political work. But these difficulties, it may well be thought, were greatly enhanced by their unquestioning acceptance of Russian leadership and of Russian dictation of their strategy and tactics. For one thing, this acceptance lent added plausibility to the accusations that these parties were of foreign inspiration. More important was the impression which they conveyed until quite recently that Soviet experience was the ideal model in the construction of a socialist society, a notion which was bound to strike many potential supporters as not only grotesque but positively sinister.

Moreover, and largely because of this distorted focus, communist parties were greatly unhinged by alternating bouts of sectarianism and opportunism and, indeed, quite commonly, by both simultaneously. The extreme tensions which this produced inside these parties were contained, but never subdued, by a bureaucratic application of the principle of 'democratic centralism', which made so much room for centralism that it left little or no room for democracy. One result of this bureaucratic deformation was a catastrophic ideological impoverishment and the transformation of the Marxism these parties professed into a vulgarised, manipulative and sloganised phraseology, which greatly affected their intellectual and political impact and their capacity for 'raising the level of consciousness'. In short, their whole historical tradition has powerfully limited the effectiveness of their role and left a vast gap between their actual performance and the kind of ideological and political effort required of revolutionary formations.

III

In their political competition with the parties of the Left, the conservative parties have always derived a very notable amount of direct or indirect support and strength from the Churches. No doubt, advanced industrial societies have undergone a marked process of secularisation, and religious influence is a steadily diminishing factor in determining the political (and moral) options of their populations. Yet, it is still the case that no one writing about 'political socialisation' and ideological competition in these countries can afford to ignore a religious and clerical factor which varies in intensity from culture to culture but which is nowhere insignificant, and which everywhere mainly operates in favour of conservative forces. As Professor Dogan notes, 'working-class voting in favour of non-socialist parties is very often motivated by religious sentiment. The fact has been observed everywhere in Europe.'[1]

The point is of particular importance in relation to predominantly Catholic countries (but not only there – e.g. Germany)[2] where the major conservative parties have been closely associated with, and supported by, the Catholic Church. Christian Democratic parties would in any case have attracted large-scale electoral support, as conservative parties. But they have undoubtedly gained a vast amount of additional strength from the support they have enjoyed on the part of the Churches, or at least from the antagonism which the latter have expressed towards left-wing parties, particularly, as in Italy and France, towards the Communist parties. Thus one observer has written that in the decisive Italian elections of 1948 'it is generally conceded that only the extraordinary effort of organised Catholicism in 1948 – the successful creation of a "Christ or Communism" vote, prevented the extreme left from coming legally to power in the elections of that year';[3] and for Germany, it has been said that the Catholic Church's 'clear stand made it a major force on the side of the government both between elections and during the campaign' (i.e. the electoral campaign of 1957).[4]

Moreover, it has to be noted that this clerical and conservative influence is propagated not only by the Churches themselves but by a vast network of powerful organisations, which group employers and wage-earners, youth and women, doctors

[1] M. Dogan, 'Le Vote Ouvrier en Europe Occidentale', in *Revue Française de Sociologie*, 1960, vol. 1, no. 1, p. 38.

[2] It is worth noting, however, that the division of Germany in 1945 was responsible for a substantial increase in the proportion of Catholics in the Federal Republic to the population as a whole.

[3] La Palombara, *Organised Groups in Italian Politics*, p. 30. Note also that in July 1949 a Vatican decree actually excommunicated all Catholics who made profession of 'the materialistic and anti-Christian doctrine of the Communists" (Quoted in R. V. Burks, 'Catholic Parties in Latin Europe', in *Journal of Modern History*, 1952, vol. 24, no. 3, p. 269).

[4] Kitzinger, *German Electoral Politics*, p. 65.

and lawyers, and whose impact is felt in every sphere of life.[1]

One segment of the population is particularly susceptible to this influence and impact, namely women. Here too the conservative bias which has often been noted in feminine voting[2] cannot be solely attributed to the religious factor – but it certainly helps. Thus Professor La Palombara also notes that 'for the millions of Italian women who take their political leads from their confessors, and for the additional millions who are members of Catholic secondary associations, the basic process of political socialisation serves to enshrine the kind of cognition, values and attitudes that only accidentally reinforce democratic institutions'.[3] However it may be with democratic institutions, it may be taken, *a fortiori*, that this process of political socialisation is even less likely to reinforce the parties of the Left.

This picture of directly political partisanship (in the literal sense of the word) needs to be modified in regard to countries like Britain and the United States – but rather less than is often suggested. It is no longer as true as it used to be that the Church of England is 'the Conservative Party at prayer', and the observation of a former Archbishop of York that 'all through the nineteenth century the influence of the parochial clergy was on the side of the Conservatives'[4] could not be made about this century without various qualifications. What has changed is that the Church of England, and indeed all British Churches, have come, with the rise of the Labour Party as a major political formation and as a party of occasional government, to shun explicit political identification with either of the two leading

[1] For a description of these networks and of their activities by a writer sympathetic to them, see M. P. Fogarty, *Christian Democracy in Western Europe*, 1957, chapters 15–19. For the United States, it has been said that 'every interest, activity and function of the Catholic faithful is provided with some Catholic institution and furnished with Catholic direction' (W. Herberg, *Protestant-Catholic-Jew*, 1956, p. 168).

[2] 'Dans tous les pays de l'Europe occidentale, qu'ils soient protestants ou catholiques, fortement ou faiblement industrialisés, les partis communistes et socialistes sont défavorisés par le suffrage féminin' (Dogan, 'Le Vote Ouvrier en Europe Occidentale', p. 39). See also M. Dogan 'Le Comportement Politique des Femmes dans les Pays de l'Europe Occidentale', in *Cahiers de l'Institut de Sociologie Solvay*, 1956.

[3] La Palombara, *Organised Groups in Italian Politics*, p. 69. See also M. N. Pierini, 'The Catholic Church in Italy', in *International Socialist Journal*, 1964, vol. 2, no. 9.

[4] C. Garbett, *Church and State in England*, 1950, p. 106.

parties; as between these, the Churches, like top civil servants, military men and judges, are officially 'neutral', and 'non-partisan'. And much the same may be said of the Churches in the United States, where they have generally sought to avoid identification with either the Republican or the Democratic Party. There are no doubt many instances in both countries where clerics have departed from this 'neutral' stance between the main parties, but the point nevertheless stands.

However, it would be mistaken to think, because of this, that the Churches in these countries have not performed and do not continue to perform an important and generally conservative political role. Professor R.K. Merton has rightly stressed that religion and religious institutions have in many instances throughout history played a deeply 'dysfunctional' and 'non-integrative' role in their societies.[1] But just as it is proper to condemn 'the large, spaceless and timeless generalisations about the "integrative functions of religion" ',[2] so is it proper to note that Professor Merton's own 'large, spaceless and timeless generalisations' about the actual or potential dysfunctionality of religion are at least as vacuous. Thus, Professor Merton notes that 'it would be premature … to conclude that all religion everywhere has only the one consequence of making for mass apathy'.[3] This is obviously true. But what the statement obscures in relation to contemporary capitalist societies is the scarcely disputable and presumably not unimportant fact that organised religion, in most of its major manifestations, *has* played a profoundly 'functional' and 'integrative' role in regard to the prevailing economic and social system, and, with some *Kulturkampf* exceptions, to the state which has defended that social order.[4]

At the time of the Napoleonic wars, Arthur Young wrote that 'the true Christian will never be a leveller, will never listen to French politics, or to French philosophy'.[5] Ever since, the

[1] R.K. Merton, *Social Theory and Social Structure*, 1965, pp. 28ff.

[2] *Ibid.*, p. 28.   [3] *Ibid.*, p. 44.

[4] One American writer speaks of the 'fusion of religion with the national purpose', which passes over 'into the direct exploitation of religion for economic and political ends' (Herberg, *Protestant-Catholic-Jew*, p. 274). The same writer also notes that 'not to be – that is, not to identify oneself and be identified as – either a Protestant, a Catholic, or a Jew is somehow not to be an American' and 'may imply being obscurely "un-American" ' (*ibid.*, p. 274).

[5] Quoted in K.S. Inglis, *Churches and the Working Classes in Victorian England*, 1963, p. 6.

Churches have striven mightily to help turn their congregations into true Christians in this sense as in all others, perhaps above all others, and to warn them against the contemporary equivalents of 'French politics' and 'French philosophy'.

It has often been claimed for Dissent in England that, unlike the Established Church, its voice has been that of radicalism and protest. Indeed, a general secretary of the Labour Party once committed himself to a proposition which has often been reiterated, namely that 'Methodism not Marxism' had been the inspiration of the Labour movement. The proposition is more alliteratively smooth than historically accurate. For however non-Establishmentarian in a secular as well as a religious sense Methodism may have been, there is very little in its history to suggest that it was ever concerned to preach rebellion to its votaries, and much to suggest, on the contrary, that the burden of its message was adaptation and submission to the economic and political order, not challenge – let alone rebellion – and that it played a by no means inconsiderable role in reconciling those who came under its influence to the work-disciplines and the system of domination of the new industrial order.[1]

Nor, from this point of view, is very much to be made of Christian Socialism in the Established Church. It is significant, for instance, that the movement should have come into being as a conscious alternative to Chartism, and that its founder, F.D. Maurice, should have had as his prime concern 'to interpose Christianity between the workers and their wrath', and thus to help reduce militant working-class protest.[2] This does not detract from the sincerity of Christian Socialists, then and later, in their wish to improve the lot of the poor, to raise the 'social question' higher on the agenda of society, and even to help create or strengthen the defence organisations of the working class.[3] But this only represents in a more accentuated form a tradition of charitable concern for the poor which has always

[1] See, e.g. E. P. Thompson, *The Making of the English Working Class*, 1963, chapter 11.

[2] For a useful analysis of the ideology and political role of early Christian Socialism, see J. Saville, 'Christian Socialism', in J. Saville (ed.), *Democracy and the Labour Movement*, 1954; for its later evolution, see P. d'A. Jones, *The Christian Socialist Revival, 1877–1914*, 1968.

[3] See, e.g. C. E. Raven, *Christian Socialism*, 1920; and F. E. Gillespie, *Labour and Politics in England, 1850–1867*, 1927.

been true of most Churches. Such concern, however, is not in the least 'dysfunctional' and 'non-integrative'; nor, save for some notable exceptions, have most religiously-inspired movements of reform wished it to be such. While many of these have had a more or less clear vision of a cooperative society in which men's relations with each other would no longer be dominated by the 'cash nexus', they have also envisaged its coming in terms which made more than ample room for the indefinite perpetuation of the existing social order; and not the least of their concerns has been to persuade the working classes that the notion of militant hurry was not part of true Christianity.

This is manifestly unfair to a thin but persistent line of clerics, Catholic and Protestant, whose hostility to an unjust and 'un-Christian' social order has not been set in the comfortable perspective of a timeless gradualism, and whose purpose has often been highly 'dysfunctional'. This strain of militant Christian protest and affirmation does occupy an honourable place in the history of different labour movements; and it has remained a source of moral and political challenge which, as for instance in regard to the protest movement in the United States against American aggression in Vietnam, should not be overlooked or dismissed.

Even so, clerical anti-conservatism, whether militant or 'moderate', has always and in all capitalist countries been a markedly minority attitude, which has to be set against a general pattern of pronounced conservatism, often of an exceedingly reactionary kind, regarding the political and moral questions at issue in society.[1]

In countries like the United States or even Britain this, however, has been compatible with the political 'neutrality' as

---

[1] For the United States, it has been noted for instance that a majority of White Protestant ministers have a 'conservative' rather than a 'liberal' Republican bias (G. Lenski, *The Religious Factor*, 1961, p. 262); and there is no very good reason to believe that the views of the late Cardinal Spellman were unrepresentative of official Catholic opinion in that country. Note also, in a more general sense, the quietist emphasis of American 'inspirational' literature, in which, it has been observed, 'the "hero" appears more and more as the "well-adjusted" man, who does not question existing social institutions and who, ideally successful both in a business or in a professional sense, feels no emotional pain' (L. Schneider and S. M. Dornbusch, 'Inspirational Religious Literature', in L. Schneider (ed.), *Religion, Culture and Society*, 1964, p. 159).

between the major parties to which reference was made earlier. There is, after all, no reason why the Catholic Church in the United States, for instance, should risk alienating large numbers of Catholics who support the Democratic Party by expressing hostility to it, since the philosophy and purpose of that party are not such as to offend the conservative susceptibilities of the Church. Nor has it for a long time been worth while for the Churches in Britain to incur the same kind of risk in relation to the Labour Party, given the proven 'moderation' of its leaders. Indeed, neutrality and even benevolence have the positive advantage of permitting such influence as the Church and its ancillary organisations may have of being exercised to strengthen the 'moderate' elements of the party against left-wing ones. In short, whatever influence organised religion may have will, in some countries, be thrown on the side of conservative parties against the Left, or, in others, on the side of right-wing elements against left-wing ones inside a working-class party. That influence may be much greater in some countries than in others; but it is nowhere unimportant.

In a wider context it has also to be noted that the Churches in advanced capitalist countries have, in this century, provided a useful element of reinforcement to the authority of the state and of its purposes by their emphatic attitude of loyalty towards it. To quote Archbishop Garbett again, 'I doubt if in any other Church [than the Church of England] so many opportunities are given of prayer for the king. Our Church has never been ashamed of its loyalty';[1] similarly, 'all bishops, incumbents and curates must take an oath of allegiance to the king and his successors before they are consecrated, instituted, licensed or ordained'.[2] The distinction, from this point of view, between the Established Church and other denominations, or with Churches in other countries, is not of great significance. Everywhere, and save for periods of tension over specific issues of particular concern to them (e.g. education), the Churches have long enjoyed harmonious relations with the state and have been more than willing to render unto Caesar what was Caesar's. It would be agreeable to think that this was due to the fact that the state whose authority they supported was 'democratic'. Unfortun-

[1] Garbett, *Church and State in England*, p. 129.   [2] *Ibid.*, p. 136.

ately, it has to be recalled that many Churches have found no major difficulty in giving their support to regimes which were anything but 'democratic', for instance the Fascist regime in Italy, the Nazi regime in Germany, and the Vichy regime in France. There were, in these countries, a great many churchmen and lay people who found in their religious convictions the inspiration to resist the commands of regimes they found odious, and all honour to them. But they were not representative of their Churches, who not only failed to oppose these regimes but gave their blessings to the latter's enterprises. It would, without much doubt, have been otherwise had communist regimes come to power in these countries; their Churches would then have rediscovered an apostolic duty of disobedience which does not appear compelling in most other cases. It may well be that in some countries, organised religion, or at least large parts of it, *would* have fulfilled that duty in opposition to Fascist-type regimes. This must remain a matter of surmise. But it would not seem unfair to suggest that the reason why the Churches in advanced capitalist countries have been so willing to serve and support the state is not, or not so much, because of its 'democratic' character, but because the governments which have represented it have had an ideological and political bias broadly congruent with that of the Churches themselves. Given this congruity, the latter have found no difficulty in identifying obedience to the state's command with religious duty, and with very few exceptions where their hierarchies have been driven to express mild dissent, in blessing the state's enterprises, including its wars, preparations for war, colonial expeditions and internal repression.

In return, the state, within the limits set by national traditions and past conflicts, has extended sympathetic support to the Churches and welcomed whatever help they might give it in strengthening the social fabric and the authority of the state itself. That the governments of advanced capitalist countries now shun anti-clericalism and seek to identify the Churches with the state is, at least in part, grounded in the conviction that such identification, and the suffused religiosity which is a common part of official life and official ritual, form a modest but useful contribution to those habits of obedience which both the state and the Churches seek to foster.

IV

For these and related purposes, however, contemporary conservatism, whether of state or of party, has relied much less on traditional religion than on that most powerful of all secular religions of the twentieth century – nationalism. From the point of view of the dominant classes and the state in advanced capitalist countries – but not only there – this has long been the supreme 'integrative' and stabilising force in society, the 'functional' creed *par excellence*.

There have of course been many situations and circumstances where nationalism has been profoundly 'dysfunctional' to the political and social order, and turned into a formidable weapon *against* dominant classes and the prevailing political system. Thus, the will to independent statehood which is an essential ingredient of nationalist sentiment has been an enormously explosive and disruptive force in regard to colonial and imperial domination and has been mainly responsible for the end of colonial rule over large areas of the globe.

Similarly, nationalist sentiment has also been a disruptive force inside a number of established states, where distinct national or ethnic movements, for instance in Belgium or Canada, have come to claim greater independence than was afforded them by existing arrangements, or have even demanded independent statehood.

And it is also in the name of nationalism that powerful movements have on a number of occasions come into being, particularly on the morrow of defeat in war, to challenge traditional political elites, deemed incapable of defending the integrity and interests of the nation. That challenge was unsuccessful against the regime in France in the three decades before the first world war, but left a deep imprint on French life. It was, on the other hand, extremely successful in Germany in the last years of the Weimar republic, where National-Socialism made national redemption and the restoration of German 'greatness' a crucial part of its platform. Indeed, the defence of national independence against ruling classes subservient to the United States has, ever since the end of the second world war, also formed a notable (but not notably effective) element in the platform of some parts of the Left, particularly Communist parties.

However, and despite the fact that national sentiment has often been used to great effect by various forces of challenge in many different societies, it is conservative forces which, in advanced capitalist societies, have turned it in this century into one of their major allies, and pressed it into service in defence of the established order and in the struggle against the Left.

Nationalism in these countries has formed such an important part of conservative ideology for a number of obvious and related reasons.

From the point of view of dominant classes, nothing could be so obviously advantageous as the assertion which forms one of the basic themes of nationalism, namely that all citizens, whoever they may be, owe a supreme allegiance to a 'national interest' which requires that men should be ready to subdue all other interests, particularly class interests, for the sake of a larger, more comprehensive concern which unites in a supreme allegiance rich and poor, the comfortable and the deprived, the givers of orders and their recipients.

The invocation of this concept need not, and in competitive political conditions cannot, arrest opposition and challenge. But it can at least help to place them on the defensive by situating them in a perspective where they can be made to appear detrimental to the 'national interest'. This is regularly done, particularly in relation to the 'sectional' demands of the subordinate classes, and most particularly in regard to the militant advancement of these demands – for instance strikes. One of the penalties which the subordinate classes pay for their subordination – indeed what almost defines them as subordinate classes – is that *their* demands can be made to appear in this light, as injurious to the 'national interest', especially when members of these classes take it into their heads to press their demands with a vigour which is necessarily and by definition disruptive. A large-scale strike, even more a general strike, has never been denounced as detrimental to employers, but as injurious to 'the nation' and to the 'national interest'. As such, and whatever the merits of the case, it must be defeated; the benefits which employers may derive from that defeat are

purely adventitious. And, as has also been noted earlier, this is
a view which many trade union leaders and political leaders of
labour have often shared, and which has served to unman them,
with grievous consequences for their followers.

It is particularly in the competition with their opponents on
the Left that conservative parties have exploited national
sentiment, insisted on their own patriotic dedication to the
nation, and regularly, often vociferously, opposed this national
dedication to the allegedly less patriotic or positively un-
patriotic and even anti-national concerns of left-wing parties.[1]
Innumerable elections have been fought (and won) by conservative parties in which this theme, suitably adapted to
particular circumstances and issues, has played an important
and sometimes a decisive role. Never has that theme been more
thoroughly exploited than in the years following the second
world war, when the myth was successfully fostered that
Western Europe faced a real and possibly imminent threat of
Soviet military aggression.[2] The Cold War may not have been
unleashed for the purpose of strengthening the forces of conservatism in capitalist countries. But it nevertheless served the
purpose admirably and gave a new dimension to the appeal for
'national unity' in a time of allegedly dire military peril.
William James once pleaded for a 'moral equivalent of war'.
From a conservative point of view this was found, in the late
1940s and 1950s, in the Cold War. From that point of view too,
its much reduced effectiveness in more recent years presents a
serious problem.

In the exploitation of national sentiments, conservative parties
are powerfully helped by innumerable agencies of civil society
which are, to a greater or lesser degree, involved in the propagation of a 'national' view and of a 'national interest' defined in
conservative terms – the press and other mass media, educational institutions, youth organisations, ex-soldiers' associations
and leagues, specifically nationalist organisations, the Churches,

[1] Thus, McKenzie and Silver note, with reference to the Conservative Party
in Britain, that 'few democratic political parties can have so systematically and
ruthlessly called into question the integrity, the devotion to the constitution of the
country, and the patriotism of its opponents' (*Angels in Marble*, p. 49).

[2] For the ways in which that myth was fostered, see D. Horowitz, *The Free World
Colossus*, 1965.

business,[1] its association and lobbies, etc. Nor certainly is the conservative drift of the propaganda for which these agencies are variously responsible less pronounced because so many of them claim to be 'non-partisan' and 'non-political'. The claim may be sincerely made, but it is nevertheless most often quite spurious; there are many more ways of advancing the conservative cause than by urging support for a particular conservative party.

This, however, is one of the areas in which the agencies of civil society have by no means been alone in their task of 'political socialisation'. The state itself, through a variety of its institutions and by a variety of means, has also played a notable and ever-growing part in the fostering of a view of national allegiance eminently 'functional' to the existing social order, since it has required, as one of its main elements, the rejection of 'extreme' and 'alien' doctrines which might pose a serious challenge to it.

Here too the vocabulary is very often 'non-political'. As the spokesmen of the nation, and of the 'national interest', presidents and prime ministers easily assume a 'non-partisan' stance and address themselves to the people, particularly on occasions of crisis or solemnity, not as the leaders of particular parties but as representatives of the nation at large, with *its* interest as their only point of reference. But as has already been noted in an earlier chapter, this does not preclude – and indeed generally comprehends – the advocacy of policies and actions which *do* have a very marked political bias and intent. In fact the more 'national' the stress, the more conservative the intent is likely to be.

Similarly, the kind of nationalist indoctrination in which armies engage is normally free from explicit 'partisan' bias; those, in uniform or out, who are subjected to that indoctrination are not normally urged explicitly to favour or to reject this or that party. *That* would be 'politics', which armies must not 'indulge' in. But it would be a very stupid recruit indeed who

---

[1] Note, for instance, the considerable amount of support which American businessmen have given to stridently nationalist groups of the 'radical Right'. Nor were these businessmen simply status-starved Texan oil millionaires: three former vice-presidents of the National Association of Manufacturers served on the First Governing Council of the John Birch Society (see F.J. Cook, 'The Ultras', in *The Nation*, 30 June 1962).

would find in that 'non-political' propaganda much encouragement to support parties of the Left, or to espouse left-wing ideas. Armies may or may not be particularly effective schools of ideological conformity. But if they are not, it cannot be for want of trying by their officer class.

In this area of 'political socialisation' the state and other institutions are able to make use of a panoply of ideas and symbols of proven appeal, to which the national and often the imperial history of these countries has added even greater potency. Thus the collective memory of past struggles and the constant celebration of past sacrifices and heroic deeds, irrespective of the occasion or cause, are not generally calculated to foster a particularly critical view of the social order for whose existence much blood has been spilt. Even the dead are here called into service once again to help legitimate the regimes for which they have died. Also, 'functional' nationalist emotions are further stirred by an accumulation of symbols and the performance of a variety of ceremonies and rituals associated with past struggles and sacrifices, all of which are of undoubted value in a process of 'political socialisation' of a mainly conformist kind.

In this connection, mention may also be made of the useful role which, at least in some countries, monarchy has continued to play in that process. The unifying and socially emollient role of the British monarchy, for instance, has long been recognised and understood, never more so than since the coming into being of 'popular politics'.[1] And it is the same recognition which was largely responsible for the decision of the American occupying power in Japan at the end of the war to maintain the imperial institution, since this, it was felt, 'was an instrument to ensure the smooth transition during limited revolution directed from above, an inhibition preventing revolutions from below'.[2]

Of course, monarchs and monarchies may well become

---

[1] For a fairly recent view of the value of the British monarchy in fostering a 'common sentiment of the sacredness of communal life and institutions', see E. Shils and M. Young, 'The Meaning of the Coronation', in *The Sociological Review*, 1953, vol. I, no. 2; but see also N. Birnbaum, 'Monarchs and Sociologists. A Reply to Professor Shils and Mr. Young', *ibid.*, 1955, vol. 3, no. 1.

[2] A. B. Cole, *Japanese Society and Politics: The Impact of Social Stratification and Mobility on Politics*, 1956, p. 13.

highly 'dysfunctional' and serve as a focus of dissension rather than as an element of national unity, even to the point of threatening the national fabric itself.[1] But where this is not the case, the monarchy is not simply another element of the constitutional system; much more important at the present time is what Bagehot called its 'dignified' function which, properly understood, means the element of reverence which it helps to create towards the state and the traditional order of things, and the sense of national unity, beyond the 'mere' conflicts of class, which it is intended to foster.

V

The point was made in the previous chapter that, as a pressure group *vis-à-vis* the state, business enjoys a vast degree of superiority over all other groups and interests. In part at least, this must be related to the vast ideological, political and, in the broadest sense, cultural influence which it wields on society at large.

I am not here referring to business influence on political parties, which was discussed earlier; or to its influence on the mass media and other agencies of 'political socialisation', which will be considered later. I mean rather the effort business makes to persuade society not merely to accept the policies it advocates but also the ethos, the values and the goals which are its own, the economic system of which it forms the central part, the 'way of life' which is at the core of its being. In so far as the belief in capitalist enterprise is an essential part of conservative ideology, business itself plays an important part in propagating it. And in so far as the countries of advanced capitalism are 'business civilisations', permeated by a business culture and a business ethos, business itself has played a crucial role in making them so.

First, business has set up or at least has mainly financed 'promotional groups' which, in conjunction with the particular defence organisations of business discussed earlier, are

---

[1] As, for instance, happened in Belgium with regard to Leopold III in the years after the war.

specifically concerned with the dissemination of free enterprise propaganda and the defence and celebration of the capitalist economic system.

Once again it must be noted that there are many other 'promotional groups' in the pluralist societies of advanced capitalism and that the aims of some of them are opposed or at least unrelated to those of business. But here too the point has also to be made that the resources of the groups concerned to promote free enterprise are vastly superior to those of the groups concerned to oppose it. Thus to take an instance from Britain, Professor Rose notes that one of the most important pro-business 'promotional groups', Aims of Industry, has an annual income of about £100,000;[1] and he also notes that 'in their role expectations the officials of Aims are not unlike the left-wing weekly *Tribune*'.[2] This may well be true. But the idea which might be derived from such a contraposition that here are organisations in any sense equivalent in resources may be dismissed out of hand.

In any case, Aims of Industry is only one among many pro-business 'promotional groups'. Another one is the Economic League which was formed in 1919 and which, Professor Harrison notes, 'had a full-time staff of 180 in 1955. It distributes journals to management, supervisors and apprentices, and claimed to have given out 19,200,000 leaflets, held 8,932 outdoor and 9,388 indoor meetings and 33,700 group talks'.[3]

Similar 'promotional groups' exist of course in all other capitalist countries, with equally large, or as in the case of the United States, larger resources, and with the same kind of record of activity. There is simply no comparison between the efforts such groups are able to deploy by way of propaganda and the efforts of 'promotional groups' concerned to propagate anti-business, anti-free enterprise sentiments. Such groups are uniformly poor in staff, and in resources for propaganda activities; in no field is the imbalance between business and its opponents more marked.

[1] Rose, *Influencing Voters*, p. 98.   [2] *Ibid.*, p. 98.
[3] M. Harrison, 'Britain', in Comparative Studies in Political Finance, *Journal of Politics*, p. 667. But note also the efforts deployed by individual firms themselves, for instance by way of 'Company publications', of which there were some ten thousand in the United States by the early sixties (T. Peterson, J. W. Jensen, W. L. Rivers, *The Mass Media and Modern Society*, 1965, p. 176.)

Nor of course are 'promotional groups' which are concerned with other issues than the celebration of business enterprise precluded from making that celebration a main theme of their propaganda. Thus the vast number of nationalist organisations in the United States do in fact engage in precisely such celebration as part of their defence of true Americanism, and derive at least part of their financial resources from business. And obviously, *any* 'promotional group' with a more or less pronounced anti-socialist bias is by definition, and whether explicitly or not, engaged in the defence of one form or other of free enterprise.

In the second place, there are the campaigns which business firms themselves, alone or in conjunction with business associations or other bodies, occasionally wage for or against particular policies, but which have a much larger ideological and political resonance. Thus individual steel companies and the Steel Federation in Britain spent £1,298,000 in opposition to steel nationalisation before the 1964 election campaign.[1] But that propaganda was not simply focused on the technical merits or demerits of private versus public ownership of the steel industry. It was the Labour Party which, deeply concerned not to appear a 'doctrinaire' party, bent on nationalisation on principle, sought to confine its advocacy of steel nationalisation to technical considerations. The steel interests, for their part, widened the debate to encompass the general virtues of free enterprise, the evils of state control and bureaucracy, freedom, individual rights and what not. This pattern is typical of the encounters between reforming governments and business interests. The former place great stress on their purely pragmatic, empirical, undoctrinaire, in no sense 'anti-business' purpose. It is the business interests themselves which widen the debate, and aggressively invoke larger ideological and political issues.

Nevertheless, it is useful to be reminded that despite their vast resources and campaigns the steel interests in Britain were not able to prevent steel nationalisation. This may serve as a necessary corrective to the notion that interests such as these are

[1] Rose, *Influencing Voters*, p. 130. Professor Rose also notes that 'the expenditure is enormous when compared to the resources of the political parties, exceeding that of Conservative Central office by nearly one-third, and totally more than four times that of Transport House (*ibid.*, p. 130). See also G. W. Ross, *The Nationalisation of Steel: one step forward, two steps back?*, 1965.

by virtue of their resources all-powerful. As has been stressed before, they are not, and can be defeated. This, however, hardly negates the fact that they *are* powerful, that they do wield vast political influence, and that they are able to engage in an effort of ideological indoctrination which is altogether beyond the scope of any other interest in society.[1]

This effort has gone furthest in the United States where, it has been noted,

> ... the attitudes, opinions, arguments, values and slogans of the American business community are a familiar part of the landscape of most Americans. In recent years, the business point of view has found abundant expression in every kind of medium: placards in buses on the economics of the 'miracle of America', newspaper and magazine advertisements on the perils of excessive taxation; speeches of business executives on the responsibilities and rights of management; editorials deploring the size of the national debt; textbooks sponsored by business associations, explaining the workings of the free enterprise economy; pamphlets exposing the dangers of unwise political intervention in business affairs; testimony by business spokesmen before Congressional committees on a host of specific issues of public policy.[2]

Another American writer, Professor Heilbroner, makes the same point more specifically.

> The striking characteristic of our contemporary ideological climate [he writes] is that the 'dissident' groups, labour, government, or academics, *all seek to accommodate their proposals for social change to the limits of adaptability of the prevailing business order.* There is no attempt to press for goals that might exceed the powers of adjustment of that order. Indeed, all these groups recoil from such a test ... Thus, it falls to the lot of the business ideology, as the only socio-economic doctrine of consequence, to provide for non-business groups and, in particular, for the intellectual community the sense of mission and destiny that is the part usually emanated from rival ideologies.[3]

---

[1] Nor should it be overlooked that defeat in this kind of campaign has certain compensations. The intensity of the campaign helps to unnerve the reforming government and leads it to be 'reasonable' as to the terms on which it carries out the contested policy. Defeated on the main issue, powerful interests can still achieve a great deal by way of limiting and even almost nullifying the damage.

[2] Sutton, *et al. The American Business Creed*, pp. 11–12.

[3] R. L. Heilbroner, 'The View from the Top. Reflections on a Changing Business Ideology', in Cheit, *The Business Establishment*, p. 2 (italics in text).

In other advanced capitalist countries a combination of historical, economic, cultural and political circumstances has assured 'rival ideologies' of a rather better hearing; and even conservatism is there much less narrowly defined in terms of business ideology and values. But this, of course, need not be disadvantageous to business. On the contrary, the enduring strength of social values drawn from a pre-capitalist age, as in Britain, or from other historical and cultural values, may help to obscure the reality of business power and fuse its values with more ancient and more hallowed ones.

In any event, business, in all these countries, has a third and enormously important means of making its impact felt upon society, namely its power of advertisement, which is also self-advertisement.

Business advertising may, notably in the United States but occasionally also in other countries, have directly political and ideological connotations, but the defence of capitalist enterprise and the propagation of its values need not be less effective, and may even be more effective, for being free from such overt connotations, and for being much more diffuse and indeed wholly 'non-political'.

For a considerable time now, and ever more emphatically, advertising by business, particularly by the largest enterprises, and the activities of the public relations industry, have not been simply concerned to sell products,[1] but to sell to the public business itself, as an activity wholly beneficial not only to those who own it but to those who work for it, to those who buy from it, and to society at large. As Mr David Ogilvy, one of the leading figures in the mid-Atlantic advertising world once put it, 'advertising is a place where the selfish interest of the manufacturer coincides with the interests of society'.[2] What he meant of course was that advertising (and public relations) are intended to make it *appear* that the two coincide. Here, indeed, and much more effectively than through the after-dinner speeches of corporation executives, or in the propaganda of pro-business groups, is where the giant enterprise becomes

---

[1] A good deal of advertising, in fact, cannot in the nature of the product – for instance, fighter aircraft and nuclear power stations – be intended to advance sales. The purpose is rather to build good-will for the company and its other products – and for business enterprise generally.

[2] M. Mayer, *Madison Avenue, U.S.A.*, 1958, p. 59.

'soulful', public-oriented, socially responsible, and all but literally obsessed with the welfare and well-being of you, the customer. Here is where the corporation is most concerned with service, least with profit, and *only* concerned with profit because it affords the corporation a better chance to serve the customer and the community. As Raymond Williams has remarked about much business advertising, 'the borderline between this and straight political advertising is often quite difficult to see'.[1] Moreover, and at the risk of wearying the reader, the point has to be made again that business is almost alone in thus being able to use advertising: unions do not normally employ public relations firms to celebrate the product *they* sell.

Even more diffuse but no less notable is the persistent effort of corporate enterprise to associate not only its products, but itself and free enterprise generally, with socially approved values and norms: integrity, reliability, security, parental love, childlike innocence, neighbourliness, sociability, etc.; as well, of course, as the desires and drives which the 'motivational research' of the 'hidden persuaders' may find worth enhancing and exploiting. Even so, the corporation may remain unloved. But it is scarcely a matter of doubt that it, and the system of which it is a part, would be even less loved and therefore more vulnerable to the attacks of counter-ideologies, if business was not able to deploy so vast an effort in building a favourable image of itself.

Finally, and self-image apart, business advertising powerfully contributes to the fostering of values associated with what Tawney called 'the acquisitive society'. This is not to attach moral reprobation to the comforts and pleasures which are to be derived from a large variety of 'gadgets' – a word which has acquired an undeservedly pejorative connotation. Nor is even the main point here that so much advertising is devoted to the creation of wants whose fulfilment is altogether irrelevant to, or incompatible with, the fulfilment of genuine and urgent human needs, which remain largely or wholly unmet because it is not in the interests of private enterprise that they should be met.[2] This is only another manifestation of a fundamentally

[1] Williams, *Communications*, p. 40.
[2] On this, see e.g. Baran and Sweezy, *Monopoly Capital*, chapter 5.

irrational system, able to impose its irrationality upon the societies in which it thrives.

The point is rather that business is able freely to propagate an ethos in which private acquisitiveness is made to appear as the main if not the only avenue to fulfilment, in which 'happiness' or 'success' are therefore defined in terms of private acquisition, in which competition for acquisition, and therefore for 'happiness' and 'success' is treated as, or assumed to be, a primary law of life, and in which concerted and rational action for humane ends is at best an irrelevance. The *firm* is soulful, benevolent, public-spirited and socially responsible. This being so, the *individual* may, therefore, safely remain private-oriented, acquisitive, predatory, and be content to enjoy the blessings which are showered upon him.

People may react differently to this and other related kinds of 'message', and it would not do to raise advertising to the status of a *decisive* influence upon the manner in which those who are subjected to it see the world. But neither would it be at all appropriate to belittle the *contribution* which business, by its power of advertising, is able to make to what must, in an anthropological if in no other sense, be called the cultural climate of their societies. Advertising, it is always said in its defence, is a necessary and valuable part of an advanced economic system. The point need not be disputed. The real issue lies elsewhere, namely that advertising, in *this* particular kind of economic system, assumes certain characteristics which are not inherent in the activity itself (not least its debasement of language and meaning, and its generally idiot triviality), and that among these characteristics is the intention to manipulate people into buying a 'way of life' as well as goods.

The various agencies of political persuasion which have been discussed in this chapter do not work in concert. Many of them are not even 'political', and resolutely shun 'politics'. And none of them, whether 'political' or not, propagates a closely defined and tightly-woven conservative ideology, let alone an officially sanctioned one. Yet however loose, diverse and even discordant the voices may be, they speak the language of adaptation to capitalist society, and do so no less when they speak of reforms which are usually conceived as part of that adaptation. This is why, despite the diversity of forms and idioms their language may assume, they must be seen as engaged, together with the state, in a combined and formidable enterprise of conservative indoctrination. That enterprise however is made immeasurably more formidable by the help it receives from other agencies of 'political socialisation', namely the mass media and education, which will be considered in the next chapter.

8

The Process of Legitimation–II

I

In no field do the claims of democratic diversity and free political competition which are made on behalf of the 'open societies' of advanced capitalism appear to be more valid than in the field of communications – the press, the written word generally, radio, television, the cinema and the theatre. For in contrast to Communist and other 'monolithic' regimes, the means of expression in capitalist countries are not normally monopolised by, and subservient to, the ruling political power. Even where, as is often the case for radio and television, agencies of communication are public institutions, or mixed ones, they are not simply the mouthpieces of the government of the day and exclusively the organs of official policy or opinions; opposition views are also heard and seen.

Nor, as occurs in many regimes where communications are *not* monopolised by the state, do those who work for them have to fear extreme retribution because what they communicate or allow to be communicated happens to offend their government or other public figures or bodies. No doubt they are subject to various legal and other official restraints and pressures, sometimes of a severe kind. But these restraints and pressures, which will be considered presently, only qualify the notion of independence of the communications media from state dictation and control; they do not nullify it.

Indeed, it cannot even be said that views which are profoundly offensive to various 'establishments', whether they concern politics or culture or religion or morals, are narrowly confined to marginal and *avant-garde* channels of expression, patronised only by tiny minorities.

Such 'controversial' views do find their way, in all these countries, in mass circulation newspapers and magazines; they are presented in book form by large publishing houses, often in vast paperback editions;[1] they are heard on the radio and seen expressed on television; they inspire films which are shown by major cinema circuits, and plays which are performed in the 'commercial' theatre – and no one (or hardly anyone) goes to jail.

The importance and value of this freedom and opportunity of expression is not to be underestimated. Yet the notion of pluralist diversity and competitive equilibrium is, here as in every other field, rather superficial and misleading. For the agencies of communication and notably the mass media are, in reality, and the expression of dissident views notwithstanding, a crucial element in the legitimation of capitalist society. Freedom of expression is not thereby rendered meaningless. But that freedom has to be set in the real economic and political context of these societies; and in that context the free expression of ideas and opinions *mainly* means the free expression of ideas and opinions which are helpful to the prevailing system of power and privilege. Indeed, Professor Lazarsfeld and Professor Merton once went as far as to suggest that:

Increasingly the chief power groups, among which organised business occupies the most spectacular place, have come to adopt techniques for manipulating mass publics through propaganda in place of more direct means of control ... Economic power seems to have reduced direct exploitation [?] and turned to a subtler type of psychological exploitation, achieved largely by disseminating propaganda through the mass media of communication ... These media have taken on the job of rendering mass publics conformative to the social and economic status quo.[2]

---

[1] Writing of the efflorescence of 'legal Marxism' in the Russia of the 1890s, B. Wolfe notes that 'finding Marxism a saleable and distinguished commodity, publishers contracted for translations of the classics and of contemporary German and French Marxist works' (*Three Who Made a Revolution* (1966) p. 140). The same phenomenon, which might be described as commercial Marxism, also occurred, on a vastly larger scale, in advanced capitalist countries in the 1960s.

[2] P. F. Lazarsfeld and R. K. Merton, 'Mass Communication, Popular Taste and Organized Social Action', in B. Rosenberg and D. M. White (eds.), *Mass Culture. The Popular Arts in America*, 1957, p. 457.

The ideological function of the media is obscured by many features of cultural life in these systems, for instance the absence of state dictation, the existence of debate and controversy, the fact that conservatism is not a tight body of thought and that its looseness makes possible variations and divergencies within its framework, and much else as well. But obscured though it may be, the fact remains that the mass media in advanced capitalist societies are mainly intended to perform a highly 'functional' role; they too are both the expression of a system of domination, and a means of reinforcing it.

The press may be taken as the first and most obvious example of this role. Newspapers everywhere vary enormously in quality, content and tendency. Some are sober and staid, others sensational and shrill; intelligent or stupid; scrupulous or not; reactionary, conservative, liberal or 'radical'; free from outside allegiance, or vehicles of a party faction or interest; critical of authority or blandly apologetic; and so on. But whatever their endless differences of every kind, most newspapers in the capitalist world have one crucial characteristic in common, namely their strong, often their passionate hostility to anything further to the Left than the milder forms of social-democracy, and quite commonly to these milder forms as well. This commitment finds its most explicit expression at election time; whether independent of more or less conservative parties or specifically committed to them, most newspapers may be relied on to support the conservative side or at least to be deeply critical of the anti-conservative one, often vociferously and unscrupulously so. This conservative preponderance is normally overwhelming.

At the core of the commitment lies a general acceptance of prevailing modes of thought concerning the economic and social order and a specific acceptance of the capitalist system, even though sometimes qualified, as natural and desirable. Most newspapers accept a certain degree of state intervention in economic and social life as inevitable and even praiseworthy; and some, greatly daring, may even support this or that piece of innocuous nationalisation. Even so, most organs of the press have always been utterly dedicated to the proposition that the enlargement of the 'public sector' was inimical to the 'national interest' and that the strengthening of private enterprise was the condition of economic prosperity, social welfare, freedom, democracy, and so forth.

Similarly, and consistently, the press for the most part has always been a deeply committed anti-trade union force. Not, it should be said, that newspapers in general oppose trade unions as such. Not at all. They only oppose trade unions, in the all too familiar jargon, which, in disregard of the country's welfare and of their members' own interests, greedily and irresponsibly seek to achieve short-term gains which are blindly self-defeating. In other words, newspapers love trade unions so long as they do badly the job for which they exist. Like governments and employers, newspapers profoundly deplore strikes, and the larger the strike the greater the hostility: woe to trade union leaders who encourage or fail to prevent such manifestly unsocial, irresponsible and *obsolete* forms of behaviour. The rights and wrongs of any dispute are of minor consequence; what counts is the community, the consumer, the public, which *must* be protected, whatever the cost, against the actions of men who blindly obey the summons of misguided and, most likely, evil-intentioned leaders.

In the same vein, most newspapers in the capitalist world have always had the 'extreme' Left, and notably communists, on the brain, and have only varied in their attitude to that part of the political spectrum in the degree of virulence and hostility which they have displayed towards it. It is also the case that for such newspapers the history of the world since 1945 has largely been a Manichean struggle imposed upon the forces of goodness, led by the United States, against the forces of evil, represented by aggressive communism, whether Soviet or Chinese. Revolutionary movements are almost always 'communist-inspired', and by definition evil, however atrocious the conditions which have given rise to them; and in the struggles of decolonisation of this century, the attitude of the vast majority of newspapers has always ranged from strong antipathy to passionate hostility towards movements and leaders (or rather terrorists) seeking independence.

All this, it should be stressed, has not been and is not simply *a* current of thought among many; it has been and remains *the* predominant, generally the overwhelming, current of thought of the national (and local) press of advanced capitalist countries.

As has also been stressed repeatedly in preceding chapters, this profoundly conformist outlook admits of many variations and deviations: it certainly does not preclude a critical view of this or that aspect of the existing order of things. And while social-democratic governments, however conservative their policies, must expect very much rougher treatment at the hands of the press than properly conservative ones, the latter are not at all immune from press criticism and attack. In this sense the press may well claim to be 'independent' and to fulfil an important watchdog function. What the claim overlooks, however, is the very large fact that it is the Left at which the watchdogs generally bark with most ferocity, and that what they are above all protecting is the *status quo*.

Many 'popular' newspapers with a mass circulation are extremely concerned to convey the opposite impression and to suggest a radical impatience with every kind of 'establishment', however exalted, and a restless urge for change, reform, progress. In actual fact, most of this angry radicalism represents little more than an affectation of style; behind the iconoclastic irreverence and the demagogic populism there is singular vacuity both in diagnosis and prescription. The noise is considerable but the battle is bogus.

For their part, radio and television similarly serve a mainly though again not exclusively conformist purpose. Here too the appearance is of rich diversity of views and opinions, of ardent controversy and passionate debate. These media, moreover, whether commercially or publicly owned, are either required, or in any case wish to suggest, a high degree of political impartiality and objectivity. Newspapers can be as politically involved and partisan, as biased in their presentation of news and views, as they choose. But radio and television must not.

In most ways, however, this assumed impartiality and objectivity is quite artificial. For it mainly operates in regard to political formations which while divided on many issues are nevertheless part of a basic, underlying consensus. Thus, radio and television in such countries as Britain and the United States may preserve a fair degree of impartiality between the Conservative, Liberal and Labour parties, and the Republican and Democratic parties, respectively; but this hardly precludes a steady stream of propaganda adverse to all views which fall outside the consensus. Impartiality and objectivity, in this sense, stop at the point where political consensus itself ends – and the more radical the dissent, the less impartial and objective the media. On this view it does not seem extravagant to suggest that radio and television in all capitalist countries have been consistently and predominantly agencies of conservative indoctrination and that they have done what they could to inoculate their listeners and viewers against dissident thought. This does not require that all such dissent should be prevented from getting an airing. It only requires that the overwhelming bias of the media should be on the other side. And that requirement has been amply met.

In countries where political life is dominated by parties which operate in a framework of consensus, this bias, to which otherwise opposed parties make a joint contribution, is easily overlooked. In countries such as France and Italy, where large Communist parties form the main opposition, the notion of political impartiality is more difficult to sustain. In the former countries, a general ideological bias has fewer immediately obvious political connotations, since the parties and movements which most suffer from hostility and discrimination form a small and even negligible political factor. In the latter, radio and television are much more directly involved in the political struggle and are in effect the instruments of the government parties, to be used against the opposition, with no nonsense about 'equal time' or any such liberal luxury which political circumstances renders inappropriate. In France, both radio and television have been quite deliberately turned into Gaullist institutions, to be used to the advantage of the general, his government, and the party which supports them;[1] and similarly in Italy, these media have predominantly been the instruments of Christian Social-Democracy and its governments.

In strict *political* terms, this is a very different situation from that which has prevailed in a country like Britain, where the

[1] Which is not to say that the governments of the Fourth Republic did not exercise pressure to achieve favourable presentation of their policies by radio and television. (For this, and for examples of the very much more sustained effort of the Gaullist regime, see the debate in the National Assembly on 24 April 1968, *Le Monde*, 25 April 1968).

Labour leaders have been assured since the war of some kind of parity with their Conservative opponents. In larger *ideological* terms, however, the contrast has been rather less dramatic; and the point applies with even greater force to the United States where, it has been said, 'organised business and such lesser interests as the major political parties and church groups have virtually a "psychological monopoly" of the media. News and comment, entertainment, advertising, political rhetoric and religious exhortation alike are more concerned with channelling existing beliefs than with radically changing them'.[1] As between all shades of the consensus on the one hand, and all shades of counter-ideology on the other, radio and television in all capitalist countries have ensured that the former had by far the best of the argument.

So far the mass media have been discussed as if their sole concern was with politics and ideology. This is of course not the case. Mainly political magazines and books form a very small part of the total, and all newspapers devote much space to matters which bear no direct or even indirect relation to politics – many newspapers in fact devote much more space to such matters than to political ones. Similarly, radio, television, the cinema and the theatre are not run *as* agencies of political communication and indoctrination; they are also, and even predominantly, concerned with 'entertainment' of one sort or another. Indeed, in the case of the mass media which are privately owned and controlled, the overriding purpose and concern is with profit. This is also true of newspapers. Lord Thompson was not expressing a unique and eccentric view when he said that what he wanted from his newspapers was that they should make money.

On the other hand, making money is not at all incompatible with making politics, and in a more general sense with political indoctrination. Thus the *purpose* of the 'entertainment' industry, in its various forms, may be profit; but the *content* of its output is not therefore by any means free from political and ideological connotations of a more or less definite kind.

The mass media are often attacked for their cultural poverty,

[1] T. Peterson, J. W. Jensen, W. C. Rivers, *The Mass Media and Modern Society*, p. 26.

their debased commercialism, their systematic triviality, their addiction to brutality and violence, their deliberate exploitation of sex and sadism, and much else of the same order. The indictment is familiar and largely justified.

But that indictment also tends, very often, to understate or to ignore the specific ideological content of these productions and the degree to which they are used as propaganda vehicles for a particular view of the world. 'A superficial inventory of the contents and motivation in the products of the entertainment and publishing worlds in our Western civilisation', Professor Lowenthal has observed, 'will include such themes as the nation, the family, religion, free enterprise, individual initiative'.[1] Such an inventory would in fact do more than include these and other highly 'functional' themes; it would also have to note the marginal place allowed to themes of a 'dysfunctional' kind. Professor Meynaud has said, in regard to the world of magazines that 'ils contribuent par la structure de leurs rubriques et l'apparente neutralité de leurs articles à la formation de ce climat de conformisme qui est l'un des meilleurs atouts du capitalisme contemporain. A cet égard, le rôle des hebdomadaires féminins qui donnent, sans en avoir l'air, une vue entièrement falsifiée de notre monde est capital'.[2] The point is of more general application, and so is Raymond Williams's remark about what he calls 'majority television', namely that it is 'outstandingly an expression of the false consciousness of our particular societies'.[3]

Furthermore, it is worth noting that much of the 'message' of the mass media is not diffuse but quite specific. It would of course be ridiculous to think of such authors as Mickey Spillane and Ian Fleming (to take two writers whose sales have been astronomical) as political writers in any true sense. But it would also be silly to overlook the fact that their heroes are paragons of anti-Communist virtues and that their adventures, including their sexual adventures, are more often than not set in

---

[1] L. Lowenthal, 'Historical Perspective of Popular Culture', in Rosenberg and White (eds.), *Mass Culture. The Popular Arts in America*, p. 50.

[2] Meynaud, *Rapport sur la Classe Dirigeante Italienne*, p. 192.

[3] R. Williams, 'Television in Britain', in *The Journal of Social Issues*, 1962, vol. 18, no. 2, p. 11. For a classic analysis of the reactionary values of boys' magazines in Britain in an earlier period, see G. Orwell, 'Boys' Weeklies', in *Collected Essays*, 1962.

the context of a desperate struggle against subversive forces, both alien and home-grown. As has been said about the anti-communism of the Spillane output, 'it is woven into the texture of assumptions of the novel. Anyone who thinks otherwise is taken to be either treasonable or hopelessly naïve.'[1] This kind of crude 'ideology for the masses' does not permeate the whole field of 'mass culture'; but it permeates a substantial part of it in most media. Nor of course is the rest of 'mass culture' much permeated by counter-ideological material. There are not, on the whole, many left-wing and revolutionary equivalents of James Bond. It may be that the *genre* does not lend itself to it; and the political climate of advanced capitalist societies certainly does not.

II

The nature of the contribution which the mass media make to that political climate is determined by the influences which weigh most heavily upon them. There are a number of such influences – and they all work in the same conservative and conformist direction.

The first and most obvious of them derives from the ownership and control of the 'means of mental production'. Save for state ownership of radio and television stations and of some other means of communications, the mass media are overwhelmingly in the private domain (and this is also true of most radio and television stations in the United States). Moreover, these agencies are in that part of the private domain which is dominated by large-scale capitalist enterprise. Ever more notably, the mass media are not only business, but big business. The pattern of concentration which is evident in all other forms of capitalist enterprise is also evident here: the press, magazines and book publishing, cinemas, theatres, and also radio and television wherever they are privately owned, have increasingly come under the ownership and control of a small and steadily declining number of giant enterprises, with combined interests in different media, and often also in other areas of capitalist

[1] S. Hall and P. Whannel, *The Popular Arts*, 1964, p. 148.

enterprise. 'The Hearst empire', it has been noted, 'includes twelve newspapers, fourteen magazines, three television stations, six radio stations, a news service, a photo service, a feature syndicate, and Avon paperbacks'; and similarly, 'in addition to magazines, *Time, Inc.*, also owns radio and television stations, a book club, paper mills, timber land, oil wells, and real estate'.[1] The same kind of concentration is increasingly found in all other capitalist countries: the Axel Springer empire, for instance, alone controls over 40 per cent of German newspapers and magazines, and close to 80 per cent of Berlin newspapers. As for films, it has been observed that 'in Britain, for example, film distribution is virtually dependent on two companies which run the circuit cinemas, and since films can normally be financed only on guarantees of distribution, this means that two companies have almost complete control over what films are to be made, and what subjects are acceptable'.[2] And it is also noteworthy that new ventures in the mass media are easily captured by existing interests in these or in other fields. Thus, Mr Hall and Mr Whannel, speaking of commercial television in Britain, note that 'rather than spreading power into new hands, it has increased the power of those already holding it. More than half the resources of commercial television are owned in part by newspapers, the film industry and theatrical interests'.[3]

Rather obviously, those who own and control the capitalist mass media are most likely to be men whose ideological dispositions run from soundly conservative to utterly reactionary; and in many instances, most notably in the case of newspapers, the impact of their views and prejudices is immediate and direct, in the straightforward sense that newspaper proprietors have

[1] G. W. Domhoff, *Who Rules America*, 1967, p. 81.

[2] A. Hunt, 'The Film', in D. Thompson (ed.), *Discrimination and Popular Culture*, 1964, p. 101.

[3] Hall and Whannel, *The Popular Arts*, p. 343. One of the main promoters of commercial television in Britain, Mr Norman Collins, described this process as follows: '. . . the viewer has found himself offered a service that is the expression of the combined experience of those men who for years have run the nation's theatres, cinemas, concert halls and newspapers. It is also a healthy and democratic [*sic*] thing that financial interests in the Independent Television should be spread so widely. It is gratifying that so many branches of industry and the press and entertainment can participate in Independent Television' (*ibid.*, p. 344). Gratifying the venture has undoubtedly been for the participants: it is the 'democratic' bit which is rather less obvious.

often not only owned their newspapers but closely controlled their editorial and political line as well, and turned them, by constant and even daily intervention, into vehicles of their personal views.[1] In the case of Axel Springer's newspaper empire, it has been remarked that 'he runs his papers like a monarch. He denies that there is any kind of central ideological control, and certainly such control is not formalised in any way. But Herr Springer is a man of the strongest political views. Deeply religious, a militant anti-communist, he has also a sense of mission. He may not direct his papers openly but his ideas seep downwards'.[2] Much the same may be said of many newspaper owners in all advanced capitalist countries. The right of ownership confers the right of making propaganda, and where that right is exercised, it is most likely to be exercised in the service of strongly conservative prejudices, either by positive assertion or by the exclusion of such matters as owners may find it undesirable to publish. Censorship is not, in a free enterprise system, purely a state prerogative. No doubt, private censorship, unlike state censorship, is not absolute. But where no alternative source of newspaper information or views is readily available – as is mostly the case in many towns, cities and regions in the United States,[3] and elsewhere as well[4] – such censorship is pretty effective all the same, particularly where other media such as radio and television are, as often in the United States, also under the same ownership and control.[5]

However, it is not always the case that those who own or ultimately control the mass media do seek to exercise a direct and immediate influence upon their output. Quite commonly, editors, journalists, producers, managers, etc. are accorded a considerable degree of independence, and are even given a free

[1] As Lord Beaverbrook told the Royal Commission on the Press, 'I run the paper purely for the purpose of making propaganda, and with no other motive.' Quoted in R. M. Hutchins, *Freedom, Education and the Fund*, 1956, p. 62.

[2] *The Times*, 15 April 1968.

[3] Only 6 per cent of all the daily newspaper cities in this country now have competing dailies' (W. Schramm, ' Its Development', in C.S. Steinberg (ed.), *Mass Media and Communication*, 1966, p. 51). These figures refer to 1953–4.

[4] Thus for France, it has been noted that 'en province, les habitants d'une trentaine de départements n'ont à leur disposition qu'un seul journal' (F. Goguel and A. Grosser, *La Politique en France*, 1964, p. 157).

[5] For the use of television and radio for anti-communist and related purposes by wealthy men in the United States, see F. Cook, 'The Ultras', in *The Nation*, 30 June 1962.

hand. Even so, ideas do tend to 'seep downwards', and provide an ideological and political framework which may well be broad but whose existence cannot be ignored by those who work for the commercial media. They may not be *required* to take tender care of the sacred cows that are to be found in the conservative stable. But it is at least *expected* that they will spare the conservative susceptibilities of the men whose employees they are, and that they will take a proper attitude to free enterprise, conflicts between capital and labour, trade unions, left-wing parties and movements, the Cold War, revolutionary movements, the role of the United States in the world, and much else besides. The existence of this framework does not require total conformity; general conformity will do. This assured, room will be found for a seasoning, sometimes even a generous seasoning, of dissent.

In 1957 Mr James Wechsler, the editor of the New York *Post*, delivered himself of some remarks about the American press which are worth quoting at some length, since they are of wider application:

The American press [he said] is overwhelmingly owned and operated by Republicans who fix the rules of U.S. political debate. And I use the words 'fix' advisedly.

I know it is a freer press than any prevailing in Communist or Fascist countries; but that is nothing to be complacent about. It is a press that has generally grown comfortable, fat and self-righteous; and which with some noteworthy exceptions voices the prejudices and preconceptions of entrenched wealth rather than those qualities of critical inquiry and rebellious spirit we associate with our noblest journalistic traditions.

It is a press that is generally more concerned with the tax privileges of any fat cat than with the care and feeding of any underdog.

It is a press that sanctimoniously boasts of its independence and means by that its right to do what its Republican owners damn please. The press used to be regarded as a public trust, not a private playground.

It is a press that is far more forthright and resolute in combating Communist tyranny in Hungary than in waging the fight for freedom in the United States.[1]

---

[1] Quoted in J. E. Gerald, *The Social Responsibility of the Press*, 1963, p. 108. Or, as Robert Hutchins put it, 'Of course we have a one-party press in this country, and we shall have one as long as the press is big business, and as long as people with

With appropriate local variations, and with some few exceptions,[1] these strictures would not seem irrelevant to the press of other capitalist countries.

A second source of conformist and conservative pressure upon newspapers and other media is that exercised, directly or indirectly, by capitalist interests, not as owners, but as advertisers. The direct political influence of large advertisers upon the commercial media need not be exaggerated. It is only occasionally that such advertisers are able, or probably even try, to dictate the contents and policies of the media of which they are the customers. But their custom is nevertheless of crucial importance to the financial viability, which means the existence, of newspapers and, in some but not all instances, of magazines, commercial radio and television. That fact may do no more than *enhance* a general disposition on the part of these media to show exceptional care in dealing with such powerful and valuable interests. But that is useful too, since it provides a further assurance to business interests in general that they will be treated with sympathetic understanding, and that the 'business community' will, at the least, be accorded a degree of indulgence which is seldom if ever displayed towards the labour interest and trade unions: *their* displeasure is a matter of no consequence at all.

Moreover, the point made in the last chapter concerning the vastly superior resources which capitalist interests, as compared with any other, are able to deploy in the field of public relations is here acutely relevant. For these resources are also used to 'soften up' the appropriate mass media, notably the press, which further contributes to the representation of the 'business case' in the best possible light.

Professor Meynaud has suggested that the control which capitalist interests exercise over a large part of the press in Italy produces an 'exemplary docility' on its part towards their 'theses and preoccupations'.[2] For France, it has been suggested that 'les consignes que l'argent fait peser sur la presse consiste beaucoup plus en interdits, en sujets à ne pas évoquer qu'en

money continue to feel safer on the Republican side' (Hutchins, *Freedom, Education and the Fund*, p. 61).

[1] For instance *Le Monde*, which provides a daily example of what a really great newspaper looks like.

[2] Meynaud, *Rapport sur la Classe Dirigeante Italienne*, p. 192.

instructions sur ce qu'il faut dire'.[1] The emphasis is bound to vary from country to country and from paper to paper. But whether the direct pressure of business interests is great or small, or even nonexistent, it is greatly to the financial disadvantage of newspapers and magazines everywhere to be 'anti-business'. Not surprisingly, organs of the extreme left, even where, as occasionally happens, they enjoy a substantial circulation, cannot rely on much advertising revenue from business sources[2] – or from government.[3]

A third element of pressure upon the mass media stems from government and various other parts of the state system generally. That pressure, as was noted earlier, does not generally amount to imperative dictation. But it is nevertheless real, in a number of ways.

For one thing, governments, ministries and other official agencies now make it their business, ever more elaborately and systematically, to supply newspapers, radio and television with explanations of official policy which naturally have an apologetic and tendentious character. The state, in other words, now goes in more and more for 'news management', particularly in times of stress and crisis, which means, for most leading capitalist countries, almost permanently; and the greater the crisis, the more purposeful the management, the evasions, the half-truths and the plain lies. In addition, governments now engage more extensively than ever before in cultural management, particularly abroad, and use education and culture as instruments of foreign policy. By far and away the greatest effort in this field since the war has of course been made by the United States whose endeavours, notably in the Third World, have given

---

[1] Goguel and Grosser, *La Politique en France*, p. 156.

[2] 'The primary reasons for the financial troubles of the Communist press [in Italy] does not seem to lie in an insufficient circulation, but rather in the almost complete lack of paid advertising, as a comparison with the largest and most influential independent papers clearly shows. While *Il Corriere della Sera* dedicates 45 per cent of its space to advertisements and other paid announcements, and *La Stampa* 42 per cent, *L'Unità* can count on merely 6 per cent.' (S. Passigli, 'Italy', in Comparative Studies in Political Finance, *The Journal of Politics*, p. 722).

[3] Note, in this connection, the systematic exclusion of the Communist *Morning Star* from government advertising, which produces a situation where a Labour government, while penalising an extreme left-wing paper, distributes vast subsidies to its most bitter critics on the Right.

an entirely new dimension to the notion of 'cultural imperialism'.[1] Not, it should be said, that these endeavours, as shown
by the uncovering of CIA activities in the cultural field, have
neglected the advanced capitalist world, including the United
States.

As far as newspapers are concerned, governments and other
agencies of the state system may, in their desire to manage the
news, resort to a variety of pressures and blandishments[2] –
even threats[3] – which may be more or less effective. But they
are, for the most part, forced to rely very largely on the cooperation and good-will of publishers, editors and journalists.
In many cases, that cooperation and good-will are readily
forthcoming, since a majority of newspapers tend, broadly
speaking, to share the view of the national interest held by
governments which are mostly of the conservative persuasion.
But where newspapers are recalcitrant, as is often the case for
one reason or another, there is relatively little that governments can do about it. In this sense too, newspapers are independent institutions; and for all their shortcomings, that
remains an important fact in the life of these countries.

Publicly owned radio and television, on the other hand, are
'official' institutions, and as such much more susceptible than
newspapers to a variety of official pressures. They may well,
as in Britain, enjoy a high degree of independence and autonomy from government, but they remain nevertheless steeped
in an official environment and permeated by an official climate,
which ensure that in political and general ideological terms
these media fulfil a conformist rather than a critical role. This
does not prevent governments and official policies from being
criticised and attacked. But criticism and attack tend to remain
within a safe, fairly narrow spectrum. To paraphrase Lord

[1] See, e.g. 'The Non-Western World in Higher Education', in *The Annals of the
American Academy of Political and Social Science*, vol. 356, 1964.

[2] Sometimes, as in Federal Germany, of a rather direct kind: 'In the budget of
the chancellor, there is a secret fund of 13 million DM, which seems to serve
partially to support government-friendly newspapers and journalists, and partially
for more honorable purposes' (V. Dueber and G. Braunthal, 'West Germany', in
'Comparative Studies in Political Finance', *Journal of Politics*, p. 774).

[3] As, for instance, in the case of the German government's attempt to crush the
awkwardly critical *Der Spiegel*. See O. Kirchheimer and C. Menges, 'A Free Press
in a Democratic State? The *Spiegel* Case', in G. M. Carter and A. F. Westin,
Politics in Europe, 1965.

Balfour's remark about the House of Lords, whether the
Conservative or the Labour Party is in office, it is generally the
conformist point of view which prevails. At the time of the
General Strike, John Reith, as he was then, wrote to the Prime
Minister in his capacity of General Manager of the BBC that,
'assuming the BBC is for the people and that the government is
for the people, it follows that the BBC must be for the government in this crisis too'.[1] Things may have moved somewhat
since then, but not as dramatically as is often claimed or as the
notion of independence and autonomy would suggest. Writing
of BBC Television in recent years, Mr Stuart Hood has noted
that judgments of what is to be produced 'are based on what
can be described as a programme ethos – a general view of what
is fitting and seemly, of what is admissible and not admissible,
which is gradually absorbed by those persons involved in
programme-making'.[2] This 'programme ethos' is much more
likely to produce controversy within the consensus than outside
it. And where programmes are consistently, or appear to be
consistently anti-Establishmentarian, official pressures come
into effective operation, not necessarily from the government
itself, but from such bodies as the board of governors of the
BBC (and the Independent Television Authority). The latter
are impeccably Establishment figures, whether Conservative,
Liberal, Labour or 'non-political'.[3] Thus, it was 'on his personal
responsibility' that the Director General of the BBC took a
sharply satirical programme such as *That Was the Week that
Was* off the air. But, as Mr Hood also notes, 'no one with
knowledge of the strength of feeling on the part of some governors at that time can doubt that the Director-General had no
real alternative if he wanted to continue in his post'.[4] It is also

---

[1] J. W. C. Reith, *Into the Wind*, 1949, p. 108.

[2] S. Hood, *A Survey of Television*, 1967, p. 50.

[3] 'At the top of the BBC hierarchy is the Board of Governors, appointed by the
government, consisting of nine men and women of ability, standing and distinction. Generally speaking they represent the upper class of British society, which is
to say, the "Establishment", the British equivalent of America's "Power Elite".
There is no special attempt to appoint governors with trade union or working-
class backgrounds, and very seldom do members have experience in broadcasting,
journalism or related fields' (B. Paulu, *British Broadcasting in Transition*, 1961, p. 17).
For the class composition of BBC Governors and of the 'Cultural Directorate'
generally in the 1950s, see Guttsman, *The British Political Elite*, pp. 342ff.

[4] Hood, *A Survey of Television*, p. 49.

worth noting that, for all its irreverence and bite, *TW3* eschewed any political commitment; indeed it was largely constructed around the notion that any such commitment was absurdly *vieux jeu*. Had it been otherwise, it may be surmised that it would not have lasted as long as it did.

The general point about governmental and official pressures on the mass media is not simply that they occur, and are more or less intense; it is rather that, given the usual political and ideological coloration of governments and state elites, these pressures reinforce the tendencies towards conservatism and conformity which already exist independently of them.

Yet an explanation of the character and intended role of the mass media in terms of the pressures, private and public, so far considered is inadequate. For it suggests that those who are actually responsible for the contents of the mass media – producers, editors, journalists, writers, commentators, directors, playwrights, etc. – are the unwilling tools of conservative and commercial forces, that they are suppressed rebels, cowed radicals and left-wingers, reluctant producers and disseminators of ideas and opinions which they detest, angry dissenters straining at the capitalist leash.

This is not a realistic picture. There *are* of course a good many such people working in and for the mass media, who suffer various degrees of political frustration, and who seek, sometimes successfully, often not, to break through the frontiers of orthodoxy. But there is little to suggest that they constitute more than a minority of the 'cultural workmen' employed by the mass media. The cultural and political hegemony of the dominant classes could not be so pronounced if this was not the case.

A realistic picture of the ideological tendencies of those who work for the mass media would divide them into three broad categories: those just referred to who belong to various shades of the Left; people with a more or less strong conservative commitment; and a third group, which is probably the most numerous, whose political commitments are fairly blurred, and who wish to avoid 'trouble'. In effect, such people occupy one part or other of the spectrum of conformity and can accommodate themselves fairly easily to the requirements of their employers. Like their committed conservative colleagues, they mostly 'say what they like'; but this is mainly because their employers mostly like what they say, or at least find little in what they say which is objectionable. These 'cultural workmen' are unlikely to be greatly troubled by the limitations and constrictions imposed upon the mass media by the prevailing economic and political system, because their ideological and political make-up does not normally bring them up against these limitations. The leash they wear is sufficiently long to allow them as much freedom of movement as they themselves wish to have; and they therefore do not feel the strain; or not so as to make life impossible.

There is nothing particularly surprising about the character and role of the mass media in advanced capitalist society. Given the economic and political context in which they function, they cannot fail to be, predominantly, agencies for the dissemination of ideas and values which affirm rather than challenge existing patterns of power and privilege, and thus to be weapons in the arsenal of class domination. The notion that they can, for the most part, be anything else is either a delusion or a mystification. They can, and sometimes do, play a 'dysfunctional' role; and the fact that they are allowed to do so is not lightly to be dismissed. But that, quite emphatically, is not and indeed cannot, in the given context, be their main role. They are intended to fulfil a conservative function; and do so.

This, however, is not to suggest that the control of the mass media and the 'mobilisation of bias' which it makes possible guarantee success to conservative parties in electoral competition, or effectively ensure ideological attunement.

In regard to the first point, it has been noted that in the British General Election of 1966, only one newspaper, the *Sunday Citizen*, with a circulation of 232,000 was 'unreservedly on the outgoing government's side' (i.e. the Labour Government), while the rest of the press (38,000,000) was more or less critical'.[1] The figures tend to give an exaggerated view of the specific commitment of most newspapers to the Conservative Party. But the fact remains that the general bias of the press, then as always, was against Labour. Yet this did not prevent the

[1] *The New Statesman*, 25 March 1966.

Labour Government from increasing its parliamentary majority from six to a hundred. And it has similarly often been noted that while the vast majority of American newspapers are Republican-oriented, the Democratic Party, in electoral terms, has not suffered particularly as a result. Again, the Gaullist control of television and the conservative bias of the larger part of the French press did not prevent the opposition from making substantial electoral gains in a number of elections,[1] just as the even more pronounced anti-communist bias of most of that press at all times has not prevented the Communist Party from retaining a remarkably stable share of popular support; and the same point applies even more strongly to the Italian Communist Party. It is simply not the case that the mass media can be counted on to deliver the votes to the conservative camp.

Nor, in larger ideological and cultural terms, is it realistic to believe that nonconformity and dissent can be finally nailed on television aerials. In the article already quoted, Professor Lazarsfeld and Professor Merton speak of the 'narcotising dysfunction' of the mass media.[2] The reason why they speak of 'dysfunction', they explain, is based 'on the assumption that it is not in the interests of modern complex society to have large masses of the population politically apathetic and inert'.[3] This is a very large assumption. For whatever may be 'the interests of modern complex society', it is certainly in the interests of dominant classes in advanced capitalist societies that very large masses of the population *should* be politically apathetic and inert, at least in regard to issues which are, from the point of view of these classes, politically dangerous. But while the purpose of the mass media may be a 'narcotising' one, their impact, from this point of view, may leave much to be desired. Indeed, that impact may be the reverse of the one intended. Thus, the portrayal by American television of daily slaughter in Vietnam was certainly not intended to arouse feelings of revulsion for American intervention in that country. But it has probably played, all the same, a considerable part in opening the eyes of many people to the crimes that were being

---

[1] See, e.g. R. Rémond and C. Neuschwander, 'Télévision et Comportement Politique', in *Revue Française de Science Politique*, 1963, vol. 13.

[2] 'Mass Communication, Popular Taste and Organized Social Action', p. 464.

[3] *Ibid.*, p. 464.

committed in their name, and strengthened the resistance movement to the war. Similarly, television has in recent years
conveyed with dramatic effect an international pattern of police
violence against demonstrators (and others) which has brought
home to millions of viewers one important aspect of state power,
whose display 'the authorities' have often found embarrassing.

This, however, is not what television is intended to achieve.
Mr Hood has also suggested that 'one of the broadcasters' main
difficulties when dealing with controversy springs from the
tendency of viewers to seek primarily from the medium confirmation of their own strongly held attitudes'; and he suggests
that 'this general law holds good for all parts of the political
spectrum whether the viewers are tough or soft, radical or
conservative'.[1] This is rather ingenuous. For while the 'general
law' may well hold good, the important point is that there is
immeasurably more about television, public and commercial,[2]
to confirm conservative-minded viewers in *their* attitudes than
is the case for 'radical' ones; as far as the latter are concerned,
television, in any serious meaning of the word 'radical', is a
permanent exercise in dissuasion.

But even if this is discounted, and even if it is true that 'what
we know in general about the mass communication media
indicates that they are much more important in confirming or
reinforcing existing opinions than they are in changing
opinions',[3] the advantage this affords to the established order
is still considerable, since its purpose must precisely be to
prevent a radical shift away from 'existing opinions' which are
predominantly cast in a conformist mould. The mass media
cannot ensure complete conservative attunement; nothing can.
But they can and do contribute to the fostering of a climate of
conformity, not by the total suppression of dissent, but by the
presentation of views which fall outside the consensus as curious
heresies, or, even more effectively, by treating them as irrelevant
eccentricities, which serious and reasonable people may dismiss as of no consequence. This is very 'functional'.

[1] Hood, *A Survey of Television*, p. 63.
[2] 'The advent of commercial television, so runs the legend, was to bring into
British television a brash, classless, nose-thumbing spirit. Now under the aegis of
the ITA, it is more closely shackled to the Establishment than the BBC, being more
conformist, more conservative, less adventurous' (*ibid.*, p. 62).
[3] L. Epstein, *Political Parties in Western Democracies*, 1967, p. 237.

III

However much argument there may be about the actual political influence of the mass media, or about their bias, or whether they have any marked bias at all, no one would deny that they have a concern with politics, and that they play *some* part in the political process of advanced capitalist societies. There would be no such agreement about the character of education in these societies. On the contrary, the view most commonly and most strongly held about education is that 'politics has no place in it', and that political indoctrination of any kind ought to be, and indeed is, utterly alien and abhorrent to educational theory and practice in Western-type regimes.

On any serious consideration however, neither the practice nor even the theory are quite so straightforward.

In the case of education even more than in that of the mass media, it is essential to make a distinction between political indoctrination in a narrow, explicit and party sense, and a much broader, more general and diffuse degree of 'political socialisation'. As for the first, it may readily be granted that schools and teachers do generally – though by no means always – try to steer clear of overt party bias and cling, in this sense, to a formal stance of impeccable political neutrality. In the second and broader sense, on the other hand, schools may or may not *consciously* engage in 'political socialisation' but cannot in any case avoid doing so, mostly in terms which are highly 'functional' to the prevailing social and political order. In other words, educational institutions at all levels generally fulfil an important conservative role and act, with greater or lesser effectiveness, as legitimating agencies in and for their societies.

There is one type of school in which this function, far from being performed furtively, or from being shunned, has always constituted one of its main and stated purposes. These are the schools which cater mainly for the children of the privileged classes, and of which the public schools in England are the pre-eminent example. 'Taken together', it has been remarked, 'the attitudes and values inculcated by the Victorian public schools

very nearly comprise a definition of conservatism'.[1] That
definition may have undergone modifications in content and
emphasis over the years but the bias remains. Today as in the
past, elite schools consciously seek to instil into their charges a
conservative philosophy whose themes remain tradition,
religion, nationalism, authority, hierarchy and an exceedingly
narrow view of the meaning of democracy, not to speak of a
marked hostility to socialist ideas and purposes. Here as in
many other cases, the process of indoctrination may have its
failures, but not for want of trying.

Nor should the point be overlooked that these elite schools
exercise a considerable influence on many less exalted educational institutions; in England, for instance, the public school
purpose and spirit, and even its customs and traditions, have
often been aped by 'ordinary' grammar schools, and served as
shining exemplars for much of the whole educational system.

Until the relatively recent past, moreover, it was not only the
public schools which were conceived as agencies of indoctrination; so, to a large extent, were the schools for 'the masses'.[2]
Such education had more than one purpose; but not the least
important of these was to instil in those subjected to it a sub-
missive acceptance of the social order of which they were, no
doubt with exceptions, destined to form the base.

It is only with the growing strength of labour movements, the
extension of political rights, the rise of important working-class
parties, the coming into being of 'popular politics' and the
irresistible spread of a democratic and egalitarian rhetoric, that
the school too came to support and propagate a concept of
'democratic citizenship' at odds with an earlier concept of 'my
station and its duties'.

This, however, does not mean that the schools ceased to be
agencies of 'political socialisation' and of affirmation of the
status quo. It means rather that they came to perform this role
much less explicitly and directly though not necessarily less
effectively.

The legitimation of the social order by the school system in

---

[1] R. Wilkinson, *The Prefects*, 1964, p. 110.
[2] See, e.g., D. V. Glass, 'Education' in M. Ginsberg (ed.), *Law and Opinion in
England in the 20th Century*, 1959, pp. 324ff; and H. Silver, *The Concept of Popular
Education*, 1965.

advanced capitalist countries may be said to proceed at three levels, which are closely related, but which it is useful to distinguish for the purpose of analysis.

In the first instance, education, as far as the vast majority of working-class children are concerned, performs an important *class-confirming* role. Professor Talcott Parsons has described the school as 'an agency through which individual personalities are trained to be motivationally and technically adequate to the performance of adult roles ... the socialisation function may be summed up as the development in individuals of the commitments and capacities which are essential prerequisites of their future role-performance'.[1] But while the point itself is perfectly valid, the formulation of it is an excellent example of ideological obfuscation. For what the vocabulary obscures is the fact that, for most working-class children, the 'commitments and capacities' which their schools 'develop' (a word which is not, in its concrete context, without ironic connotations) are those appropriate to a 'future role-performance' as low-skilled wage-earners. It is obviously true that the schools, for some children of the working classes, are a means of upward mobility: after all, advanced capitalist society does need to draw on a constantly larger pool of more or less trained personnel. For the vast majority, however, the schools play a crucial role in *confirming* their class destiny and status. They do so, most effectively, by virtue of the starved education which they provide and by the *curtailment* rather than the 'development' of further educational opportunities which, combined with unfavourable environmental circumstances, they ensure. And the very fact that some working-class children are able to surmount these handicaps serves to foster the notion that those who do not are themselves, because of their own unfitness, the architects of their own lowly fate, and that their situation is of their own making. The educational system thus conspires to create the impression, not least among its victims, that social disadvantages are really a matter of personal, innate, God-given and insurmountable incapacity. As two French writers put it, 'l'autorité légitimatrice de l'Ecole peut redoubler les

---

[1] T. Parsons, 'The School Class as a Social System: Some of its Functions in American Society', in Halsey, Floud and Anderson (eds.), *Education, Economy, Society*, pp. 434–5.

inégalités sociales parce que les classes les plus défavorisées, trop conscientes de leur destin et trop inconscientes des voies par lesquelles il se réalise, contribuent par là à sa réalisation'.[1] Not only do *others* believe, in Aristotelian fashion, that the fact of slavery proves that some men are natural slaves; large numbers of the latter's modern equivalents believe it too, and also believe in consequence that they are the prisoners, not of a social system, but of an ineluctable fate.

At a second level, this sense of personal inadequacy is powerfully reinforced by the fact that for the majority of working-class children education, such as it is, is experienced as an imposition of an alien culture, values and even language,[2] as an almost traumatic disjunction from family and environment. 'The teacher in Britain', one writer notes, 'has become an agent by which the attempt is made to transmit the typical middle-class values. Since the educational system did not grow from the community, but was imposed from above, it is the values of those in positions of higher status that were considered, usually unconsciously, as worth inculcating'.[3] And for the United States, Margaret Mead has suggested that 'when the American hears the word "school-teacher" ... he will think of a grade-school teacher who teaches perhaps the third or fourth grade; this teacher will be a woman of somewhat indeterminate age, perhaps in the middle thirties, neither young nor old, of the middle class, and committed to the ethics and manners of a middle-class world';[4] and 'the teacher in the overcrowded city school', she adds, 'teaches her pupils to acquire habits of hygiene and of industry, to apply themselves diligently to prepare to succeed, and to make the sacrifices necessary to success, to turn a deaf ear to the immediate impulse, to shatter any tradition which seems to block the path to the

[1] Bourdieu and Passeron, *Les Héritiers*, p. 117.

[2] For which, see e.g. B. Bernstein, 'Some Sociological Determinants of Perception', in *British Journal of Sociology*, 1958, vol. 9, no. 2 and 'Language and Social Class', *ibid.*, 1960, vol. 11, no. 3. Two French authors also note that 'à une époque où le travail collectif prend une importance considérable, le système d'enseignment est encore centré sur la réussite individuelle, sur une forte valorisation des qualités d'expression et d'abstraction, plus développés chez les enfants d'origine bourgeoise' (Bon and Burnier, *Les Nouveaux Intellectuels*, p. 259).

[3] P. W. Musgrave, *The Sociology of Education*, 1965, p. 227.

[4] M. Mead, *The School in American Culture*, 1951, p. 5.

goal, *but to shatter it in a way and with the sanctions of the entre-preneur*.[1] The idea is to 'integrate' the working-class child into the *given* society; those who are 'bright' are helped to prepare their escape from their working-class condition; the rest are helped to accept their subordination.

That help, at a third level, tends to assume a fairly strong ideological and political form. The educational system does not merely seek to instil 'middle-class values' in general, but a rather more particular view of the given society and of the world. Durkheim once stressed the need which society had of socialisation through education in terms of the transmission of 'fundamental values', what he called 'essential principles' – 'the respect of reason, of science, of the ideas and sentiments which are at the root of democratic morality'.[2] He was no doubt right; societies do need to transmit 'fundamental values' and 'essential principles'. The point however is that the values and principles which are generally deemed 'fundamental' and 'essential' are those which are sanctioned by the dominant forces in society; and 'democratic morality' can, without too much difficulty, be adapted to profoundly conformist ends.

Professor Dore has, in relation to Japan, written in contrasting terms of 'national unity' and 'class division', and noted that 'the modern Japanese educational system has worked in a number of ways to prevent the development of class consciousness in Japan'.[3] But much the same, despite differences of approach, culture and traditions, may also be said of other advanced capitalist countries. Mr Martin Mayer, for instance, has noted about American education that 'there are many different ways to assert ethnocentricity – to insist that the best place is here, and the best people is us. Except in moments of crisis, the community does not care how the assertion is made, but there must be no nonsense about making it'.[4] And making it, it should be noted, does not require instructions and directives from a Ministry of Education. Lesser educational authorities also play their part, particularly in times of crisis.[5] And

[1] *Ibid.*, p. 25 (My italics).

[2] E. Durkheim, *Education et Sociologie*, 1922, p. 62.

[3] R. E. Ward and D. W. Rustow (eds.), *Political Modernization in Japan and Turkey*, 1964, p. 199.   [4] Mayer, *The Schools*, p. 48.

[5] Robert Hutchins quotes the following passages 'from a letter addressed to all the teachers in a Middle Western city by the superintendent of schools, who,

even without any instructions and directives, the schools themselves, though with important differences in the degree of
emphasis and shrillness, are willing to involve themselves in the
nationalist celebration, not in opposition to but in defence of
'democratic morality'. It was said in the previous chapter that
nationalism has been a powerful force in sustaining capitalist
regimes; the schools have been an important channel for its dissemination and for the internalisation of values associated with it.

What other elements of conservative ideology are particularly stressed varies from country to country. In the United
States, it has been noted that 'through its schools the society
teaches the dominant economic ideology in America, a variant
of capitalism [*sic*] often called the free enterprise system'.[1]
In regard to Italy, it has been said that the educational system

... retains a strong Roman Catholic orientation. Highly centralised under a Ministry of Public Instruction in Rome, it still serves to
inculcate a system of values that is more attuned to conservative
Catholic, even Fascistic, doctrine than the central idea of the 'new
deal' approach to social, political, and economic problems that is
favoured by the left wing of Christian Democracy. It need scarcely
be added that the schools – largely staffed with teachers who are
pro-Catholic – are anything but breeding grounds for the political
ideas of the extreme Left.[2]

Yet while the emphasis and the content may vary, the total
message is one of attunement to and acceptance of the prevailing economic and social order, and of its main institutions and
values. The schools may not always *induce* acceptance of the
prevailing system of power; but they *teach* it, in a multitude

under the law of the state, has the power to oust any of them from their jobs':
'The threat to American institutions by international Communism makes imperative
that greater emphasis be given in our schools to the study of the meaning, significance and the value of American Democracy. Indoctrination has never been in
good repute among educationalists in the United States ... It now appears necessary for the schools in the United States to indoctrinate American youth for
American Democracy ... In our present confused world, it is essential that we
teach our young people that American Democracy is the best government in the
world and that we explain why it is the best ... They must understand that
American Democracy was founded on private enterprise and that this economic
system has brought forth a great and powerful nation which will continue to grow
even stronger by perpetuating and protecting private enterprise' (*Freedom, Education and the Fund*, p. 110).

[1] R. J. Havighurst and B. L. Neugarten, *Society and Education*, 1957, p. 146.
[2] La Palombara, *Interest Groups in Italian Politics*, p. 68.

of both diffuse and specific ways. Of course exceptions to this pattern are to be found everywhere. But they *are* exceptions to a pattern of general conformity.

One important reason for this is that in all systems of education, whether centralised or not, those responsible for the appointment of teachers and headmasters are normally concerned to avoid the recruitment of teachers, and even more so of headmasters, who may be too acutely 'controversial'; and while this does not only cover politics, it certainly includes 'controversial' political views and mainly means advanced left-wing views.

One country where this has most notably affected recruitment is the United States, where

... in the period after 1945, several states passed laws requiring non-membership in the Communist Party or in the organisations that were designated by the Attorney-General as subversive. One effect of such requirements is to bar from teaching a few people who may hold subversive political views. Another effect is to bar from teaching a larger number whose political and economic views, when judged a few years earlier or a few years later, might be seen neither as subversive nor dangerous, but merely as unpopular or non-conformist.[1]

But whether institutionalised or not, and with many different degrees of strictness, the bias everywhere naturally and inevitably operates against teachers whose views and attitudes fail to conform to prevailing modes of thought; and the knowledge or even the suspicion that the bias exists, and may very adversely affect career prospects, is itself a powerful inducement to the avoidance of views and activities which would cause offence or displeasure to superior authority. The inducement is often and honourably resisted. But there is no strong evidence that teachers are in general more immune from it than other men and women.

IV

Attention, in the context of the present chapter, must also be paid to universities. There are of course many obvious and

[1] Havighurst and Neugarten, *Society and Education*, p. 267.

profound differences between the schools, not to speak of the mass media, on the one hand, and universities on the other. But there are also, in relation to the legitimation process, more similarities between them than many academics would readily admit, or than many would perhaps even be aware of. For universities do, in a variety of ways, play an important part in that process. This is not their main function, just as it is not the explicit function of the schools or the mass media. But it is a function which with different degrees of intensity and success they do nevertheless perform, and it is the more necessary to stress it because so much that is said and written about the 'role of the university in the modern world' obscures the fact. In part, they perform that function because of the external pressures and influences to which they are subjected; and in part also, independently of these pressures.

There is no dispute about the fact – it is indeed the merest commonplace – that with the exception of some private institutions of higher learning, notably in the United States, the universities are very largely dependent upon the state for finance in the pursuit of their main activities, namely teaching and research. One obvious consequence of that fact is that the state has come to have an increasing say, directly or indirectly, in the manner in which the universities use the funds which are allotted to them. For the United States, Professor Clark Kerr has noted that, in 1960, 'higher education received about 1·5 billion [dollars] from the federal government – a hundredfold increase in twenty years';[1] and he further observes that 'clearly, the shape and nature of university research are profoundly affected by federal monies'.[2] Indeed, in his valedictory 'military-industrial complex' speech, President Eisenhower went as far as to suggest that 'the free university, historically the fountainhead of free ideas and scientific discovery, has experienced a revolution in the conduct of research. Partly because of the huge cost involved, a government contract becomes virtually a substitute for intellectual curiosity'.[3] This is probably somewhat overdrawn; more apposite is the notion that a government contract, and subsidies generally, tend to *direct* intellectual

[1] Clark Kerr, *The Uses of the University*, 1963, p. 53.
[2] *Ibid.*, p. 53.   [3] Quoted in Cook, *The Warfare State*, p. 3.

curiosity in certain fields rather than in others, notably that of 'defence'. The point also applies in full measure to universities in other countries; the state everywhere now plays an important, even a decisive part in determining how, both in teaching and research, universities may play their part in 'serving the community'. Thus, quite apart from the government itself, the University Grants Committee in Britain has come to assume a much more positive role than in the past and now views it as its task 'to assist, in consultation with the universities and other bodies concerned, the preparation and execution of such plans for the development of the universities as may from time to time be required to ensure that they are fully adequate to national needs'.[1] The degree of control, intervention and direction which this implies may confidently be expected to grow.

But while such a development is inevitable, and may in certain limited respects be even deemed desirable, it has also in the particular context in which it occurs certain important implications which advocates of state intervention tend to ignore.[2] Professor Clark Kerr also suggests that 'the university has become a prime instrument of national purpose';[3] and this is echoed by a former Rector of the University of Orléans, who speaks of the university as the 'collectivité responsable de la mission la plus essentielle à l'avenir national – avec la Défense *et faisant d'ailleurs de plus en plus partie de celle-ci*'.[4] But the 'national purpose' or the 'mission' of which the universities become an instrument, 'prime' or otherwise, is something to the determination of which they themselves, as universities, naturally make no contribution. In other words, what they serve is, using the word literally, an alien purpose, that of the state. And not only do they serve it; by so doing, they identify themselves with it, and accept it as legitimate, worthy of support.

Universities and their spokesmen very often seek to eschew such an explicit commitment. Lord Robbins, in an address delivered to the assembly of European rectors and vice-chancellors at Göttingen in 1964 may well have been expressing

[1] W. Mansfield Cooper, 'Change in Britain', in W. Mansfield Cooper *et al.*, *Governments and the University*, 1966, p. 7.

[2] See, e.g., R. O. Berdahl, 'University-State Relations Re-examined', in P. Halmos (ed.), *Sociological Studies in British University Education*, 1963.

[3] Kerr, *The Uses of the University*, p. 87.

[4] G. Antoine and J. C. Passeron, *La Réforme de l'Université*, 1966, p. 25. (my italics).

a common sentiment when he said that the duty of universities was to advance

> ... the habit of social judgement in terms of consequences rather than categories. We must assess the value of actions, not in terms of pre-established classification according to this or that *a priori* ethic, but rather in terms of their effect on human happiness. We must teach that the maxim, *let justice be done if the skies fall*, comes from the childhood of the race; and that, on any civilised assessment, the falling of the skies is one of the consequences which have to be taken into account before we can say whether a certain course of action is, or is not, just.[1]

But the 'civilised assessment' of which Lord Robbins speaks is much more likely to be interpreted in conservative ways than in dissenting ones. On the whole, the university, as an institution, has seldom refused to serve the 'national purpose', as defined by the state, and has found it relatively easy to rationalise its acceptance in terms of its own proclaimed ideals. From this point of view, the notion that universities, as distinct from some of those who work in them, are centres of dissent is a piece of mythology. If anything, the university, including the majority of its teachers, has always tended, particularly in times of great national crisis, and precisely when acute moral issues were involved, to take a poor view of its dissenters, staff and students, and quite often to help the state by acting against them. As Professor MacIver has noted, 'there is no evidence to confirm the charge that educators are markedly radical. On the contrary, such evidence as we have suggests that they tend on the whole to the conservative side'.[2] This is not to underestimate the minority, sometimes the sizeable minority, which has, as in the United States in regard to the war in Vietnam, refused to identify itself with the 'national purpose' as defined by the state. In fact, that minority everywhere is now probably larger, proportionately, than at any time in the past. As higher education expands to meet the needs of the economic system, so does it also come to include more and more teachers who do conceive their vocation as requiring them to insist that 'let justice be done if the skies fall', and who do therefore find themselves at odds with an unjust society and

[1] Lord Robbins, *The University in the Modern World*, 1966, p. 15 (italics in text).
[2] R. MacIver, *Academic Freedom in our Time*, 1955, p. 132.

with a state which expresses its injustices. Nevertheless, it is still the case that the great majority of academics in these countries have found little or no difficulty in reconciling their vocation with support for the 'national purpose', whatever that purpose may have been.[1] Indeed, many American academics have been not only willing but eager to place their skills at the service of *any* policy their government has chosen to pursue. As Professor Riesman has noted, 'American scholars, despite our country's tradition of pluralism and foreign study, are for the most part readily enlisted in an era of total war and total loyalty'.[2] But it bears repeating that academics elsewhere are no different, in this respect, from their American counterparts – American academics have only, in recent years, had greater opportunities.

This points to another large change which has come over university life. Not only is the state more involved in the university; academics are also immeasurably more involved than ever before in the life of the state. Lord Bowden has said of the United States that

... dons are everywhere in Washington – they run the science policy committees, they advise the president himself and most of his department heads ... The universities themselves are an essential component of this new machine. The system depends on free and frequent interchange of staff between the government, business and the academic world.[3]

Quoting this, Professor McConnell has a comment which seems singularly apposite:

In this interchange [he writes] ... the universities have almost certainly lost some of their prerogative to criticise, some of their freedom to speak out on controversial political and economic issues. President Clark Kerr of the University of California, as did President Eisenhower when he left office, warned that the alliance between industry and the Department of Defence might exert excessive influence on national policy. President Kerr might also have

[1] For a useful discussion of the moral and political postures of American social scientists in recent years, see T. Roszak (ed.), *The Dissenting Academy*, 1967; C. W. Mills, *The Sociological Imagination*, 1959; and P. Lazarsfeld and W. Thielens Jr, *The Academic Mind. Social Scientists in a Time of Crisis*, 1958.

[2] D. Riesman, *Constraint and Variety in American Education*, 1956, p. 90.

[3] T. R. McConnell, 'Governments and University – A Comparative Analysis', in Mansfield Cooper *et al.*, *Governments and the University*, pp. 89–90.

warned of the possible dangers to the integrity of the university from the military-industrial-university complex.[1]

This is not, it should be clear, simply a matter of academics producing material which may be of use in the determination of public policy, but of the assumption by academics of an official role, of their entry into government service on a part-time or, temporarily, on a full-time basis. There may well be academics whose independence of mind and whose critical powers – assuming they were there in the first place – are not eroded by this involvement with the world of office and power. But it is at least as likely that, for most academics, that involvement produces an 'understanding' of the 'problems' of government which makes for a kind of 'responsible' criticism that bears a remarkable resemblance to more or less sophisticated apologetics. Such men are often senior and eminent academics; their contribution to the 'officialisation' of university thought and behaviour ought not to be underestimated.

Apart from the state, the most important influence on universities is that of the business world. This is so for many reasons. For one thing, more and more academics are now drawn into that world as consultants and advisers; and just as those academics who are involved with the state may be expected to import into their universities a 'responsible' appreciation of the official point of view, so may those who have close contact with the world of business be expected to exhibit, in their work as academics, a lively appreciation of the virtues and purposes of private enterprise. Like their 'officialised' colleagues in relation to government, they too are most likely to show an acute 'understanding' of the 'problems' of business. As Professor McConnell puts it in regard to both:

> Some of the dangers of allying the university with government and industry are obvious. Others are subtle. I believe a careful study would show that, increasingly, the values of the academic man have become the values of the market place or the governmental arena and not the values of the free intellect. The age of faculty and university affluence has exalted economic advantage at the expense of human and humane values.[2]

[1] *Op. cit.*, p. 90.   [2] *Op. cit.*, pp. 90–1.

Secondly, private institutions of higher learning, notably in the United States, are largely dependent for financial support on wealthy individuals, either businessmen or others, and on corporate enterprise. But even universities which rely mainly on financial support from the state find benefactions, gifts and endowments very useful, and these similarly come mainly from the world of business and from members of the dominant classes. The largesse which private benefactors have displayed towards universities has often been celebrated as a tangible proof of the sense of social responsibility and 'soulfulness' of corporations, and of wealthy men generally. But however this may be, the impact of such benefactions, and the knowledge that they are to be had, is not likely to produce among the actual or potential recipients an attitude of critical independence towards the benefactors or towards the activities which make the benefactions possible in the first place. Thus a Business School largely endowed by business, and whose teachers enjoy a close and cordial relation to the world of business, cannot be expected to find much that is radically wrong with private enterprise – even though the endowment is altogether without strings. Similarly a university research project sponsored and financed by business is most likely to be conducted within the framework of assumptions and values of the 'business community'; and its results are equally unlikely to be of a kind acutely displeasing to the sponsors.

Thirdly, businessmen and other 'leaders of the community', whose ideological dispositions are not likely to run to radicalism, dominate the boards of trustees, regents or governors in whom the ultimate control of universities is vested; and while the point has been most often made in regard to the United States, it applies with equal force to other systems where lay governors play a role in institutions of higher learning. For the United States, Professor MacIver has noted that 'in the non-governmental institutions, the typical board member is associated with large-scale business, a banker, manufacturer, business executive, or prominent lawyer. His income falls in a high bracket'.[1] An older study, published in 1947, noted also that the 734 trustees of thirty leading universities were 'divided about equally between the professions on the one hand, and

[1] MacIver, *Academic Freedom in Our Time*, p. 78.

proprietors, managers and officials on the other'. Of the latter group, 'bankers, brokers and financiers' and 'manufacturing entrepreneurs and executives' were by far the largest group; and for the professional group, lawyers and judges were the largest element, followed by clergymen.[1] As far as known party preferences are concerned, 61 per cent were Republicans and 35 per cent Democrats, the likelihood being that the percentage of Republicans was higher for the total group.[2] This study was based upon the years 1934–5. But, as Professor Domhoff has recently argued,[3] 'there is no reason to believe that the dominance of the elite universities by members of the power elite has diminished' in the intervening years.

The degree of actual control of university life which this 'dominance' entails no doubt greatly varies, and may well in normal circumstances be of a formal kind. But circumstances often tend not to be normal; and whatever that degree of control may be at any time, the influence of lay governors is almost certain to be exercised in conservative directions, and to reinforce in whatever measure is possible the conformist tendencies of the university.[4]

Moreover, in so far as university heads, administrators and teachers are susceptible to other 'outside' influences, these influences are also likely to encourage such tendencies. To quote Professor MacIver again, 'our colleges and even more our schools are the targets of a tremendous volume of protestations, charges and appeals'.[5] He might have added that such protestations, charges and appeals are seldom if ever based on the view that universities are too conservative; it is for their liberalism and their 'leniency' towards the dissenters in their midst that university authorities must expect, particularly in times of crisis, to come under attack from the press and a variety

[1] H. P. Beck, *Men Who Control our Universities*, 1947, pp. 51ff.

[2] *Ibid.*, p. 103.

[3] Domhoff, *Who Rules America?*, p. 79.

[4] A distinguished American educator wrote in 1930 that 'their indirect and, I believe, largely unconscious influence may be and often is, however, considerable ... In the social and economic realms they create an atmosphere of timidity which is not without effect in critical appointments and in promotion' (A. Flexner, *Universities: American, English, German*, 1930, p. 180, in Beck, *Men Who Control Our Universities*, p. 34). This too is unlikely to have been rendered obsolete with the passage of the years.

[5] MacIver, *Academic Freedom in Our Time*, p. 62.

of other conservative forces – and not only in the United States.

Fourthly, the growth of corporate enterprise, quite apart from the influence of businessmen, has itself had a profound impact upon the universities. Professor Galbraith has observed that 'modern higher education is, of course, extensively accommodated to the needs of the industrial system';[1] and Mr William Whyte has demonstrated one aspect of this 'accommodation' by reference to the fact that, of all the American students who graduated in 1954–5, the largest single group of all (19·4 per cent), had been studying business and commerce, *'more than all of the men* in the basic sciences and the liberal arts put together. (And more than all the men in law and medicine and religion ...)'.[2] Other advanced capitalist countries have still a long way to go before business studies assume so prominent a place in their universities. But the proliferation of business administration departments, industrial relations departments, graduate business schools and the like suggests that some of the ground at least is being made up.

There is one characteristic of this type of study which is seldom accorded the attention which it deserves, namely that what it provides for its students is not simply a training in the 'techniques of management' and other assorted skills, but also a training in the ideology, values and purposes of capitalist enterprise. Those engaged in such studies, as teachers and students, may conceivably be pursuing the kind of intellectual inquiry which is supposed to be the characteristic of university work: but they are also the servants of a cult, the cult of Mammon.

The university also 'accommodates' itself to the demands of business in other ways. 'In some cases', Mr Whyte has also noted, 'the business demand has also influenced them in the type of man they favour in the selection of students and the awarding of scholarships. One dean of freshmen told me that in screening applicants from secondary schools he felt it was only common sense to take into account not only what the college wanted but what, four years later, corporations' recruiters would want'.[3] In this respect too, other advanced capitalist

---

[1] Galbraith, *The New Industrial State*, pp. 370–1.

[2] W. H. Whyte, Jr., *The Organisation Man*, 1956, p. 88 (italics in text). See also his chapter 8, 'Business Influence on Education'.

[3] Whyte, *The Organisation Man*, p. 116.

countries may be lagging behind. But here too there is every reason to believe that universities and their students are becoming increasingly aware of the requirements of business, not only in technical but also in ideological terms.

It is in this perspective that the role of universities as teaching institutions must be set. Both in the appointment of their teachers and in the content of their teaching, universities in the countries of advanced capitalism do retain a very wide degree of formal and actual autonomy – very often an all but absolute autonomy. But that autonomy all the same is exercised within a particular economic, social and political context which deeply affects the universities. This is not to suggest that university authorities and teachers are the bullied victims of outside pressures who are only allowed to exercise their autonomy on condition that they do not do so in ways which offend the powers that be. It may sometimes be so. But it is much more often the case that both university authorities and teachers endorse the context, are *part* of it, and exercise their autonomy in ways which are congruent with that context, not because they are compelled to do so but because they themselves are moved by conformist modes of thought. Thus, in an address delivered in 1961 to the Alumni Association of Harvard and entitled 'The Age of the Scholar', we find Dr Pusey, then President of Harvard, defending his Economics Faculty and other teachers in the following terms:

Can anyone seriously charge that these men and the others in their departments are subverting the American way of life? And can one seriously charge the same of the university as a whole, taking note of its programme in history, government, public administration and social relations, and its far-reaching effort in business, which is almost completely directed toward making the private enterprise system continue to work effectively and beneficially in a very difficult world?[1]

There are some who might find this kind of grovelling utterly incompatible with the ideals associated with a university. But there is nothing to suggest that its expression did violence to

[1] N.M. Pusey, *The Age of the Scholar*, 1963, p. 171. It may be stressed that this address *was* delivered in 1961, and not at the height of the McCarthy era.

Dr Pusey's ideas and beliefs, or that he was not presenting an accurate view of the ideology of his teachers.

The point is directly relevant to the appointments policies of the universities. For the tragedy of American universities in the McCarthy era – and after – is not only that many of them were debarred from employing communists and other 'subversives'; an equal or even greater tragedy, is that they mostly found little difficulty in endorsing 'loyalty' requirements; and that those who were not so debarred used their autonomy and freedom in appointments similarly to exclude such men and often to get rid of them if they had them. It is illuminating in this respect to follow the tortured hesitations of as liberal and humane a university administrator as Dr Hutchins. On the one hand, 'convinced and able Marxists on the faculty may be necessary if the conversation about Marxism is to be anything but hysterical and superficial'. On the other, 'it may be said that a Marxist cannot think [*sic*] and that therefore he is not eligible for membership in a university community according to my definition of it. *I admit that the presumption is to that effect.*' But then yet again, 'I must add that regarding the presumption as irrefutable comes dangerously close to saying that anybody who does not agree with me cannot think'. And after seeking to draw a distinction between good members of the Communist Party (i.e. those who, despite the 'strong presumption' that there are 'few fields in which a member of the Communist Party can think independently', yet may do so) and bad members (i.e. a communist who could not demonstrate his 'independence in the field in which he teaches and conducts his research'), Dr Hutchins goes on to say that:

Whether I would have had the courage to recommend to our board the appointment of a Marxist, or a bad member of the Communist Party, or a good member whose field was not affected by the Party line *is very dubious indeed.* But *in the most unlikely event* that such persons ever came over my academic horizon, *uniquely qualified* to conduct teaching and research in their chosen fields, I *ought to have had* the courage to say that they should be appointed without regard to their political views or associations.[1]

---

[1] Hutchins, *Freedom, Education and the Fund*, 1956, pp. 158–9 (my italics). Yet Dr Hutchins also regretfully notes that 'nobody would argue that all professors must be members of the Republican Party; but we seem to be approaching the point

Such criteria are sufficiently stringent to make it indeed 'most unlikely' that Dr Hutchins would have had an opportunity to test his 'courage'. At least Dr Hutchins had qualms. There have always been many others in a similar position to his whose behaviour has suggested that they suffered from fewer inhibitions.

But the matter, to repeat, is not only one of 'courage' in the face of external pressure. It is also, and outside the United States much more often, one of quite autonomous suspicion and hostility towards certain forms of intellectual or political unorthodoxy, easily rationalised into a sincerely held belief that such forms of unorthodoxy must, 'on academic grounds', at least cast grave doubt on a person's suitability for an academic post, particularly a senior academic post. Most academic economists, for instance, are likely to believe that Marxist economics is nonsense. Their reluctance to see a Marxist economist appointed in their department is therefore not, God forbid, based on anything as vulgar as prejudice, but on the view that no such person could conceivably be a 'good economist', not surprisingly since good economists are by definition not Marxists. Such processes of thought, and others akin to them, are a familiar part of the university scene in all advanced capitalist countries. They do not produce anything like an absolute bar on the appointment, and even on the promotion to senior posts, of acutely deviant academics. But they help in the formation of a climate in which certain deviant modes of thought and of political commitment find, to put it mildly, very little encouragement indeed – without any external pressure.

The fact that universities are on the whole strongly conformist institutions, most of whose teachers are likely to dwell in their ways of thought within the prevailing spectrum of consensus, cannot but affect the manner in which they fulfil their teaching function.

In the address already quoted, Lord Robbins told the European rectors and vice-chancellors that 'we are the universities of free societies; and nothing would be more alien to the spirit of such societies than that we should again become the

where they will all be required to be either Republicans or Democrats' (*ibid.*, p. 153).

instruments for the inculcation of particular dogmas or creeds'.[1] But, Lord Robbins added, 'there is, however, one exception to this rule. There is one creed which the free society cannot repudiate without decreeing its own abdication – the creed of freedom itself.'[2]

This is fine but the point needs to be taken further. For the creed of freedom is understood by many people who subscribe to it to include, and even to require, a certain view of the economic, social and political arrangements appropriate to a 'free society'; and this, not unnaturally, is very often accompanied by an exceedingly negative approach to all ideas which run counter to that view. In other words, if a man who subscribes to the creed of freedom also believes that free enterprise is an essential part of it, he will find abhorrent all theories of society which posit its abolition. On this view, the creed of freedom holds no guarantee that it will foster among its subscribers the 'habit of critical objectivity' which Lord Robbins sees as one of its basic ingredients.[3] After all, it is precisely in the name of freedom that many American universities have engaged, with the utmost sense of rectitude, in the virtual elimination, in terms of appointments, of certain forms of dissent. Mme Roland's bitter lament, 'Liberty, how many crimes have been committed in thy name', might here be rephrased to read, 'Freedom, how many orthodoxies have been defended in thy name', and in the name of democracy too.

There are certainly some important senses in which it is true to say that most universities in the countries of advanced capitalism are not 'instruments for the inculcation of particular dogmas or creeds'; in the sense for instance that neither teachers nor students are generally required to make obeisance to any particular doctrine, party or leader; in the sense that argument is not normally stifled, and is indeed often encouraged; and also because students, in most respectable university institutions, do have access to views and ideas different from and oppoesd to those offered them by most of their teachers.

These are indeed admirable and precious features of university life. Yet, without in the least belittling them, it has

---

[1] Robbins, *The Universites in the Modern World*, p. 14.
[2] *Ibid.*, p. 14.   [3] *Ibid.*, p. 15.

to be noted, in this as in other realms, that the pluralism and diversity which they suggest are not quite as luxuriant as they might at first sight appear to be. For while universities are centres of intellectual, ideological and political diversity, their students are mainly exposed to ideas, concepts, values and attitudes much more designed to foster acceptance of the 'conventional wisdom' than acute dissent from it. Many universities may harbour and make available to their students every conceivable current of thought; but everywhere too some currents are very much stronger than others.

Nevertheless, young men and women do often leave their university in a frame of mind more rebellious than when they entered it; and large numbers of students in all capitalist countries (and non-capitalist ones as well for that matter) have dramatically demonstrated that as agencies of socialisation universities have distinct limitations. Students are much more likely to be taught to understand the world in ways calculated to diminish rather than enhance their propensities to change it. Yet the purpose is often defeated by the determination of growing numbers of students to escape the conformist net woven for them by their elders.

This, however, does not affect the point that the pressures towards conformity generated by the university are very strong; and the degree to which universities do remain elite institutions tends to foster among many of those who have gained access to them, not least among students from the working classes, a sense of alienation from the subordinate classes and of empathy with the superior classes, which is not conducive to sustained rebelliousness. Nor certainly is the knowledge that such rebelliousness may well jeopardise the prospect of a career for which, in many cases, particularly in regard to children of the working classes, great personal and parental sacrifices have often been made. Even where such pressures, and many others, are resisted in the course of a university career, the stern expectations of the 'outside world' after graduation are such as to induce in many graduates a sense that rebelliousness and nonconformity are expensive luxuries with which it may be prudent to dispense until some future date. But very often, somehow, the future in this sense never comes; instead, erstwhile rebels, safely ensconced in one part or other of the 'real world', look back with a mixture of amusement and nostalgia at what they have come to see as youthful aberrations.

The question of the role of the universities in the legitimation process is in many ways connected with the more general question of the role of intellectuals (who may not, of course, be academics, just as all academics are not intellectuals) in the fashioning, as distinct from the transmission, of ideas and values.

In *The German Ideology*, Marx, it will be recalled, speaks of intellectuals as 'the thinkers of the [ruling] class (its active, conceptive ideologists, who make the perfecting of the illusion of the class about itself their chief source of livelihood)',[1] that illusion being the view of 'its interest as the common interest of all members of society, put in an ideal form; it [the ruling class] will give its ideas the form of universality, and represent them as the only rational, universally valid ones'.[2] This view of the function of intellectuals in bourgeois society is only partially qualified in *The Communist Manifesto* by the notion that 'in times when the class struggle nears the decisive hour ... a portion of the bourgeoisie goes over to the proletariat, and in particular, a portion of the bourgeois ideologists who have raised themselves to the level of comprehending theoretically the historical movement as a whole'.[3]

Since then, the world at large has tended to view the role of intellectuals in very different fashion indeed, and so have many intellectuals themselves. The word itself came into being at the time of the Dreyfus Affair, and was then used in a pejorative sense to describe some of those who refused to accept the national and patriotic view of the issue.[4] 'Intellectual' has ever since continued to bear the mark of its origin, and to be associated, not with an apologetic vocation, but with a dissenting one; and the role which many intellectuals have played in working-class movements and parties has greatly served to confirm this view. And so has the strong 'anti-intellectualist' bias which has been characteristic of most movements of the Right.

[1] Marx, *The German Ideology*, p. 40.   [2] *Ibid.*, p. 41.
[3] Marx and Engels, *The Communist Manifesto*, in *Selected Works*, vol. 1, pp. 41–2.
[4] L. Bodin and J. Touchard, 'Définitions, Statistiques et Problèmes', in *Les Intellectuels dans le Société Française Contemporaine, Revue Française de Science Politique*, 1959, vol. 9, no. 4, pp. 836ff.

But this view of the intellectual as a 'natural' dissenter is to a large extent an optical illusion, produced by the greater visibility of dissenting intellectuals, by the very fact that they stand out as dissenters. The real picture is rather different. Even those who most virulently attacked pro-Dreyfus intellectuals in the name of nationalism were often themselves intellectuals. As René Rémond observes, 'cet acharnement contre les intellectuels ne doit pas dissimuler que le nationalisme a lui-même un caractère intellectuel prononcé: ses pères sont des écrivains, Barrès, Maurras. Le nationalisme est pour une part une invention littéraire.'[1] The point may be taken much further. Not only is it intellectuels who have fashioned and formulated the various versions of conservative ideology – that after all is not surprising. More important is the fact that what may properly be described as conservative intellectuals have always greatly outnumbered dissenting ones. History mainly remembers the Voltaires, Rousseaus and Diderots; and thus makes it easier to forget that until quite late in the France of the Age of Reason, these men were not only fighting the Ancien Régime, but also the vast army of its *intellectual* supporters. So it has remained since then. And quite naturally, it is the intellectual supporters of every Ancien Régime who have access to the major means of ideological influence. As Professor Porter observes, 'By definition those intellectuals who are powerful within the ideological system are the traditionalists, the clerisy, the ideologists, the conservatives ... the utopians, the rebels, or the avant-garde find themselves more or less excluded from the means of communication, except under controlled situations when they are presented as curiosities'.[2]

However, the contribution of intellectuals to the stability of the existing social order – their role, in Gramsci's phrase, as 'experts in legitimation' – has assumed many other forms than the straightforward and explicit conservative defence of it.

Quite clearly, the greatest of all dangers to the capitalist system is that more and more people, particularly in the subordinate classes, should come to think as both possible and desirable an entirely different social order, based upon the social ownership of at least a predominant part of the means of

[1] R. Rémond, 'Les Intellectuels et la Politique', in *ibid.*, p. 870.
[2] J. Porter, *The Vertical Mosaic*, 1966, p. 493.

economic activity, and dedicated to the elimination of privilege and unequal power; and that 'the masses' should also seek to give expression to this belief in terms of political action.

The main purpose of the process of legitimation which has been described here is precisely to prevent the spread of such consciousness. But that purpose is not only served by the insistence on the virtues of the capitalist *status quo*. It is also served, at least as effectively, by criticism of many aspects of existing economic, social and political arrangements, coupled, however, with the rejection of the socialist alternative to them. That rejection may be based on many different grounds; for instance that the deficiencies of capitalist society, however real, are remediable within its ambit, and without recourse to revolutionary change; or that common ownership affords no guarantee of democracy and equality, which is true, and that it is not necessary to their achievement, which is not; that common ownership is in any case irrelevant to the problems of an 'industrial system', which has made the notion of 'capitalism' itself obsolete; and so on.

Provided the economic basis of the social order is not called into question, criticism of it, however sharp, can be very useful to it, since it makes for vigorous but safe controversy and debate, and for the advancement of 'solutions' to 'problems' which obscure and deflect attention from the greatest of all 'problems', namely that here is a social order governed by the search for private profit. It is in the formulation of a radicalism without teeth and in the articulation of a critique without dangerous consequences, as well as in terms of straightforward apologetics, that many intellectuals have played an exceedingly 'functional' role. And the fact that many of them have played that role with the utmost sincerity and without being conscious of its apologetic import has in no way detracted from its usefulness.

V

There is one last aspect of the process of legitimation to which reference must be made, and which is of crucial importance, since it underlies all others. This is the degree to which capitalism as an economic and social system tends to produce, in itself, by its very existence, the conditions of its legitimation in the subordinate classes, and in other classes as well.

In the classical Marxist scheme, it is precisely the reverse process which was held to occur: capitalism, out of its own contradictions and derelictions, breeds in the proletariat the conditions which makes it will its own emancipation from it. As Marx put it in 1867:

Along with the constantly diminishing number of the magnates of capital, who usurp and monopolise all advantages of this process of transformation, grows the mass of misery, oppression, slavery, degradation, exploitation; but with this too grows the revolt of the working class always increasing in numbers, and disciplined, united, organised by the very mechanism of the process of capitalist production itself.[1]

Since then, many people have derided these predictions as having been manifestly falsified by the evolution of capitalism, and attributed to that evolution the failure of the working classes to rise in revolt against it.

On the other hand, many others, notably on the Left, have found an explanation, or an additional explanation, of that failure, in the cultural hegemony of the dominant classes over the subordinate ones – in the manufacture, as it were, of a false consciousness by the former for the latter. And indeed, as has been argued in this and in the previous chapter, the control over the 'means of mental production' has been of great importance in legitimating capitalist rule.

Yet, the attribution of that legitimation to the ameliorative capacities of capitalism, which is a highly relative matter, or to the manipulative and persuasive powers of the dominant cultural apparatus, leaves something of major consequence out of account.

That something, as it happens, was noted by Marx himself, who wrote, also in *Capital*, that 'the advance of capitalist production develops a working class, which by education, tradition, habit, looks upon the conditions of that mode of production *as self-evident laws of nature* ... the dull compulsion of economic relations completes the subjection of the labourer to the capitalist'.[2]

---

[1] Marx, *Capital*, vol. 1, p. 763. [2] *Ibid.*, p. 737 (my italics).

Here, indeed, is 'socialisation', produced by the operation of the system itself and only enhanced by the legitimation process.

This 'natural' subordination does not, most emphatically, exclude the will to improve the conditions in which it occurs. But it does, in general, establish formidable mental barriers against the will to remove these conditions altogether. This is of course what Lenin meant when he wrote, in a famous passage of *What is to be Done?*, that 'the history of all countries shows that the working class, exclusively by its own effort, is able to develop only trade union consciousness'.[1]

The simple but crucial fact is that subordinate status tends, not always but more often than not, to breed its qualified acceptance rather than its total rejection. George Orwell wrote in 1937 that 'this business of petty inconvenience and indignity, of being kept waiting about, of having to do everything at other people's convenience, is inherent in working class life. A thousand influences constantly press a working man down into a *passive* role'.[2] The passage of some thirty years, for all the changes in working-class life which have been so loudly celebrated, has hardly pushed that observation into the realm of history.[3]

Moreover, classes, including the working classes, do not only reproduce themselves physically, but mentally as well, and tend to instil in their children the consciousness, expectations and mental habits associated with their class. Of all the socialisation functions which the family performs, there is none which is more 'functional' than this one; for in the present context, it means that the working-class family tends to attune its children in a multitude of ways to its own subordinate status. And even where, as is now ever more frequently the case, working-class parents are ambitious for their children, the success for which they hope and strive is mostly conceived in terms of integration at a higher level within the system and on the latter's own terms; and this is also most likely to lead them to try to persuade their children that the path to success lies not in rebellion

[1] V. I. Lenin, *What is to be Done?*, 1942, pp. 33–4.

[2] G. Orwell, *The Road to Wigan Pier*, 1937, p. 49 (italics in text).

[3] For a useful survey of recent European investigations in working-class 'resignation', see S. Herkommer 'Working Class Political Consciousness', in *International Socialist Journal*, 1965, vol. 2, no. 7.

against but in conformity to the values, prejudices and modes of thought of the world to which entry is sought.

In short, the condition of the working class is itself a major element in its 'political socialisation', and provides fertile ground for all the other forces which seek to enhance that process.

And yet, this is not by any means the whole of the story. Certainly the forces of attunement at work in advanced capitalist society, whether they are the result of deliberate striving or of the weight of the system itself, are indeed formidable. But this is not at all the same as saying that their combined impact is finally compelling, that they spell with inexorable finality the death-knell of socialist challenge, that they herald the arrival of 'one dimensional' man. They constitute one major factor in the equation of class conflict. But the hopes of some and the laments of others that they are powerful enough, together with the 'affluent society', to bring it to an end, to ensure the evacuation of the battlefield by the working classes, and to leave only small and easily manageable bands of guerillas on the terrain – all this constitutes a fundamental underestimation of the profoundly destabilising forces at work in capitalist society, and an equally fundamental overestimation of its capacity to cope with them. The realistic perspective which advanced capitalist societies offer is one not of attunement and stability, but of crisis and challenge. What this suggests for the character of their political regimes in the coming years is discussed in the next and last chapter.

9
Reform and Repression

The most important political fact about advanced capitalist societies, it has been argued in this book, is the continued existence in them of private and ever more concentrated economic power. As a result of that power, the men – owners and controllers – in whose hands it lies enjoy a massive preponderance in society, in the political system, and in the determination of the state's policies and actions.

Given this permanent preponderance, the familiar claim, indeed the familiar assumption, that these are countries which have long achieved political equality, whatever may be the case in regard to economic and social equality, constitutes one of the great myths of the epoch. Political equality, save in formal terms, is impossible in the conditions of advanced capitalism. Economic life cannot be separated from political life. Unequal economic power, on the scale and of the kind encountered in advanced capitalist societies, inherently *produces* political inequality, on a more or less commensurate scale, whatever the constitution may say.

Similarly, it is the capitalist context of generalised inequality in which the state operates which basically determines its policies and actions. The prevalent view is that the state, in these societies, can be and indeed mostly is the agent of a 'democratic' social order, with no inherent bias towards any class or group; and that its occasional lapse from 'impartiality' must be ascribed to some accidental factor external to its 'real' nature. But this too is a fundamental misconception: the state in these class societies is primarily and inevitably the guardian and protector of the economic interests which are dominant in them. Its 'real' purpose and mission is to ensure their continued predominance, not to prevent it.

However, the manner in which the state fulfils that role and the degree to which it manifests its bias differ greatly according to place and circumstance. The maintenance of a social order characterised by class domination may require the dictatorship of the state, the suppression of all opposition, the abrogation of all constitutional guarantees and political freedoms. But in the countries of advanced capitalism, it generally has not. With occasional and notable exceptions, class rule in these societies has remained compatible with a wide range of civil and political liberties; and their exercise has undoubtedly helped to mitigate the form and content of class domination in many areas of civil society. The main agent of that mitigation has been the state, which helps to explain why it has been able to present itself, and why it has been widely accepted, as the servant of society. In fact, this mitigating function does not abolish class rule and even serves, at a price, to guarantee it. But this does not detract from its importance to the subordinate classes.

It is perfectly true that civil and political liberties in advanced capitalist regimes have been severely circumscribed by the economic, social and political framework in which they have existed; that they have often been infringed in practice and, particularly in times of crisis, even more drastically narrowed; that constitutional guarantees have not prevented the systematic discrimination and oppression of such minorities as the black people in the United States; that the liberties enjoyed by the citizens of metropolitan capitalist countries were more often than not conspicuous by their absence in the territories which succumbed to imperialist occupation; and that, for all their democratic and liberal rhetoric, these regimes have shown themselves capable of massive crimes in the protection of sordid interests.

Yet, when all this and more has been said about the limits and contingent character of civic and political liberties under 'bourgeois democracy', and when the fact has been duly noted that some of these liberties are a mere cloak for class domination, it remains the case that many others have constituted an important and valuable element of life in advanced capitalist societies; and that they have materially affected the encounter between the state and the citizen, and between the dominant classes and the subordinate ones. It is a dangerous confusion to believe and claim that, because 'bourgeois freedoms' are inadequate and constantly threatened by erosion, they are therefore of no consequence. For all its immense limitations and hypocrisies, there is a wide gulf between 'bourgeois democracy' and the various forms of conservative authoritarianism, most notably Fascism, which have provided the alternative type of political regime for advanced capitalism. The point of the socialist critique of 'bourgeois freedoms' is not (or should not be) that they are of no consequence, but that they are profoundly inadequate, and need to be extended by the radical transformation of the context, economic, social and political, which condemns them to inadequacy and erosion.

Indeed the largest of all questions about Western-type regimes is how long their 'bourgeois-democratic' framework is likely to remain compatible with the needs and purposes of advanced capitalism; whether its economic, social and political contradictions are of such a kind as to render unworkable the political order with which it has, in general, hitherto been able to accommodate itself.

This was the question which was asked, with anxious insistence, about capitalist regimes in the late twenties and thirties, when Fascism and Nazism appeared to many people on the Left, and not only on the Left, to foreshadow the direction in which 'liberal capitalism' in many countries other than Italy and Germany was likely to travel. That question was, in subsequent decades, buried deep beneath the celebration of Western democracy, the free world, the welfare state, the affluent society, the end of ideology and pluralistic equilibrium. To have posed it again even a few years ago would have appeared ludicrous or perverse but at any rate distinctly obsolete. Whatever might be said about the economic, social and political deficiencies of Western capitalism (and the tendency was in any case to sing its praises, or rather the praises of 'post-capitalist' society), at least its 'democratic' and 'liberal' foundations were held to be secure and beyond challenge, save of course for the threat posed to them from the Left.

In the recent past, however, that old question has again come to the surface, and been posed with growing frequency, again by no means exclusively on the Left. Nor is this surprising, given the tendencies which advanced capitalism and the political system associated with it have increasingly exhibited. The point is not that 'bourgeois democracy' is imminently likely to move towards old-style Fascism. It is rather that advanced capitalist societies are subject to strains more acute than for a long time past, and that their inability to resolve these strains makes their evolution towards more or less pronounced forms of conservative authoritarianism more rather than less likely.

There are many reasons for taking this view of the political prospects of these societies. But the most fundamental of them all lies, by a fatal paradox, in their productive success. For as the material capacity of the economic system unfolds at an ever-increasing pace its immense promise of human liberation, so does its inability to match performance with promise become more blatant and obvious. The contradiction is not new: but it reveals itself more plainly with every productive and technological advance.

In order to fulfil their human potentialities, advanced industrial societies require a high degree of planning, economic coordination, the premeditated and rational use of material resources, not only on a national but on an international scale. But advanced capitalist societies cannot achieve this within the confines of an economic system which remains primarily geared to the private purposes of those who own and control its material resources.

Similarly, and relatedly, these societies require a spirit of sociality and cooperation from their members, a sense of genuine involvement and participation, which are equally unattainable in a system whose dominant impulse is private appropriation. It is forever said that industry is a partnership, a cooperative enterprise, a social venture, and so forth. This is certainly what it needs to be, yet which the very nature of the capitalist system renders impossible. The 'two sides of industry' remain two conflicting sides, in permanent and inevitable opposition. Indeed, the whole of society, steeped as it is in a miasma of competition and commercialism, is a battlefield, now more active, now less, but with no prospect of genuine peace.

No doubt, the transcendence of capitalism – in other words, the appropriation into the public domain of the largest part of society's resources – cannot by itself resolve all the problems associated with industrial society. What it can do, however, is to remove the greatest of all barriers to their solution, and at least create the *basis* for the creation of a rational and humane social order.

It is the need for this transcendence of capitalism which all the agencies of legitimation seek to obscure. Yet they cannot obscure the discrepancy between promise and performance. They cannot obscure the fact that, though these are rich societies, vast areas of bitter poverty endure in them; that the collective provisions they make for health, welfare, education, housing, the social environment, do not begin to match need; that the egalitarian ethos they are driven to proclaim is belied by the privileges and inequalities they enshrine; that the structure of their 'industrial relations' remains one of domination and subjection; and that the political system of which they boast is a corrupt and crippled version of a truly democratic order.

The consciousness of these discrepancies does not by any means automatically lead to a rejection of the social system which produces them; and even where it does lead to it, the rejection may often be in favour of pseudo-alternatives which are perfectly 'functional' and therefore self-defeating. In fact, experience has sufficiently shown that the translation of a consciousness of deep ills into a will for *socialist* change is a painful, complex, contradictory, 'molecular' process, which can be greatly retarded, deflected and distorted by an endless variety of factors of the kind which were discussed in earlier chapters.

Yet, a deep malaise, a pervasive sense of unfulfilled individual and collective possibilities penetrates and corrodes the climate of every advanced capitalist society. Notwithstanding all the talk of integration, *embourgeoisement*, and the like, never has that sense been greater than it is now; and never in the history of advanced capitalism has there been a time when more people have been more aware of the need for change and reform. Nor has there ever been a time when more men and women, though by no means moved by revolutionary intentions, have been more determined to act in the defence and the enhancement of their interests and expectations. The immediate target of their demands may be employers, or university authorities, or political parties. But as was noted at the very beginning of this study, it is the state which men constantly encounter in their relations with other men; it is towards the state that they are increasingly driven to direct their pressure; and it is from the state that they expect the fulfilment of their expectations.

Faced with this pressure, and conscious of the general malaise which produces it, power-holders respond in two ways. First, they proclaim their own will to reform. Never, it is safe to say, has the language of orthodox politics been more generous with words like reform, renewal, even revolution. No politician, however reactionary, is now simply 'conservative'. We may not all be socialists now: but we are all ardent social reformers. Much of the crusading rhetoric which is now part of the common currency of politics is no doubt utterly bogus. But some of it is not. It would be trivial to depict the men in whose hands state power lies as entirely indifferent to poverty, slums, unemployment, inadequate education, starved welfare services, social frustration, and many other ills which afflict their societies. To take such a view would be to engage in a crude and sentimental demonology, which conceals the real issue.

The trouble does not lie in the wishes and intentions of power-holders, but in the fact that the reformers, with or without inverted commas, are the prisoners, and usually the willing prisoners, of an economic and social framework which necessarily turns their reforming proclamations, however sincerely meant, into verbiage.

The point has often been made in regard to under-developed countries, for instance the countries of Latin America, that even if they were to receive wholly disinterested aid, which they do not, that aid would be stultified by the economic, social, political and administrative structures which dominate their existence, and which those who give the aid are indeed concerned to preserve. It is a point which has much validity in regard to state action for the purpose of reform in the context of advanced capitalism. For that action has to be confined within the structural limits created by the economic system in which it occurs. These are often described as the inevitable limits imposed upon state action by a 'democratic' political system: much more accurately, they are the limits imposed by property rights and unequal economic power, and which the state readily accepts and defends.

Reform, in such circumstances, is, of course, possible. But save in exceptional cases, when popular pressure is unusually strong, it is also stunted, inadequate, incapable of resolving the problems and removing the grievances which gave rise to the pressure for change in the first place. Even this kind of reform may help to mitigate some at least of the worst 'dysfunctionalities' of capitalist society; and, as has been stressed here repeatedly, this mitigation is indeed one of the most important of the state's attributions, an intrinsic and dialectical part of its role as the guardian of the social order. Nevertheless, reform always and necessarily falls far short of the promise it was proclaimed to hold: the crusades which were to reach 'new frontiers', to create 'the great society', to eliminate poverty, to abolish the class struggle, to assure justice for all, etc., etc. – the crusades regularly grind to a halt and the state comes under renewed and increased pressure.

In order to meet it, the state then exercises a second option, namely repression; or rather, reform and repression are tried simultaneously. These are not alternative options but complementary ones. However, as reform reveals itself incapable of subduing pressure and protest, so does the emphasis shift towards repression, coercion, police power, law and order, the struggle against subversion, etc. Faced as they are with intractable problems, those who control the levers of power find it increasingly necessary further to erode those features of 'bourgeois democracy' through which popular pressure is exercised. The power of representative institutions must be further reduced and the executive more effectively insulated against them. The independence of trade unions must be whittled away, and trade union rights, notably the right to strike, must be further surrounded by new and more stringent inhibitions. The state must arm itself with more extensive and more efficient means of repression, seek to define more stringently the area of 'legitimate' dissent and opposition, and strike fear in those who seek to go beyond it.

This process has strongly cumulative tendencies. For no more than reform does repression achieve its purpose. On the contrary, the more the state seeks to repress, the greater is the opposition it is likely to engender; and the more opposition it engenders, the greater are the powers which it must invoke. It is along that road that lies the transition from 'bourgeois democracy' to conservative authoritarianism.

This transition need not assume a dramatic character, or require a violent change in institutions. Neither its progression nor its end result need be identical with the Fascism of the inter-war years. It is indeed most unlikely to assume the latter's particular forms, because of the discredit which has not ceased to be attached to them, and of the loathing which Fascism has not ceased to evoke. In fact, the usage of Fascism as a reference point tends dangerously to obscure the less extreme alternatives to it, which do not require the wholesale dismantling of all democratic institutions, the total subversion of all liberties, nor certainly the abandonment of a democratic rhetoric. It is easily possible to conceive of forms of conservative authoritarianism which would not be 'Fascist', in the old sense, which would be claimed to be 'democratic' precisely because they were not 'Fascist', and whose establishment would be defended as in the best interests of 'democracy' itself. Nor is all this a distant projection into an improbable future: it describes a process which is already in train, and which is also, in the condition of advanced capitalism, more likely to be accentuated than reversed. The gradual transition of capitalism into socialism may be a myth: but the gradual transition of 'bourgeois democracy' into more or less pronounced forms of authoritarianism is not.

This view of the evolution of advanced capitalist regimes appears to leave out of account the forces of the Left, working-class movements and parties, and the strength of their 'countervailing power' in these societies. Unfortunately, it is precisely the present condition of these forces, the crisis in which they find themselves, which provides an additional element of likelihood to this evolution.

Historically, labour and socialist movements have been the

main driving force for the extension of the democratic features of capitalist societies; and it is also they who, from very necessity, have been the strongest defenders of civil and political liberties against infringements primarily directed at them, and at their capacity to act as agencies of counter-pressure. But their performance of this role has been very substantially and very negatively affected by the constantly more pronounced ideological and political integration of social democratic leaders into the framework of capitalism.

Social democratic parties, or rather social democratic leaders, have long ceased to suggest to anyone but their most credulous followers (and the more stupid among their opponents) that they were concerned in any sense whatever with the business of bringing about a socialist society. On the other hand, they – and their counterparts in the Democratic Party in the United States – have continued to proclaim their dedication to reform and radical change and made this the main element of differentiation between themselves and their conservative opponents.

But social democratic leaders in government illustrate particularly clearly the limits of reform. For while they raise great hopes among their followers and many others when in opposition, the constrictions under which they labour when in government, allied to the ideological dispositions which lead them to submit to these constrictions, leave them with little room to implement their promises. This, however, is only one half of the story. The other half consists in the fact that, confronted with demands they cannot fulfil, and with pressures they cannot subdue by reform, they too turn themselves into the protagonists of the reinforced state. Like their conservative opponents, they too seek to undermine the strength of the defence organisations of the working class, for instance, as in the case of the Labour Government in Britain, by the legislative curb of trade union rights, or, as in the case of German social-democratic ministers inside the 'Grand Coalition', by endorsing and supporting the promulgation of emergency laws principally designed to deal more effectively with opposition from the Left. Wherever they have been given the chance, social-democratic leaders have eagerly bent themselves to the administration of the capitalist state: but that administration increasingly requires the *strengthening* of the capitalist state, to which purpose, from a conservative point of view, these leaders have made a valuable contribution.

By thus turning themselves into the pillars of the established order, social democratic leaders produce two contradictory reactions. On the one hand, they produce in some of their supporters, and among others, notably in a younger generation, who might have become their supporters, the reaction which Raymond Williams expressed when he wrote, on the basis of four years' experience of Labour Government: 'A definition has failed and we are looking for new definitions and new directions.'[1] In so far as this helps to dissipate long-held illusions, and produces a search for genuine alternatives, there is much about this which is hopeful, even though the search is likely to be slow and difficult, with innumerable diversions and false trails.

On the other hand, social democratic failures and derelictions also produce, and more commonly, a marked movement away from the Left, and an increased vulnerability to the blandishments of the Right. The failure of social-democracy implicates not only those responsible for it, but all the forces of the Left. Because of it, the path is made smoother for would-be popular saviours, whose extreme conservatism is carefully concealed beneath a demagogic rhetoric of national renewal and social redemption, garnished, wherever suitable, with an appeal to racial and any other kind of profitable prejudice.

The failure of social democracy would present much less sombre perspectives if the traditional alternatives to social democratic parties, namely Communist ones, were not themselves, with hardly any exception, afflicted by certain profound weaknesses, of which the gravest is their lack of genuine internal democracy.

A serious revolutionary party, in the circumstances of advanced capitalism, *has* to be the kind of 'hegemonic' party of which Gramsci spoke, which means that it must be capable of 'creating a unity, not only of economic and political aims, but an intellectual and moral unity, posing all the issues which arise, not on the corporative level but on the "universal"

[1] R. Williams, *The May Day Manifesto*, 1968, p. 14.

level', and 'coordinated concretely with the general interests of subordinate groups'.[1] But the creation of such a party is only possible in conditions of free discussion and internal democracy, of flexible and responsive structures.

Nor is this essential only as a means of obviating ideological anaemia and political sclerosis. It is equally essential as a demonstration of the kind of social and political order which such a party seeks to bring into being. It is in its own *present* structures, in its own *present* modes of behaviour, attitudes, and habits that it must prefigure the society to which it aspires. For it is only by so doing that it can convince the vast majority of the population whose support it requires that its purpose is not to replace one system of domination by another, conceivably worse. If socialist democracy is its aspiration for tomorrow, so must internal socialist democracy be its rule today. Mere proclamations of future intentions are not enough.

Whether existing Communist parties can ever turn themselves into agencies appropriate to a new socialist politics is a matter of conjecture. But even if the answer were to be in the affirmative, it is only in Italy and France that such a transformation could be expected to help resolve the problems of the Left. Everywhere else, these parties, whatever they may do, are bound to remain for a very long time political formations of secondary consequence – vanguard parties without the vast armies of members and supporters which revolutionary change in these societies clearly requires; and the same is even more evident in regard to other groupings to the left of social democracy. For the foreseeable future at any rate, no formation of the Left will be in a position seriously to place the question of socialism on the agenda of most advanced capitalist societies. Nor certainly is this to be achieved by spontaneous eruption. The events of May–June 1968 in France showed well enough the yearning for fundamental change which simmers beneath a seemingly placid political surface, and to use Régis Debray's phrase, the degree to which the 'small motor' of a student movement may activate the 'big motor' of the working class. But these events showed equally well that, in the absence

[1] Quoted by Merrington, 'Theory and Practice in Gramsci's Marxism', in *The Socialist Register, 1968*, p. 154. See also A. Gorz, 'Reform and Revolution', in *ibid.*, pp. 131 ff.

of appropriate political organisation, what is possible is turmoil and pressure but not revolution.

It is the absence, for the present and for a long time to come, of such appropriate political agencies, paralleled by the existence of deep troubles and discontents, which makes the movement of 'bourgeois democracy' towards authoritarianism more rather than less likely. A common belief about the propensities of capitalist regimes in that direction is that they come to the surface at the point where dominant interests and the power-holders which protect them are faced with a revolutionary movement which appears to be on the way to the achievement of power. Faced with such a threat, it is often said on the Left, these interests opt for the authoritarian response to it, and accept or support the destruction of the constitutional framework in order to save themselves from revolution.

This is a possible scenario. But reflection suggests that whatever dominant classes, economic elites and conservative forces in general may wish, such a moment is one of the least likely to make this kind of response viable. For by the time a socialist movement has reached such a commanding position, which means, in the conditions of advanced capitalism, that it has become a vast popular movement, extending well beyond the working classes, it may be *too late* for the forces of conservatism to take up the authoritarian option with any real chance of success. It is when labour movements and socialist parties are divided and unsure of themselves and of their purpose that the realisation of that option becomes possible. Historical antecedent would seem to confirm this view. For in practically all cases where conservative authoritarianism, and Fascism, have replaced 'bourgeois democracy', the labour and socialist movements, far from constituting a genuine threat to the capitalist order, were in fact bitterly divided and deeply confused. This is surely what Marx meant when, writing about the Bonapartist regime in France, he said that 'it was the only form of government possible at the time when the bourgeoisie had already lost, *and the working class had not yet acquired*, the faculty of ruling the nation'.[1]

Sooner or later, and despite all the immense obstacles on the

[1] K. Marx, *The Civil War in France*, in *Selected Works*, vol. 1, pp. 469–70 (my italics).

way, the working class and its allies in other classes will acquire that faculty. When they do, the socialist society they will create will not require the establishment of an all-powerful state on the ruins of the old. On the contrary, their 'faculty of ruling the nation' will, for the first time in history, enable them to bring into being an authentically democratic social order, a truly free society of self-governing men and women, in which, as Marx also put it, the state will be converted 'from an organ superimposed upon society into one completely subordinated to it'.[1]

[1] K. Marx, *The Critique of the Gotha Programme*, *ibid.*, vol. 2, p. 29.

Index